Online Coaching

Elke Berninger-Schäfer

Online Coaching

Foreword by Peter Meyer and Harald Geißler

Springer

Elke Berninger-Schäfer
Karlsruher Institut
Karlsruhe, Germany

ISBN 978-3-658-39132-4 ISBN 978-3-658-39133-1 (eBook)
https://doi.org/10.1007/978-3-658-39133-1

Responsible Editor: Eva Brechtel-Wahl
This Springer imprint is published by the registered company Springer Fachmedien Wiesbaden GmbH, part of Springer Nature.
The registered company address is: Abraham-Lincoln-Str. 46, 65189 Wiesbaden, Germany

Foreword 2

For a long time, modern communication media have been an integral part of our lives. Not only in our professional lives, but also in our private lives. Today, if you stroll down a busy street, sit in a train or visit a department store, you will see people everywhere using their mobile phones to make calls, surf the Internet or check their e-mails. "Handyfreie Zonen" (mobile phone free zones), on the other hand, are becoming increasingly rare. And if they exist, there must be good reasons for this, such as at a concert.

Against this background, with regard to coaching, it is first of all noticeable that—at least in the German-speaking world—coaching with modern media is still a rarity and by no means a mass phenomenon. Secondly, it is apparently *not*necessary to have good reasons for this abstinence. It seems rather to be an undisputed self-evident truth that coaching must be carried out face-to-face. The question of the use of modern media in coaching is obviously still largely taboo.

As powerful as this normality has been so far, it is slowly but surely coming to an end. Because in the last decade, not only have various Internet tools been developed for coaching. The publication of articles dealing with the possibilities of how coaching can use modern media has also now reached a considerable level.

It was therefore only a matter of time before the first monograph on coaching with modern media would appear, which would also address coaching practice in particular. This time has now come with the publication of the present book. Its peculiarity lies in the fact that the long-term work of the author with the Internet platform "CAI World" developed conceptually and communicatively by her is reflected in it. This development work, which I was able to experience as a long-time companion, was driven by a vision that gave the author the strength and courage to go her—often stony—way with admirable perseverance. Because in the development of her coaching platform and the conceptual ideas and argumentative connections underlying it, which are unfolded in the present book, she was neither deterred by the—especially initial—practice pressure of the prevailing coaching scene nor by the not inconsiderable economic development risks. This achievement deserves the highest recognition.

The present book sets an important milestone in the history of coaching. Because it shows that coaching with modern media opens up a variety of possibilities for the development of completely new coaching formats and will thus be able to open up new fields of practice and target groups. This will be all the better if this development work is conceptually systematically reflected and empirically carefully checked.

In this sense, I would like to congratulate Elke Berninger-Schäfer on the publication of her book and wish it intensive reception and effectiveness.

Prof. Dr. Harald Geißler
Professor of General Pedagogy with a focus on Vocational and Business Education at the University of the Bundeswehr Hamburg until 2016
Owner of Virtual Coaching
Hamburg
in June 2017

Foreword 1

Dear readers,
The digitization of the world began a few years ago—from Internet 1.0 to the current version 4.0, it was only about 20 years. How does this change affect us as human beings, employees and leaders? Is everything just faster or just different or worse? Does this online world open up completely new possibilities beyond the obvious ones like Amazon, Facebook and Twitter?

The online world with its huge data streams of news through different channels, such as online news, social media (e.g. Facebook) and the classic e-mail, makes it increasingly difficult to assess which information corresponds to the truth or is post-factual in nature. In times of Big Data, there is also the danger of manipulation by and with information (an example of this can be found here: ▶ https://www.dasmagazin.ch/2016/12/03/ich-habe-nur-gezeigt-dass-es-die-bombe-gibt/).

On the other hand, the online world offers us new possibilities. In this book, Ms. Berninger-Schäfer goes into detail about the possibilities of online coaching. She explains which online skills are necessary for experienced coaches to make online coaching with all its opportunities efficient and effective for the customer.

"In the customer's interest"—what do I mean by that? Ms. Berninger-Schäfer opens up completely new possibilities for cooperation worldwide for leaders with the CAI-World—complex topics professionally moderated and solutions viewed from different perspectives, to be processed, and this both on- and offline—wow!

For a leader who leads his teams on a trust basis, the CAI-World is a highly effective and very efficient way to complex tasks across hierarchies in a virtual space. They use scientifically proven methods for changing perspectives and visualization, and the teams become more creative and productive.

The business world in the age of digital leadership needs such virtual work spaces and methods in order to meet the increased demands for speed and complexity in global collaboration networks—in order to secure competitiveness.

Peter Meyer
Senior Vice President Purchasing Automotive Business DS (CP/AB1), Robert Bosch GmbH
In autumn 2017

Preface

When I was asked by the German Association of Psychologists (BDP) many years ago whether I would conduct psychological counseling online, I rejected this idea outright. It was inconceivable to me that I could use my psychological expertise without being able to see the person I was interacting with in front of me. In addition, my computer affinity was very limited.

And yet, the request increasingly evoked fantasies about how my professional work could be expanded through online support. One reason for this were computer games that my son played at the age of around twelve. I looked over his shoulder and was fascinated by the possibilities that arise when a player (as an avatar) can design himself, when he can build entire worlds and act in them. I asked myself how it would be if my clients could represent their life and work worlds in a colorful, possibly three-dimensional world, or if they could visualize and explore problems or issues that concern them in this way. How would it be if we could "trial and error" in these virtual worlds and directly "experience" the effect of this behavior? How much more effective would our work together be than the reflection, goal-setting and planning that takes place in my office, in a setting and context that does not match the client's context of action? These creative design options inspired many ideas that, at first, remained in the realm of the fantastic.

These ideas were given further impetus in 2008 by the development of "blended learning seminars" in the coaching courses that I initially designed and implemented on behalf of the Leadership Academy Baden-Württemberg and later as a cooperating partner. It was very exciting to experience how my concepts delivered as Word files were interactively implemented by the team responsible for this on the computer. The implementation of online seminars in coaching continuing education posed new challenges for online group moderation, reading and writing skills.

Another important milestone was the first implementation of the virtual Collegial Coaching Conference®, a method of collegial group coaching, which was developed by me and T. Berg at the Leadership Academy Baden-Württemberg and is carried out by the participants in groups of usually 8–10 people after a one-time training. In these groups, a group member receives coaching from the remaining participants. This is done within the framework of a methodologically and temporally structured approach, which greatly facilitates virtual implementation. With the implementation of the Collegial Coaching Conference ®in a virtual variant, we thus created a first prototype in 2008, with which virtual coaching was possible.

The 2nd LOCCS symposium took place at Ludwig Maximilian University in Munich in May 2011. LOCCS stands for "The **L**inguistics **o**f **C**oaching, **C**onsulting & **S**upervision" and uses discourse analytical methods to research the specific communication between clients and coaches/consultants/supervisors. The aim of LOCCS is to contribute to the connection of theory and practice in the field of coaching, consulting and supervision. At this symposium I had the opportunity to present the virtual Collegial Coaching Conference®and to get into conversation with other interested parties. Since then, there has been an exchange with Prof. Dr. Harald Geißler, the pioneer of virtual coaching in Germany. The networking of the actors in the field of virtual coaching progressed and has been further developed since then.

The next important milestone for me was the visit to the Learntec in 2012, an annual IT education fair in Karlsruhe, where I came into contact with providers of 3-D worlds that were not only suitable for training, but also for coaching. The fascination that was originally triggered by the mentioned computer games now led to the fact that I wanted to carry out coaching in 3-D worlds. First attempts to meet my client's avatar as an avatar, to have coaching rooms and landscapes equipped according to my instructions and to design coaching sessions there led to very encouraging and exciting experiences. A great challenge were the technical hurdles that came with the installation of the 3-D worlds. This was confirmed by a master's thesis that was carried out at the Zurich University of Applied Sciences (ZHAW) under the direction of Prof. Hansjörg Künzli. This work showed the great potential of 3-D coaching, but also the technical hurdles and obstacles that significantly reduced the use of this potential.

Encouraged and disappointed at the same time, I decided to set up my own platform that would allow me to realize my ideas. This led to the foundation of the CAI GmbH, of which I share the management as a shareholder with Heidi Kupke, my valuable supplement on the IT and business know-how side. To have experienced, knowledgeable, interested and open-minded IT employees who are willing to engage in this new product development, as well as a pool of coaches who are willing to go down this pioneer path, realize our slogan "Coaching meets IT". This is done in the CAI ®World, an online platform that allows me to meet clients multimedially, i.e. either or both in writing and/or by listening, speaking and seeing. As a coach, I have an integrated systemic-solution-oriented coaching process, various tools such as question sets, constellation figures, image material, the inner team, the resource tree, a whiteboard, etc. at my disposal. All coaching sessions are automatically documented. I can manage my clients, offer clients and coaches a database and train coaches in online coaching. Various coaching formats can be carried out and evaluated, such as business coaching, health coaching, transfer coaching, group coaching, etc. A special value is the possibility to provide authentic, anonymized data material for scientific research.

The reactions of companies, coaches and individual clients confirm this development path in that, after initial great skepticism, an increasing openness to professional online formats in coaching has become apparent. This may be because life and work on the Internet have become a matter of course and the generation that grew up with the Internet has arrived in the working world and already in management positions. In this respect, the professionalization of online coaching is an essential step for the future viability and future-proofing of coaching.

This book is aimed at both people who work as coaches and people who work in the fields of therapy, counseling, supervision and training or are interested in such tasks. Many approaches in online coaching can also be used in other contexts, e.g. in everyday management or in the field of digital collaboration. In addition, there is a lot of information for personnel and organizational developers who are responsible for coaching in their organizations.

Elke Berninger-Schäfer

Acknowledgments

I would like to thank all those who were willing to support and shape the development path in online coaching, the clients and colleagues, the clients and especially the CAI and KIC team.

I would like to thank Mr. Klockenbusch and Ms. Brechtel-Wahl for creating the opportunity for this book to be published by Springer-Verlag.

I would like to thank the pioneers, in particular Prof. Dr. Harald Geißler, and my teachers, in particular Dr. Gunther Schmidt.

Likewise, a big thank you to the scientific community, here in particular Prof. Hansjörg Künzli and Prof. Dr. Eva-Maria Graf, who contribute to the professionalization in online coaching and with whom the exchange is just a pleasure.

My development path was significantly shaped by the valuable cooperation partners in our coaching further education. Here I would like to warmly thank Mr. Thomas Berg, Secretary General of the Leadership Academy Baden-Württemberg, and Mr. Prof. Dr. Michael Nagy, President of the University of Economics for Management in Mannheim.

Elke Berninger-Schäfer
Karlsruhe
in October 2017

Contents

About the author

Prof. Dr. Elke Berninger-Schäfer

Elke Berninger-Schäfer is the owner of the Karlsruher Institut (KI), managing shareholder of CAI GmbH, Diplom-Psychologin, Senior Coach DBVC, lecturer, Lehrcoach, supervisor BDP, approved psychotherapist, provider of DBVC recognized coaching training for business coach and health coach, the training for online coach, as well as in digital leadership & coaching.

Contact: info@karlsruher-institut.de, ► www.karlsruher-institut.de

List of Figures

List of Tables

Introduction

E. Berninger-Schäfer, *Online Coaching*,
https://doi.org/10.1007/978-3-658-39133-1_1

Coaching as a professional format is enjoying increasing popularity, is scientifically researched all the while being carried out in different contexts. Yet, coaching is an unprotected term, with a plethora of different services that operate under its label. A separation of professional and non-professional coaching can only be achieved through the delineation of quality standards and requirements for quality assurance, ethical guidelines and scientific foundation. Universities and associations contribute to this, as well as larger organizations that have defined their own quality requirements, commissioning processes, process structures and evaluations.

In this situation, online coaching is increasingly being requested by organizations due to internal digitalization strategies and processes.

Here, the clarification of a professional understanding, of quality standards, of ethical guidelines and of a necessary competence development is particularly important, since under this label the field of possibilities grows even more inflationary. This poses further great challenges for the professionalization efforts of coaching.

The increasing attention to online coaching corresponds to the social changes that are affecting all areas of life. Multimedia has long been a matter of course in private and professional life (Seel & Ifenthaler, 2009).

For example, Hinterberger and Kühne (2009) point out that in the meantime almost all areas of life can be found on the Internet with a prefix such as "cyber", "online", "tele" or "e", such as e-government, e-health, e-commerce, e-coaching, e-learning, e-therapy, e-banking, etc. (Hinterberger & Kühne, 2009, p. 16).

In ► Chap. 2 "Current situation" results of surveys are presented, which allow an assessment of the market situation of coaching and online coaching (► Sect. 2.1). These results are embedded in the topic of Internet behavior (► Sect. 2.2).

The use of the Internet can take place very differently. This affects the media used, the objectives and the competences of users. The diverse possibilities that different communication media offer create new and different forms of encounter. ► Chapter 3 "The media-based encounter" deals with this topic. First, in ► Sect. 3.1 the use of terms such as virtual-real-real is clarified, with a special focus on the word "presence". In ► Sect. 3.2 "Telematics and its risks" the social consequences of digital communication are mentioned. This raises questions about individual consequences, such as influence on perception and thinking or social consequences, such as emotional distance. In turn, these raise further questions about the limits of mediated communication in professional applications. At the same time, there are already numerous studies on interventions on the Internet in therapy, coaching and counseling, which are dealt with in the following ► Sect. 3.3.

In order to make these results also systematically usable for online coaching, in ► Chap. 4 "Coaching and its Development" coaching and coaching practice fields are first defined in more detail (► Sect. 4.1), in order to then be able to assign online coaching to the previous development phases in coaching (► Sect. 4.2). The current development is accompanied by a differentiation of topics, target groups and formats (► Sect. 4.3). This differentiation is supported and drastically extended by online coaching (► Chap. 10).

Before these explanations are made, however, an approach to the term "online coaching" is first made in ► Chap. 5. Starting from a proliferating variety of terms (► Sect. 5.1), a theoretical clarification of terms is made, which, however, does not correspond to the current market situation (► Sect. 5.2).

This is considered in ► Chap. 6 "Overview of existing offers", with an exemplary list first being made under the label "Online counseling" (► Sect. 6.1), since coaching and counseling are often used synonymously. Only in the following ► Sect. 6.2 is a professionalization understanding added, which allows a classification of online coaching offers in a staged model. The four stages of this model with an increasing demand for coaching professionalism and their technical requirements are specified in Sects. 6.2.1, 6.2.3 and 6.2.4 and illustrated with examples.

The described professionalization understanding is based on the previously evaluated success factors in coaching and online coaching. These are described in ► Chap. 7 "Success factors in coaching", by first going into the unspecific success factors in coaching (► Sect. 7.1). Special attention is paid to the change in the reference state (Sect. 7.2) as it represents a switch in the coaching process. The work with holistic, neuronal patterns and their change affects cognitive, emotional and physiological aspects and is therefore particularly exciting in the online context. Coaches and online coaches need knowledge about these factors, the latter also having to take into account the effective factors in online coaching (Sect. 7.3). These are elaborated in five subchapters (Sects. 7.3.1 to 7.3.5). For online applications in 3-D worlds, however, there are even more special features and effective factors, so that they are given their own chapter with four subchapters (Sect. 7.4 with 7.4.1 to 7.4.4).

The use of scientifically founded action factors is done by the design of the coaching conversation both face to face and online. Therefore, in ► Chap. 8 "Process Control in Coaching and Online Coaching", first the coaching conversation is dealt with in its general, constitutive elements (► Sect. 8.1). Then, some exemplary process models in coaching and online coaching are described (► Sect. 8.2), before a process model for online coaching developed by Ribbers and Waringa (2015) is presented in more detail (► Sect. 8.3). An integration of the process models and the action factors presented in ► Chap. 7 is carried out in the phase sequence of the "Karlsruhe School" (► Sect. 8.4). This sequence is controlled and implemented online in each coaching unit from the clarification of concerns, the description of the situation, the activation of resources and change of patterns, the finding and solution of goals, to the planning and evaluation of implementation.

The competence fields necessary for the professional implementation of online coaching can be derived from the explanations of the effective factors in coaching and the design of coaching processes. They are presented in ► Chap. 9 "Competencies for Online Coaching". These include media competence (► Sect. 9.1) and media communication (► Sect. 9.2) with a focus on reading and writing competence (► Sect. 9.2.1) as well as listening: acoustically conveyed communication (► Sect. 9.2.2).

A specific methodological competence (► Sect. 9.3) includes the online use of professional coaching tools. These are described in detail in nine sub-sections (Sects. 9.3.1 to 9.3.9) and illustrated with a case study in a tenth sub-chapter (► Sect. 9.3.10).

Another competence of professional coaches relates to the format competence increasingly demanded in market studies. Since online coaching represents a special enrichment here, ► Chapter 10 "Coaching formats" is dedicated to this development. To these aspects of professional coaching, which are still little described in the literature, a clarification of the terms setting and format is first carried out in ► Sect. 10.1. In further sections, various setting factors (► Sect. 10.2) and format criteria (▶ Sect. 10.3) are listed and explained. Individual formats are exemplarily presented in their online variants. This is done in eight subsections (Sects. 10.4.1 to 10.4.8). In them, online formats for group coaching, team coaching, conflict coaching, transfer coaching, "walk and talk", self-coaching with the Solution Finder, CAI ®Business Coaching and a coaching program for culture development in a globally operating corporation are described. The differentiation of coaching formats by online possibilities also includes the requirements for a design competence.

The competence fields described in ▶ Chaps. 9 and 10 have a direct influence on the quality in online coaching (▶ Chap. 11). This is represented in its structure-process and result quality (▶ Sect. 11.1). In order to realize these quality criteria, professionalization in online coaching is essential. This is addressed in the chapter on further education (▶ Sect. 11.2). Another quality feature of professional online coaching is the compliance with ethical guidelines for online applications in coaching, therapy and supervision (▶ Sect. 11.3).

Online coaching needs a technical environment. ▶ Chapter 12 "Media conception for online coaching" deals with the requirements. This includes knowledge about processes of information processing (▶ Sect. 12.1) and about media design principles (▶ Sect. 12.2). The topics of barrier-free (▶ Sect. 12.3) and data security (▶ Sect. 12.4) each have their own section, as they are associated with legal regulations and are essential for professional online applications.

Finally, in ▶ Chap. 13 the advantages (▶ Sect. 13.1) and disadvantages (▶ Sect. 13.2) of online coaching are presented. These lead to a list of recommendations (▶ Sect. 13.3), which frame the many tips that have already been given in previous passages.

In the final remarks, online coaching is placed in the current social upheavals caused by digital possibilities and a future forecast is made.

Current Situation

Contents

E. Berninger-Schäfer, *Online Coaching*,
https://doi.org/10.1007/978-3-658-39133-1_2

The situation in which online coaching is currently embedded can be described by an increasing professionalization, the emergence of platforms that mediate coaches or online working coaches and increasing surveys on this topic.

The Professional Scene

The professional scene that has developed began about 10 years ago with Prof. Dr. Harald Geißler and was continued in the pioneer phase by a few other representatives, such as Robert Griffith. This development is embedded in the large field of online counseling.

While a few years ago online counseling was still considered an supplement to face-to-face counseling, it is now an recognized, independent offer (Reindl et al., 2016). Face-to-face encounter is usually understood to mean the simultaneous, physical encounter of people in the same room.

In addition to online counseling, there are many other professional, media-based applications, also in 3-D worlds. Here are some examples.

- The Neubrandenburg University of Applied Sciences has opened a psychological counseling service in "Second Life". In a preliminary study, the users' requirements for such an offer were collected.
- Another project "Church in virtual worlds" was carried out by the Freiburg Archbishopric's Pastoral Office over a period of three years (2008–2011) and evaluated positively (Kebekus, 2011).
- In the research project "Virtual Assistants and Their Social Acceptance" (VASA) of the Federal Ministry of Education and Research, which the University of Bielefeld and the v. Bodelschwinghschen Stiftungen Bethel have been carrying out in cooperation since 2010, technical helpers (Billie as an artificial person) are used to support old people and people with physical and mental disabilities, e.g. in the care of appointments, in taking medication and in stimulating conversations with other people. (Yaghoubzadeh & Kopp, 2015).
- The professionalization of online coaching is attracting attention from associations and congress organizers (see Coaching Congress of the German Coaching Association in November 2018: "Business Coaching-The Next Level"—Coaching in the Transformation Process or the every two years Congress "Coaching meets Research" of the University of Applied Sciences Northwestern Switzerland in Olten, which will be held in 2018 under the title "Organization, Digitalization and Design").
- The Zurich University of Applied Sciences (ZHAW) has been training students in the Institute of Applied Psychology in the use of the CAI® World for 6 semesters. This was specially designed for professional online coaching and is successfully evaluated by ZHAW. Digital competence is considered an essential key qualification.

Platforms for the Placement of Coaches

On the Internet there is a sudden boom of offers under the label Online-Coaching, which however on closer inspection turns out to be primarily platforms for the placement of coaches or offers of coaching by mail or (video) telephone. Concrete examples are presented and discussed in ► Chap. 6 . In addition, individual online tools for coaching are coming onto the market, so that a classification and professional evaluation of the same is necessary for coaches as well as clients.

■ **Survey of Online Supervision and Online Coaching**
Reindl et al. (2016) carried out expert interviews in the form of a quantitative online survey in the field of supervision in order to assess the demand for online supervision, in particular also with regard to target groups, applied instruments and qualifications.

They found that the majority of supervisors are still hesitant and often not yet open to the possibilities that are contained in online applications. This is in line with experiences that we partly make in the coaching networks of the Karlsruhe Institute. For many colleagues, the need for immediate, physical contact seems to be an almost unshakeable belief, almost a dogma.

Reindl et al. (2016) explain the sparse results of their survey of online supervision by the typical characteristics of a pioneer phase, in which a few "early adopters" generate experience-based knowledge, a professional community and scientifically sound material still have to be built up, just as standards and qualification programs. This situation can be directly transferred to coaching.

The Kienbaum "Future Management Development Study 2017" reports that online formats would increase in coaching, but not for top management level. However, it should be noted that it remains unclear what is meant by online coaching. As long as there is no clear idea of professional online coaching, survey results that do not explicitly represent their understanding of it are also not interpretable.

The present book wants to remedy this and provide a basis for the professionalization of online applications in coaching, supervision, therapy and counseling, with a focus on online coaching. To what extent this effort is worthwhile depends on whether there is or will be a market for coaching and online coaching.

2.1 Market Assessment

According to the ICF[1] Global Coaching Study of 2012, there are 47,500 professional coaches worldwide. North America and Western Europe form the coaching focus with over 70%. The study found that the majority of clients, the average fees and the number of sessions have increased and that global demand is still expected to increase. The main problem of the industry is the unprotected designation "coach".

The Trigon Coaching Survey 2010, in which 297 people from Germany, Austria and Switzerland participated, describes that 64% of the respondents expect the coaching demand in companies to increase in the future and 7% to increase strongly (Vogelauer, 2010).

The Federal Association for Further Education of the Wuppertal Kreis carried out a trend survey in 2013. According to this, 30% of the training institutes surveyed expect an increase in sales of around 10% and more in the field of process accompaniment and coaching. 31% of the institutes expect trainer and lecturer fees as well as hotel and room costs to increase in 2014. Almost half of all respondents

1 ICF = International Coach Federation.

expect increases in costs for advertising, sales, customer retention and running costs (personnel, IT and administration).

The use of web-based training and mobile apps as learning media is also expected to increase (68 to 63%), as well as the use of serious games (46%) (Wuppertaler Kreis e. V., 2013).

This assessment corresponds to the digital transformation taking place globally according to the Grünbuch/Arbeiten 4.0 (2015) of the Federal Ministry of Labour and Social Affairs, which bundles a variety of changes through new information and communication technologies in the economy and society, thus changing the way we live and work fundamentally. Germany as a location must face up to this development with Industry 4.0, Big Data, Crowdworking and automation, with its opportunities and risks.

"In the service sector, an 'on-demand economy' is emerging. In this case, online platforms act as simple, fast and cost-effective intermediaries for services for companies and private households" (Grünbuch & Arbeiten, 4.0, p. 15).

On the homepage "förderland/Wissen für Gründer und Unternehmer" ("Knowledge for founders and entrepreneurs"), "online coaching" is recommended as a business idea to copy. The reason given is that online coaching is on the rise due to the rapid development of communication media. Coaching by e-mail and via the Internet is recommended under the term "online coaching". Start-up costs of an average of 16,000 € are assumed, with sales of 40,000 € in the first and 75,000 € in the second year. Investments in further education are not mentioned, nor is there any indication that coaching should be a professional service in general. The overall impression is that online coaching is a profession that anyone can pursue independently (▶ http://www.foerderland.de/gruendung/gruendungsvarianten/geschaeftsideen/idee/pc-internet/online-coaching/, accessed 05.05.2016).

Even though there are such solecisms, professional online consulting has been developing since the mid-1990s (Engelhard, 2013). Based on four surveys and their results, this situation should be briefly outlined with regard to online coaching.

▪ Survey 1

Grant and Zackson (2004) surveyed 2,529 coaches, all members of the International Coach Federation (ICF) with an online questionnaire, with the English-speaking members in a clear majority, especially with regard to Australia and North America. The majority of the coachings (63%) were conducted by telephone, 34.2% as face-to-face coaching and 1.5% by means of other electronic tools, e.g. E-mail.

▪ Survey 2

The Sherpa Coaching Survey reported on the first applications of webcams and the use of so-called instant messengers ("Skype") in coaching in the American area from 2009 onwards. Here there was a clear increase, so that in the 10th Survey 2015 it was reported that 40% of the coaches and clients use webcams at least occasionally and 20% work exclusively through this medium of communication (Sherpa Coaching Survey, 2015). The authors attribute this also to the increasing better quality of the communication media.

■ **Survey 3**

Marzschesky (2015) conducted an online survey on the acceptability of online coaching with a sample of 18 coaches and 69 clients, most of whom came from the Karlsruhe Coaching Center[2] and the CAI® database[3]. She found that on the client side, it was the younger age group (between 30 and 40 years old) that chose online coaching. Over 50% of clients who preferred face-to-face coaching were over 50 years old. On the coach side, online coaching was also less common among coaches over 50 years old. However, it must be taken into account that many of the participants in the study had never experienced online coaching before. The aspects that were prioritized as particularly important for coaching by the participants related to trust, personal contact, the openness associated with it, sustainability and data protection.

■ **Survey 4**

Hinkelmann and Enzweiler (2016) summarize the results of the 14th coaching survey conducted by Middendorf on the opportunities and risks of virtual coaching, stating that of the 454 coaches surveyed, the majority (84%) said they preferred face-to-face coaching. Next came telephone coaching (7%). A long way behind is the percentage of those who use other online coaching options. Reasons given include a feeling of strangeness towards new technologies and ignorance of their professional use.

These exemplary quoted surveys show on the one hand that the use of online coaching (in the broadest sense) has a regional component. In the USA and especially in Australia, where large spatial distances have to be bridged, online coaching (mostly telephone coaching) has long been a matter of course. On the other hand, the use of online coaching is related to the technical progress of the media that can be used. Other aspects that influence the use or acceptance of online coaching are the age of the respondents and their prior knowledge of online coaching.

The number of average monthly Google searches for online coaching and related terms can be seen in ◘ Fig. 2.1. The terms listed are used synonymously (see ► Sect. 5.1 for variety of terms). There is an increase in the first half of 2016.

Armutat et al. (2015) define Virtual Coaching as coaching with modern media. This is directly related to the spread of these media and is associated with media behavior. Since the use of the Internet has become a matter of course in professional and private life all over the world, it shapes the current social development and the personal situation of the users. The market assessment of online coaching is directly related to this.

2.2 Internet Behavior

The Initiative D21, founded in 1999, is a non-profit association to which approximately 200 member organizations belong and which implements non-profit projects in the field of information and communication technologies in a partnership of politics and business.

2 The Karlsruhe Coaching Center is operated by the Karlsruhe Institute.
3 The CAI® database lists professional online coaches.

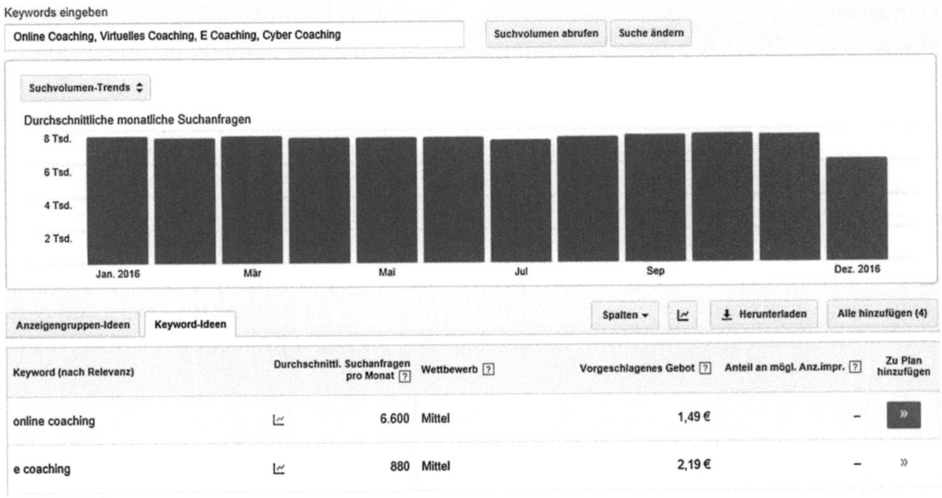

Fig. 2.1 Google searches for online coaching and related terms, viewed on 09.02.2017

Initiative D21 publishes the (N)ONLINER Atlas annually in cooperation with TNS Infratest since 2001. Due to the large number of cases, empirically sound data on Internet usage in Germany can be provided (► http://www.initiatived21.de/portfolio/nonliner-atlas/, accessed on 30.06.2015).

The (N)ONLINER Atlas 2014 (Fig. 2.2) also states that the highest relevance for users is security (93%) and simplicity (68%); if given a choice, however, security is more important than simplicity (91% to 9%).

Ribbers and Waringa (2015) speak of over 3 billion users of the Internet worldwide. According to their estimates, one person is online 23.8 h per month. Of this, 37.2 h per person per month are in North America, 26.8 h in Europe, and 17.2 h in Asia/the Pacific region. In their opinion, online coaching therefore perfectly fits the new world of work ("the New World of Work", Ribbers & Waringa, 2015, p. 7). Ribbers & Waringa explain that this means not only that coaches can expand their portfolio with online coaching (online coaching as an addition to the face-to-face format), but also that they can open up new target groups, e.g. young clients or expats who live and work abroad.

Virtual reality glasses, which create the impression of being in a three-dimensional world through the wearer's head movements, are becoming increasingly popular. A representative survey by the German digital association Bitkom showed that almost every third German over the age of 14 can imagine using such glasses. This is an increase of 10% over 2015 (► http://checkpoint-elearning.de/wissen/sporter-eignisse-in-der-virtual-reality-erleben, accessed 04.08.2016).

However, it is not only about the possibilities, but also about the awareness of the dangers that the new communication technologies bring. The psychoinformatics should be mentioned as an example.

Psychoinformatics deals as a scientific discipline with the prediction of psychological variables, such as personality traits, attitudes and preferences, based on the evaluation of data from human-machine interaction. Social media are used as data sources as well as the use of apps, vehicles or household appliances, provided they

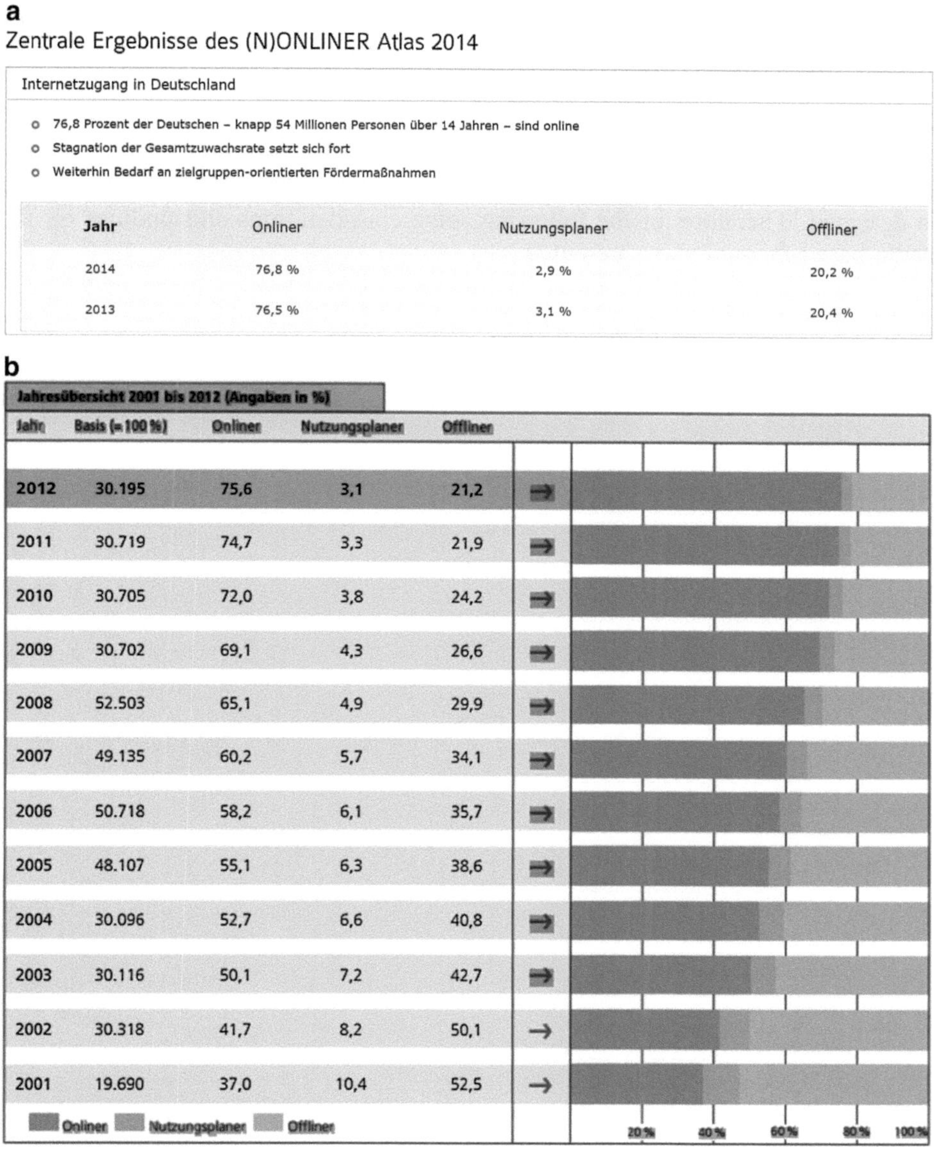

a

Zentrale Ergebnisse des (N)ONLINER Atlas 2014

Internetzugang in Deutschland

- 76,8 Prozent der Deutschen – knapp 54 Millionen Personen über 14 Jahren – sind online
- Stagnation der Gesamtzuwachsrate setzt sich fort
- Weiterhin Bedarf an zielgruppen-orientierten Fördermaßnahmen

Jahr	Onliner	Nutzungsplaner	Offliner
2014	76,8 %	2,9 %	20,2 %
2013	76,5 %	3,1 %	20,4 %

b

Jahresübersicht 2001 bis 2012 (Angaben in %)

Jahr	Basis (= 100 %)	Onliner	Nutzungsplaner	Offliner
2012	30.195	75,6	3,1	21,2
2011	30.719	74,7	3,3	21,9
2010	30.705	72,0	3,8	24,2
2009	30.702	69,1	4,3	26,6
2008	52.503	65,1	4,9	29,9
2007	49.135	60,2	5,7	34,1
2006	50.718	58,2	6,1	35,7
2005	48.107	55,1	6,3	38,6
2004	30.096	52,7	6,6	40,8
2003	30.116	50,1	7,2	42,7
2002	30.318	41,7	8,2	50,1
2001	19.690	37,0	10,4	52,5

Fig. 2.2 **a, b** Key results of the (N)ONLINER Atlas 2014

provide digital data. Monday (2016) explains how, based on such data, predictions can be made about political, sexual and religious orientation, intelligence, life satisfaction, relationship status and personality traits, such as openness, conscientiousness, extraversion, agreeableness and neuroticism.

For this purpose, for example, likes in Facebook, WhatsApp usage or speech analyses are evaluated.

The algorithms that make these predictions are of great interest for advertising and online services. But they also show how much users of free services pay with their data and how easily Internet behavior can be abused. It can therefore be concluded that data protection must play a major role in professional services in the fields of coaching, therapy, counseling and supervision.

The role the Internet plays in everyday life changes social behavior and poses legal, ethical, political and economic challenges to social development. For professional services that take place over the Internet, as is the case with online coaching, the first question is how a professional encounter that takes place medially should be designed. Therefore, in the following some considerations and findings on the media-based encounter are presented.

The Media-Supported Encounter

Contents

E. Berninger-Schäfer, *Online Coaching*,
https://doi.org/10.1007/978-3-658-39133-1_3

Thiery (2014) formulates the need to deal with media-supported encounters in professional services as follows:

> Anyone who, in view of the changed cultural situation, takes the position that psychotherapeutic work is impossible with telematic subjects should also think about the future of their professional practice. Successive generations will assume the availability of media offerings in which they can present their concerns anonymously at a distance. Especially when it comes to taboo, shameful or topics that can be consequential for their biography in a negative way (Thiery, 2014, p. 58).

So the question is no longer whether there can and should be media-supported encounters in the counseling, supervision, coaching and therapy context, but rather how they should look so that they meet a professional claim.

The question that is repeatedly asked in this context is whether the processing of personal issues that are to be accompanied by individual change is possible at all without the immediate interpersonal contact, that is, without the personal encounter.

The distinction between personal encounter and, in contrast, the accompaniment via the Internet, be it in coaching, counseling, supervision or therapy, is not tenable because whenever two or more people interact, it is always a form of personal encounter. Rather, it is exciting to find out what effects the different, media-supported forms of encounter have.

Since earlier considerations on the subject of virtual accompaniment were mainly related to mailing or chat counseling, it is usually meant that the interacting persons are not in the same room at the same time.

The variety of virtual communication possibilities that are now possible in various combinations expands our idea of personal encounter. For example, over audio connections, tone and other paraverbal signals can be perceived, over video functions facial expressions and gestures, the encounter in worlds with avatars creates the illusion of actually moving together in the same space. Organizations that operate globally design identical meeting rooms, so that during meetings via audio and video functions, the simultaneous presence in the same space is suggested. Filk speaks of social spaces of everyday life, which would arise through attribution of meaning through digital media and fundamentally shape the perception of reality (Filk, 2014).

Thus, the need arises to redefine personal encounter, to distinguish between the various media-based interaction possibilities and to investigate their effects. For this purpose, some terms must first be clarified.

3.1 Virtual—Really—Real

Often, the difference between online procedures and the simultaneous physical encounter of people in the same space is referred to as virtual vs. real or virtual vs. face-to-face or virtual vs. presence. This creates a contrast that is not tenable in the various forms of computer-aided encounter. Internet-based communication is real, which is evident from its effects. People can feel connected to each other through mediated communication, get angry, feel hurt, fall in love, etc. Even in online communication, there is a face-to-face contact via the video function. Especially in professional relationship management, such as therapy, coaching, consulting or supervision, a high presence of the persons concerned is absolutely necessary if satisfactory results are to be achieved. This does not mean the co-presence in the same space, but the willingness to engage with each other, the concentration on and readiness for this encounter. However, how the presence is conveyed is initially open. In the following, therefore, of co-presence or of face-to-face contact is meant when the simultaneous, physical presence of people in the same space is meant.

In systemic thinking, the question is rather how individual constructions of reality affect the Internet and how professional counseling formats can deal with them. The research object would be the Internet as a relationship medium, an expression used by Brunner (2009).

Constructivist theories (learning psychology, philosophy, sociology) assume that human perception cannot capture an image of an objective reality, but is influenced by physiological, social, cognitive and emotional processes to create a subjective representation of reality. Radical constructivism postulates that reality only arises through this process.

Thiery (2014) refers to Esposito when he explains that virtual reality is not a fictional reality, but the reality of fiction, an alternative construction of possibilities. He argues that with virtual worlds, new spaces of experience and knowledge would arise that would offer more opportunities for a non-dominant discourse than would be possible in the offline world.

> » Any form of influence that is based on language as an intervening medium is virtual, thus also counseling and therapy, offline as well as online. With therapeutic intent, non-existent, not yet realized (virtual) possibilities are explored that are supposed to show the clients possibilities of escape from the subjectively experienced limits (Thiery, 2014, p. 63).

It can thus be concluded that the great difference between face-to-face and online meeting forms is that neither time nor place are shared and that professional communication is mediated by the media. However, this has consequences for social interaction, for reflection processes and for language behavior.

This is also what Ribbers and Waringa (2015) refer to when they point out that in social interactions there is a common language and mutual agreement about the meaning of words that creates a shared reality. In this context, they remind us of George Orwell, who in his book "1984" describes how a totalitarian state, through the systematic limitation of allowed words, increasingly limits its citizens in their ability to express personal thoughts, ideas and feelings. In their opinion, the opposite is the goal of coaching, namely to help clients express their thoughts, feelings and insights. The Internet offers opportunities for this that it has never had before in human history. Ribbers and Waringa (2015) point out that writing-based communication in professional relationships does not go hand in hand with a supposed reduction of possibilities, but with a helpful concentration on content. This will be discussed later (Sec. 7.3).

3.2 Telematics and its Risks

Heinz Thiery (2014) speaks of telematics and thus means the change in communication through electronic media in its societal effects. This also includes the total communicative de-limitation by means of mobile communication, which is propagated by the telecommunications industry with the advertising slogan 'anywhere-anytime-anyone' (Döring, 2007, p. 299).

According to Thiery (2014), this influences the entire communication behavior, also offline. He speaks of the emergence of a telematic culture, characterized by other forms of relationship initiation.

Being online means referring to oneself, being there, solidifying with others or breaking through loneliness. In addition, identity concepts are redefined.

Thus, digitization not only changes communication behavior, but also has an impact on thinking and perception.

This results in the following basic question:

- Does digitization intensify the isolation, the self-centeredness of the postmodern human being, thus the egocentrism, and
- does it prevent the encounter that serves self-discovery and development?

Kühne and Hinterberger (2009) also describe the concerns and skepticism that arise from the use of computer-mediated counseling services with the following topics:

- Emotional impoverishment in counseling contact up to relationship impairment
- Indeterminacy due to the high anonymizability
- Fast food counseling that quickly satisfies hunger without satiating
- Protection through distance, avoidance of intensive communication

The following questions are also often asked:

- How can the lack of sensory stimuli be compensated for?
- How are emotions transported without sensory presence?
- What are the possibilities and limits of computer-mediated communication?
- How can the professionalism of the procedure be guaranteed?

A working group of CAI®certified online coaches [1]evaluated their experiences with the reservations of coaches and coachees towards online coaching in a workshop in April 2015 and came to the following collection of arguments (unpublished photo protocol):

- Uncertainty regarding the data (Who can see them? Can they be deleted?)
- The expectation of "strokes" cannot be met
- Loss of perceptual levels
- Technical dependence
- Challenge of the combination of technology + network security + professional approach
- Low trust
- Technical thresholds
- Positive and negative disinhibition by invisibility, anonymity and asynchrony

---

1 CAI®certified online coaches have completed the additional qualification in online coaching offered by CAI®World (▶ www.cai-world.com).

In order to continue to explore how, despite these concerns, professional accompaniment can be designed that is based on a respectful and empathic relationship, the following studies will be used that deal with the effect of online applications in therapy, coaching or counseling and partly make comparisons between online and face-to-face applications.

3.3 Studies on Interventions on the Internet in Therapy, Coaching and Counseling

The increase in the use of the Internet in general has also led to an increase in the use of the Internet for health-related and psychosocial issues over the past 20 years, as Reindl (2015) explains. In the German-speaking world, Reindl cites figures between 60 and 80%. Eichenberg & Ott refer to 80% of US Internet users in 2006 (Eichenberg & Ott, 2011). Accordingly, the number of therapeutic services has increased, so that they are even on the rise in Germany despite the ban on distance treatment and are part of the standard range of therapeutic care in other countries (e.g. Netherlands, Sweden) (Reindl, 2015, p. 57). Trepte et al. (2008) point out that online therapy is a widespread phenomenon in the USA, the effectiveness of which has been demonstrated in many studies. The key here is to establish a solid working relationship despite the spatial separation.

Andersson and Cuijpers (2009) carried out a meta-analysis of 12 studies on the treatment of depression involving a total of 2446 participants. Ten of the 12 studies related to therapeutic interventions via the Internet, two studies related to purely computer-mediated treatment. There was a clear superiority of the therapist-supported approaches via the Internet over the purely computer-mediated approaches.

Eichenberg and Ott (2011) found in their review of 89 controlled evaluation studies of Internet-based intervention programs (IBI) that positive efficacy evidence exists for anxiety disorders, eating disorders and substance-related disorders. The effects were less pronounced in depression and obesity. Most of the studies (73.3%) were based on cognitive-behavioral and behavioral therapy programs that used manuals, e.g. for cognitive restructuring, or were problem-solving, self-management and attention training programs. The information sections were supplemented with exercises and partly with an interactive quiz. If contacts were made with therapists, they were very minimal and consisted of weekly, short emails during the duration of the program. These contacts reduced the drop-out rate.

Wagner from the Medical School Berlin confirms positive effects in the online treatment of depressions. The 62 participants were divided into two groups equally. One group took part in an internet-based therapy program and in the other group the therapy took place in the face-to-face setting. In both cases, cognitive behavioral therapy was used over a period of eight weeks. The results showed the same good success in both groups. In contrast to the results of the face-to-face therapy, the online therapy was more stable in the long term (Wagner et al., 2014).

Ribbers and Waringa (2015) also point out that there are many studies that prove the effectiveness of online therapy, e.g. in the case of depressions, anxiety disorders, traumas, but also in the case of asthma or hypertension.

Although there are no generally binding quality standards for internet-based advice, it is attributed to a high performance in problem solving, empathetic understanding of the advisers and effective support according to Reindl (2015).

This list shows that online coaching can be based on a scientific foundation, but that a systematization of the definitions of terms, the formats or the success factors is still outstanding. An approach is made through the clarification of terms (▶ Chap. 5) and success factors in coaching and online coaching (▶ Chap. 7), as well as the definition of quality (▶ Chap. 11) in the following explanations. First, the term coaching will be dealt with in general and the historical development of coaching in order to be able to place online coaching in the development dynamics of the coaching field.

Coaching and Its Development

Contents

E. Berninger-Schäfer, *Online Coaching*,
https://doi.org/10.1007/978-3-658-39133-1_4

4.1 Coaching Concept and Practice Fields

Coaching is usually described as a consulting format, with "consulting" being considered as an overarching category (Aksu & Graf, 2011).

In contrast to organizational or expert consulting, coaching is often understood as an accompanying, person-centered approach. The pure process-accompanying approach is questioned by some authors, e.g. Böning (2014), Dehner (2009) or Schreyögg (2015). Böning, for example, clearly differentiates between different target groups and, in particular, for coaching in top management, highlights the importance of input and advice from the coaches. Online coaching offers a refreshingly charming solution to this debate, in that input parts can be provided in document form and uploaded to a virtual space, while coaches can remain in a purely process-accompanying role.

Coaching is offered by different disciplines in different areas for different target groups, which poses great challenges for the categorization, concept formation and research of coaching. Fritze et al. (2014) question whether this is more of a fashion or marketing term or a format that refers to an identifiable theoretical construct with derived methodological approaches. The authors explain that coaching is about a "success in action" primarily in the professional field. What this means in detail is determined by the respective context, e.g. when it comes to professional performance, sporting performance, leadership or personal health. Depending on the industry, target group and topic, different practice fields emerge, raising the question of the cross-practice core characteristics of coaching.

Schermuly and Graßmann (2015) list several aspects that they have found in most coaching definitions. These include:

- Reference to the work context for executives or business coaching
- Coaching as an interaction between a professional coach and a coachee
- Coaching is not for the treatment of clinical issues and mental disorders
- Coaching is for the development of options or competencies
- Coaching is for the development of personality
- Improving the satisfaction and performance of individuals and thus the performance of organizations
- The achievement of coaching goals according to Greif (2008) by systematic promotion of results-oriented self-reflection
- So-called life coaching refers to the whole life

Schermuly et al. (2014) found the following ranking of the most common coaching topics in their survey of German coaches:

1. Accompaniment in times of change
2. Personality development
3. Reflection on one's own professional role
4. Leadership style
5. Career development
6. Personal motivation
7. Interpersonal problems with superiors
8. Taking on a leadership position
9. Problems with self-worth

The authors relate these topics to phases of personal and organizational change.

In the simplest description, a coaching process is about designing a change from an undesired current state to a desired future state, which is accompanied by resource activation, potential development, and self-efficacy. So it is about a change of experience and behavior. So coaching is a psychological change accompaniment with references to the change-relevant contexts (organizations, industries, professions, roles, lifestyles, cultures, etc.).

The definition or description of coaching this book can be described as follows:

- **Coaching**

Coaching serves the reflection of topics and the clarification of change concerns, in order to find self-congruent goals in a systematic, structured accompaniment process, to activate resources and to plan and implement measures for goal achievement with the greatest possible transfer probability.

The division of coaching into different fields of practice, e.g. business coaching, health coaching or life coaching, and the coaching topics prevailing therein, as well as the formats in which coaching is carried out, are subject to permanent change. In order to classify online coaching, the previous development phases in coaching will therefore be presented first.

4.2 Development Phases in Coaching

Drath describes the historical development of coaching in his book "Coaching and its Roots", which was published in 2012. In it, he speaks of godfathers, ancestors and pioneers, of different psychological schools and integrative approaches since the beginning of coaching to the present day. In 2005, Böning and Fritschle already presented the development of coaching in the FRG from its origin to its intensive professionalization in seven phases.

Here a short overview of the individual phases of the development of coaching should be given, first as they can be found with Böning and Fritschle (2005) and Birgmeier (2011). Based on the explanations of Drath (2012) and Groß and Stephan (2015), the list is supplemented by one more phase (phase 10).

Böning and Fritschle have outlined 6 development phases of coaching (◘ Table 4.1).

Birgmeier (2011) continues the list by defining a 7th, 8th and 9th phase, which are supplemented here in part by own descriptions (◘ Table 4.2).

Birgmeier himself describes the transition from coaching research to coaching science as phase 10 and coaching ethics as phase 11, which in turn would have a reinforcing effect on phase 7, professionalization in coaching.

Further development stages result from market research. Drath (2012) predicts further segmentation of the market, whereby, according to his explanations, the service "coaching" will differ more and more within the individual market segments.

In their studies of the coaching market, Gross and Stephan (2015) also come to the conclusion that the future of coaching will be characterized by differentiation, e.g. through new formats with new media and overall through different offers.

4

Table 4.1 The first six development phases of coaching since the mid-1970s. (Based on Böning & Fritschle, 2005, p. 31)

Phase	Time period	Name	Topic
1	70s to mid-80s in the USA	The origin	Development-oriented leadership by superiors
2	Mid-1980s in USA	The extension	Career-related support
3	Mid-1980s in West Germany	The "kick"	Individual support of top managers by external consultants
4	End of the 80s in the FRG	The systematic personnel development	Internal consultation of executives of the lower and middle level
5	Beginning of the 90s	The differentiation	Group/team/project coaching, etc.
6	Middle/end of the 90s	Populism	"Everyone" consultant becomes a coach Expansion to all possible topics

Table 4.2 Development phases in coaching based on Birgmeier (2011) with own additions

Phase	Time period	Name	Topic
7	2000s	Deepened professionalization	Target group-specific and methodologically differentiated applications, quality definitions, standardization of training, association foundation, intensification of research, congresses, conferences, younger coaches taking over
8	Middle/end of the 2000s	"Professionalization" criticism	Lack of transparency of the market, "container concept", "charlatan problem"
9	End of 2000s to present	Coaching research Coaching science Ethics	Dialogue between different academic disciplines and approaches, between practice and research Academization of coaching First German-language scientific coaching journal "Coaching | Theory & Practice" since 2015

Based on the described situation and the explanations of Drath (2012) as well as of Groß and Stephan (2015), the next stage of coaching development (if stages 9, 10 and 11 of Birgmeier are summarized as coaching research, coaching science and ethics of coaching) would be phase 10 of coaching development "Digital coaching and online professionalism" (Table 4.3).

In the context, the development of coaching can be described in 10 phases over a period of 50 years (Table 4.4).

Table 4.3 The phase 10 of coaching development

Phase	Time period	Name	Topic
10	End of 2010s to 2020s	Digital coaching Online professionalism	Coaching through modern media Platforms and online tools Format extension Differentiation of topics, settings, target groups Quality dialogues Further academisation

The differentiation of coaching formats related to the current situation of coaching development is described in more detail in ▶ Chap. 10 because it has far-reaching implications for the competence fields of professional coaches. The general development of coaching described so far goes hand in hand with further differentiation within topics and target groups in the coaching field.

4.3 Differentiation in the Coaching Field

The development shown above is embedded in an already differentiated coaching field, as Böning and Kegel (2015) describe it using the metaphors of the "tree", the "fan" and the "landscape". For this purpose, coaching topics and target groups are used as systematization criteria.

The tree metaphor described by Böning & Kegel makes clear the organic, uncontrolled growth of the coaching field, which depends on environmental conditions and develops different branches. The trunk stands for what essentially characterizes the coaching approach, the roots for the conceptual origins of coaching.

The coaching tree (Fig. 4.1) was created with the online tool "Resource Tree" from the CAI®platform [1]. The representation is based on descriptions by Böning & Kegel, but deviates from them in the following points:

1. Health coaching is not considered a special form of life coaching, but as an independent field of application. On the one hand, this has an individual aspect, e.g. in the processing of topics such as personal life and work style, stress management or life balance. Health coaching is used for behavioral prevention at the personal level. On the other hand, health coaching refers to organizational relationships, e.g. by processing topics such as healthy leadership, accompaniment in the implementation of occupational health management and the development of a health-promoting organizational culture, and is thus part of the relationship prevention. (Berninger-Schäfer, 2013).
   In this understanding, health coaching is to be located between life coaching and business coaching.

1 The online tool "Resource Tree" is part of the toolbox in the CAI ®World (▶ www.cai-wold.com).

4

Table 4.4 Overall overview: the phases of coaching development

Phase	Time period	Name	Theme
1	70s – mid 80s in USA	The origin	Development-oriented leadership by superiors
2	Mid 80s in USA	The expansion	Career-related counseling
3	Middle of the 80s in BRD	The "Kick"	Individual counseling of top managers by external consultants
4	End of the 80s in BRD	The systematic personnel development	Internal counseling of middle and lower management
5	Beginning of the 90s	Differentiation	Group/team/project coaching, etc.
6	Middle/end of the 90s	Populism	"Everyone" consultant becomes a coach Expansion to all possible topics
7	2000s	Deepened professionalization	Target group-specific and methodologically differentiated applications, quality definitions, standardization of training, association foundation, intensification of research, congresses, conferences, younger coaches taking over
8	Mid/end of the 2000s	"Professionalization" criticism	Intransparency of the market, "container term", "charlatan problem"
9	End of 2000s to present	Coaching research Coaching science Ethics	Discourse between different academic disciplines and approaches, between practice and research Academization of coaching First German-language academic coaching journal "Coaching | Theory & Practice" since 2015
10	End of 2010s to 2020s	Digital coaching Online professionalism	Coaching through modern media Platforms and online tools Format extension Differentiation of topics, settings, target groups Quality dialogues Further academization

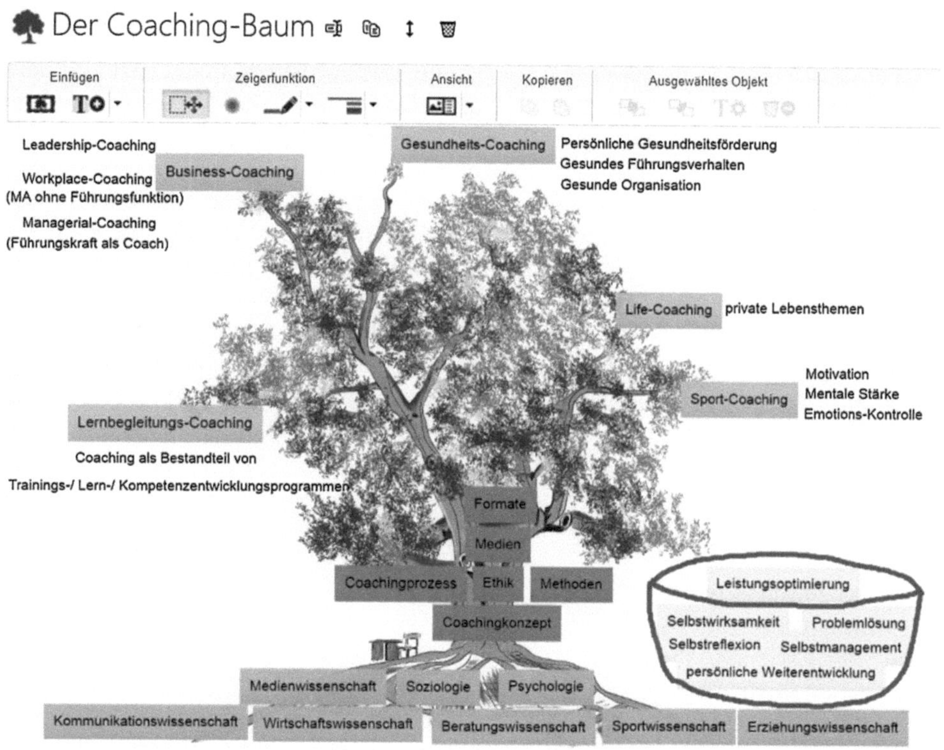

Fig. 4.1 The coaching tree, created with the tool "Resource Tree" in the CAI®World

2. Böning & Kegel speak of educational coaching and explain that this might develop as an independent field of application. Coaching is already an integral part of learning programs (trainee programs, leadership development, training) in many organizations. The increasing academization of coaching leads to students already learning coaching techniques during their studies and accompanying each other as "study coaches". Short coaching units to support learning transfer have been described, for example, by Geißler (2012). Thus, learning accompaniment coaching was included as an independent field of application (Peus et al., 2011; Berninger-Schäfer & Webers, 2010).
3. The division of application areas into business coaching and coaching in the non-profit sector certainly has well-founded historical roots. Coaching emerged in the economic context, specifically in the leadership area. In the non-profit sector, supervision was the predominant accompaniment format. This changed at the end of the 90s and the beginning of the 2000s, not least due to the coaching offers and coaching further education of the Leadership Academy Baden-Württemberg, which, among other things, specifically relate to the public sector (Arnold, 2011; Berninger-Schäfer, 2008 und 2011).
   Leadership and management techniques, change processes, marketing and employer branding, resource management and culture development are relevant in all organizations, regardless of whether they are in the profit or non-profit sector. Therefore, a distinction is made between coaching in the profit and

non-profit sector, as this is not a specific field of application, but a contextual factor that comes with certain rules, processes, values, competencies and cultures that must be taken into account in coaching and for which a coach should have field competence. Based on the "tree metaphor", these would be environmental conditions that shape the tree or setting factors (► Chap. 10).

4. Böning & Kegel describe the roots of the tree as psychology/psychotherapy, supervision, leadership training and sports, which is historically correct (see Drath, 2012; Böning & Fritschle, 2005). In the tree presented here, the roots are seen in scientific disciplines that metaphorically should "locate" and "nourish" coaching. This may still be very idealistic, but in the course of an increasingly coaching research it should form the basis for the resulting theoretical concepts and approaches in coaching. The following scientific disciplines are mentioned as examples of disciplines that deal with coaching, without claiming to be complete:
   - Psychology
   - Communication science
   - Sociology
   - Economics
   - Consulting science
   - Linguistics
   - Sports science
   - Media science
5. Böning & Kegel locate the characterization of coaching in the trunk. "The thick trunk increasingly contains genuine content, components such as self-reflection, social competence, strengthening of self-esteem, self-efficacy expectation, self-attention and work-life balance. Effective problem solving or the pursuit of performance goals also play a role" (Böning & Kegel, 2015, p. 17).
   The author and the author thus describe various consequences or results of coaching.

In the presentation chosen here, possible results of coaching are to the right of the tree, symbolized by a "harvest basket". Instead, what results from the scientific foundation of coaching is arranged in the trunk and should result. This includes the conceptual anchoring of coaching, the resulting ethical attitude of the coaches and the way in which coaching processes are controlled or which methods are used for this purpose. The implementation of concept and process takes place via different media and formats and then takes place in the respective application fields (branches).

This metaphorical representation of coaching does not yet symbolize the possible variety of formats. In ► Chap. 10 various formats are described exclusively with online examples, which make entirely new differentiations possible in the coaching field. While the explanations in ► Chap. 4relate coaching and its development to the background for the embedding of online coaching, online coaching should increasingly be placed in the center of attention in the following explanations. For this purpose, a clarification of terms (► Chap. 5) and a categorization of existing offers (► Chap. 6) will be carried out first.

The Concept of Online Coaching

Contents

E. Berninger-Schäfer, *Online Coaching*,
https://doi.org/10.1007/978-3-658-39133-1_5

5.1 Variety of Terms

While the term coaching in general is still not used uniformly (▶ Sect. 4.1), there is even greater confusion when it comes to the term online coaching and its understanding. The variety of terms with which one is confronted in this and its related fields, such as supervision, is impressive and rather represents a jungle than a differentiation. Therefore, for the derivation of the term online coaching, borrowings are made from other disciplines, in particular from online learning, as this can look back on a longer history and thus higher professionalization.

Engelhard (2013) lists the terms "internet counseling", "digital counseling", "computer-aided counseling", "e-counseling" or "online counseling" or "online supervision" for the field of supervision.

For coaching, terms such as: online coaching, e-coaching, i-coaching, cyber coaching, distance coaching, virtual coaching, digital coaching, media coaching, web coaching or remote coaching can be found in this context.

The situation represented by this variety of concepts can be described with the metaphor of the natural meadow in early spring, when it begins to sprout and grow, the most diverse plants, unordered, blooming, colorful, displacing, already dying, poisonous, healing, beautiful, smooth, rough, pleasing, wounding. Something new has begun, a colorful market of offers, partly with great packaging, partly advertised in a sensational way and still often difficult to classify. The products and procedures that serve as online coaching and equivalent terms in the broadest sense refer to coaching, a discipline that is still young itself and in need of further professionalization. On the other hand, there are quality standards, training guidelines, market observations, defined commissioning processes and evaluations, ethical norms and scientific research in the professional coaching scene. The academization of coaching is progressing by allowing coaching skills to be acquired in bachelor's and master's programs. Nevertheless, it is a relatively new profession (see Drath, 2012), which, combined with modern communication media, is already creating new formats, the professionalization of which is also in a standstill.

Therefore, a definition of terms will be given first. This will be followed by a brief overview of the existing offers in all their diversity. This reflects the situation as it is encountered by a person who is looking for meaningful offers.

5.2 Definition of Terms

Often, one of the terms listed above hides a coaching approach via telephone, chat, e-mail or video. Collaborative platforms are also used, which, for example, enable working with avatars in 3-D spaces or the use of various coaching tools (constellations, question sets, image material, etc.). This makes both synchronous and asynchronous, text-based work and also text-based work or mixed forms possible. Mixed forms also occur when online coaching is combined with face-to-face coaching, which is referred to by some authors as "blended coaching" (Geißler et al., 2013).

Seel and Ifenthaler (2009) deal with terminology that is also useful for online coaching in relation to e-learning. They justify their preference for the term online learning over e-learning because they refer to the possibilities that arise from the connection of a computer with the Internet.

» With online learning, it's all about using new multimedia and telecommunications technologies to improve learning (Seel & Ifenthaler, 2009, p. 16).

The authors describe e-learning as the use of multimedia materials and online learning as an addition to access to information and services available on the Internet, as well as communication for information exchange and collaboration in real time over spatial distances. Here, learning is supported as knowledge construction in addition to learning as retention, insofar as metacognitive strategies are developed, such as planning, evaluating, controlling and solving new tasks. Seel and Infenthaler (2009) describe the strategic and planned use of conscious learning and thinking processes as a characteristic of intelligent behaviour.

In analogy to this, the term online coaching is the designation for a computer-supported, multimedia and interactive approach in which professional coaching processes are controlled.

In contrast to online learning and online therapy, it is a non-hierarchical, non-advisory approach to self-reflection and further development that is carried out via the Internet and thus makes time and location independent (Ribbers & Waringa, 2015).

According to this understanding, online coaching corresponds to process consulting according to Schein (2003).

» Process consulting is the establishment of a relationship with the client that allows him to perceive, understand and react to the process events that occur in his internal and external environment in order to improve the situation as he defines it (Schein, 2003, p. 39).

This definition is not necessarily reflected in the offers that can be found on the market under online coaching (and its related terms). Rather, it is a collection of offers of various kinds, from pure consulting services by telephone and chat to the sending of texts or meetings in 3-D worlds. The following list therefore does not reflect professional online coaching, but the actual market situation. In the following chapters, the characteristics of professional online coaching will be worked out.

Overview of Existing Offers

Contents

E. Berninger-Schäfer, *Online Coaching*,
https://doi.org/10.1007/978-3-658-39133-1_6

Table 6.1 Internet search. (As of September 7, 2017)

Term (e)	Search engine: google	Search engine: bing
Coach	916.000.000	142.000.000
Coach Video	402.000.000	140.000.000
Coaching	332.000.000	118.000.000
Online Coach	173.000.000	197.000.000
Online Coaching	25.100.000	97.600.000
Online-Coaching	14.100.000	97.600.000
Coaching Youtube	43.200.000	69.800.000
Coaching via eMail	20.100.000	51.900.000
Coaching video	22.600.000	50.400.000
E-Coaching	27.600.000	2.030.000
Coach skype	12.300.000	24.300.000
Coaching via phone	78.4000.000	23.300.000
Coaching via skype	3.060.000	8.450.000

A complete market overview seems impossible if you look at the number of entries that can be found on the Internet under the keywords listed in Table 6.1.

In addition, online coaching, which is used synonymously with the other, above-mentioned terms, is often understood to mean telephone, email, skype, and chat, or the conduct of webinars or seminars. This would dramatically increase the number of entries.

Accordingly, there is a wide range of individual coaches, institutes and associations, up to public institutions, among the providers.

Some examples should be given here without claiming to be a comprehensive representation. Since coaching is sometimes also offered under consultation, some examples should be given first, which represent the diversity one encounters when researching. After that, a classification will be made in different stages.

6.1 Online Consultation

The portal of the umbrella association of statutory health insurance funds offers online consultation on certain topics, e.g. mobbing advice or marriage, family and life advice, in the form of e-mailing, individual chat or group chat (► www.portal-gesundheitonline.de).

The Caritas e. V. online consultation offers the opportunity to ask questions via a login, to which an answer will be given within two working days. The contact can also be continued by telephone or in person in a local Caritas advice centre. Topics are named, such as social problems, disability and mental illness, parents and family, legal guardianship and provision, debt, etc. ► http://www.caritas.de/hilfeundberatung/onlineberatung/onlineberatung.

Beranet is a platform on which service providers can carry out their advisory services. It offers mail, individual and group chat functions, document exchange, statistics and client management, as well as payment and barrier-free access. ► www.beranet.de.

Under ► www.seelsorge.net those seeking help receive assistance via email or SMS. In the 2013 annual report, an average of 150 active visitors per day were mentioned. Furthermore, it says:

> The number of requests by email increased massively, while the number of requests by SMS remained the same. In the 2013 reporting year, the Masters were able to forward an average of 4 new pastoral requests to the counsellors every day. This means that the voluntary counselling clergy answered 1200 first requests (600 in 2012). The internet ministry is therefore more popular than ever. On average, between five and six emails were exchanged per request. In individual cases, the number of emails written can be in the hundreds. The team members, at the moment there are 27 voluntary counsellors, therefore wrote several thousand emails last year, which means many days of voluntary, qualified work. An evaluation of the frequency of problem areas shows that questions and problems relating to one's own personality, relationships and partnership occur most often. Questions about the meaning of life are also common [Annual Report 2013, accessed 01.08.2016].

Young people and adults can find forums, online counselling and other information on love, friendship and sexuality at ► https://profamilia.sextra.de/.

Under ► www.liveonlinecoaching.com a seminar program on health and psychology is offered, which is carried out in the form of webinars. This program can also be found at AOK under the label AOK-LIVEONLINE.

About ► http://www.ceus-online-coaching.de/ materials can be obtained on certain topics, such as bullying, crisis management, re-entry into the workforce, money troubles, eating disorders or relationship problems, which give instructions for changing one's way of thinking and problem solving. This is done over a period of eight weeks. This approach can additionally be supported by personal coaches.

This list already gives an impression of the unsorted variety and unclear use of the term online coaching on the Internet, i.e. online coaching can mean very different things and take place at different levels of professionalism. The target groups are potential coachees or coaches who offer their services online.

What is currently also referred to as online coaching in the professional coaching scene is classified below. This classification allows for a division into four levels, which reflect an increasing level of professionalism in online coaching.

6.2 Stages Model for Classifying the Professionalism of Online Coaching

The classification of online coaching using a stages model is based on an understanding of professionalization, according to which online coaching is not simply the transfer of face-to-face coaching into virtual spaces or coaching with media-mediated communication. Professional online coaching requires knowledge of the specific success factors of online communication and accompaniment, as well as the resulting requirements for coaching behavior, coaching processes and coaching tools. Furthermore, this includes technical competence and the use of media or platforms that meet requirements for data security, quality and traceability for professional use.

From this understanding, various online requirements for professional coaching arise. These are presented in four stages and illustrated with examples (◘ Fig. 6.1).

- **Stage I:** This refers to the fact that telephony, emailing, chatting or communication via a video function are referred to as online coaching.
- **Stage II:** Here, platforms are used that offer various communication channels and even more possibilities for cooperation, but not coaching-specific.
- **Stage III:** Coaching-specific tools are used as a single tool (e.g. question set or constellation tool) or in combination, partly isolated, partly embedded in a predefined coaching process.
- **Stage IV:** This stage is reached when the various possibilities of a platform can be combined with coaching-specific tools, processes and management of the coaching activity.

6.2.1 Stage I: Medially Mediated Communication (Telephony, Video, Emailing, Chatting)

Stage I refers to the use of communication media such as emailing, chatting, forum entries, telephony, videocalling and possibly data exchange. This is simply media-mediated communication, whatever that may mean for coaching behaviour and coaching results.

▶ Examples

- On ▶ www.ecoachings.de a coaching access for 10, 20 or more days is offered. These packages always include 1 or 2 or multiple coaching hours with a coach, which are carried out via Skype, telephone or chat. In addition, a document exchange is possible, as well as the transmission of written messages, to which the coach reacts within 24 h.
- Under ▶ www.das-onlinecoaching.com a text-based coaching via Moodle is offered.
- Some online coaches work text-based via the website of the German Society for Psychosocial Online Counselling (▶ www.dg-online-beratung.de). This allows for data transmission via a secure SSL encryption.
- At ▶ http://www.bensattinger.com/online-coaching/ sessions from 1 to 60 min can be booked via Skype on the topics of fitness and nutrition.
- On the homepage of ▶ www.i-coaching.at clients can submit their topic in writing. They will receive an assessment by email as to how the topic can be processed with i-Coaching. The first request is free of charge. After a positive decision and payment, communication will take place by email.

These examples could be continued indefinitely. ◀

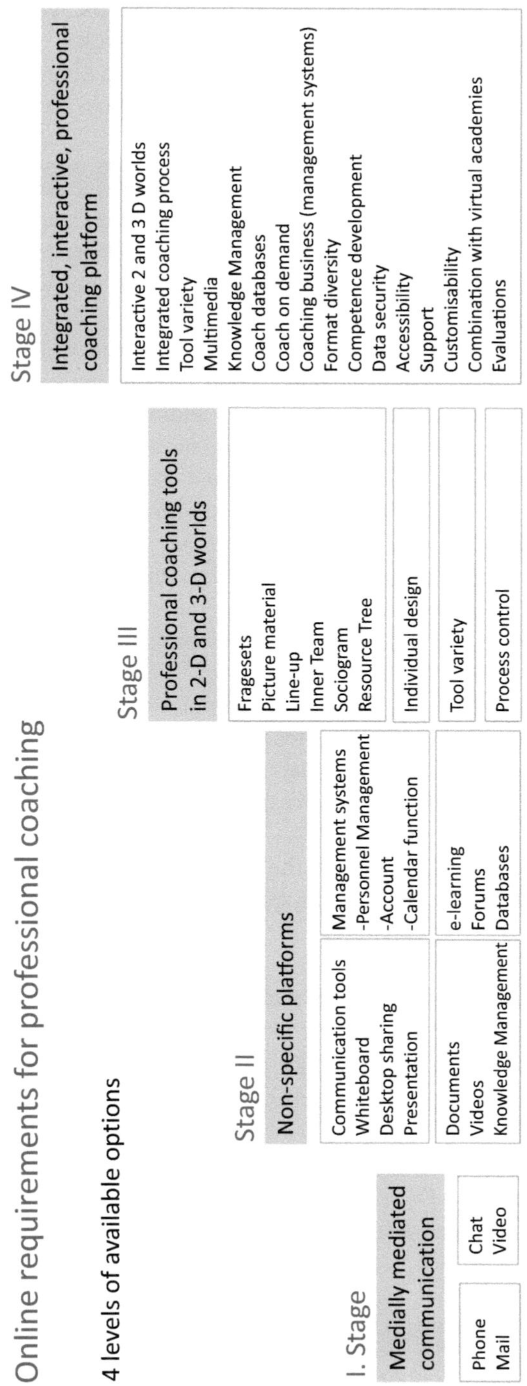

Fig. 6.1 Four stages of professionalism in online coaching. (© Berninger-Schäfer)

6.2.2 Stage II: Unspecific Platforms

In stage II, management systems are used which, for example, combine media communication with administrative, billing and calendar functions.

On these platforms, a partly written-based interaction with coachees takes place. In part, coaching tips and answers to questions (reproducible type) are provided.

6

▶ Examples

- "Jigsawbox" is a platform that allows coaches to enter their own logo, content in the form of pdf, video or audio file to pass on to individual persons or groups for self-study, as well as Paypal and written communication in individual or group setting (▶ www.jigsawbox.com).
- "Coachingcloud" is a platform with a calendar and payment function. There is the possibility to provide content (pictures, videos, etc.) to the coachees, communicate in writing and create your own branding. In addition, individual clients can choose coaches. Companies are offered a matching tool for their internal database and evaluations (▶ www.coachingcloud.com). Coaches and coachees can chat with each other.
- "Life Coach hub" is a platform from which information on various topics, such as goal achievement, time management, motivation, fitness, etc. can be purchased. Coaches can be contacted directly via a database. Online coaching takes place purely in writing (▶ www.lifecoachhub.com).
- E-learning platforms offer coaching as part of competence acquisition, for example "The LearnScape" (▶ www.thelearnscape.com).
- Other systems for client management (appointments, document sharing, goal setting, partly e-commerce) are offered, for example, by "Coach accountable" (▶ www.coachaccountable.com), "The Coaches Console" (▶ www.coachesconsole.com) or "Journal Engine" (▶ www.journalengine.com). ◀

In addition, there are now providers on the market who address coaching directly, insofar as they are developed as coaching-specific tools or platforms (stage III).

6.2.3 Stage III: Professional Tools and Process Control

Coaching professionalism only technically develops from level III onwards, when coaching-specific tools (e.g. question sets or coaching processes) are used. This phase also includes individual coaching tools which are two- or three-dimensionally mapped, or the encounter of avatars in 3-D worlds. It is possible to make a distinction here between existing 3-D worlds which are simply also used for coaching, or three-dimensional spaces, landscapes, tools and avatars which are specifically developed for coaching.

▶ Examples

- "Virtual coaching" is a tool developed by Prof. Dr. Harald Geißler, which is based in a browser and contains standardised question sets and image material. This principle applies to different coaching situations, such as needs clarification coaching, goal achievement coaching, self-coaching, etc. The coach accompanies his coachees by

telephone while they fill in the questions and thus leads the coaching process (▶ www.virtuelles-coaching.com).
- "CoachMaster" by Robert Griffiths contains a set of questions that allows a coaching process according to the Grow model. This text-based tool can also be used to support telephone or face-to-face coaching. In CoachMaster, own processes and questions can also be mapped. Therefore, Griffiths also understands the CoachMaster as a development platform (▶ www.bobgriffiths.com)
- "Ecoachpro" is a platform developed by Anne Ribbers and Alexander Waringa, in which text-based communication is carried out. In their publication published in 2015, the authors present a coaching process (ABC model, see ▶ Sect. 8.3), which they design with mails (▶ www.ecoachpro.nl, see also Ribbers & Waringa, 2015).
- The "Coaching Tools Company" sells written documents for coaching, e.g. coaching questions (▶ www.thecoachingtoolscompany.com). ◀

▪ Three-dimensional Coaching Tools

Christiane Grabow has developed the "lps cocoon" arrangement tool as interactive software for download. With symbol stones, systemic arrangements can be made in the software or on the PC during face-to-face contact (▶ http://www.lpscocoon.de).

With "CoachingSpaces", figures can be arranged on a three-dimensional surface to represent situations or inner aspects. The chat function is supplemented with a video-audio function. Participants can be invited. A small database can be used to select coaches. This tool is also offered for self-coaching (▶ www.coachingspaces.com).

With "ProReal", avatars can be placed in a landscape to which symbolic objects such as a clock, a bridge, an elephant, etc. can be added. The avatars can move and express emotions through body language, color, and size. The coach and client are connected by audio (▶ http://www.proreal.co.uk).

▪ Coaching with Avatars in 3-D Worlds

There are other providers of 3-D worlds that contain simulation spaces for various training situations in which coaching can also be carried out. However, they have not been specifically developed for coaching. Rather, it is possible to rent these spaces, as one rents office space, in order to carry out coaching there.

I myself have experience with TriCAT (▶ www.tricat.net) and Aula by vcomm solutions (▶ www.vcomm.ch). With TriCAT I was able to use geometric figures (changeable in color and size). In Aula, "avatar figures" and my coaching questions were "built in" for me.

With conventional 3-D worlds, the need for installation can be problematic, e.g. when used in companies, as company firewalls often block them.

6.2.4 Stage IV: Integrative Coaching Platform

Stage IV includes integrative platforms that combine all of the possibilities presented, show ethical conduct, quality standards and scientific evaluations, allow for data-secured procedures, provide support, and qualify coaches for online coaching. This development corresponds to the relatively short history of online coaching.

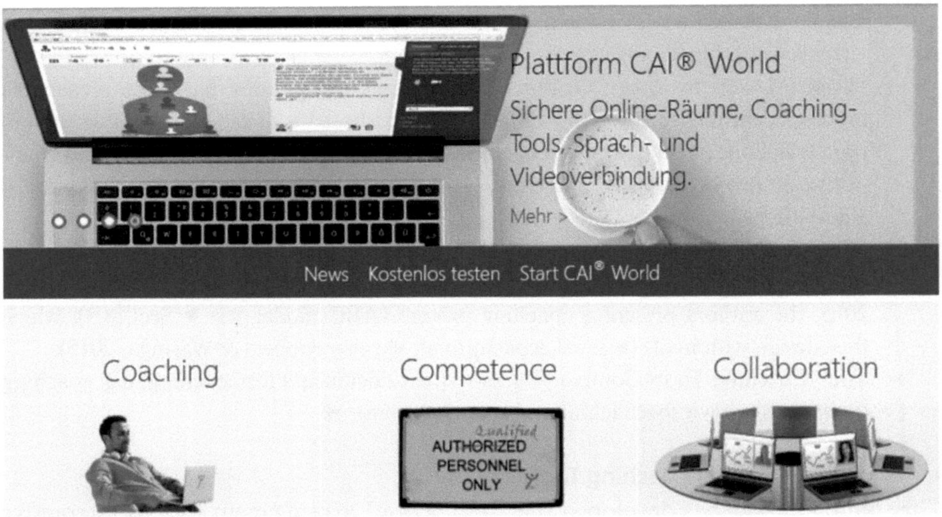

Fig. 6.2 Homepage of the CAI® platform. (© CAI GmbH)

While Prof. Dr. Harald Geißler (► www.virtuelles-coaching.com, since 2006) and Christiane Grabow (► www.lpscocoon.de, since 2008) have developed their tools as a pioneer achievement almost 10 years ago, many of the above-mentioned providers have only been on the market for a short time. This shows that a market is emerging here, which, however, in its diversity with different services, coaches the need to search, compare and take advantage of two or three offers in order to cover their own needs for professional tools, process control, client and knowledge management, networking, matching and evaluation, multimedia and data protection. This situation is unsatisfactory.

An online platform that claims to contain all the coaching-relevant features and has been set up according to professional quality standards in coaching is the CAI® World (► www.cai-world.com).

On the CAI® platform (Fig. 6.2) the CAI® World is integrated. It contains the following possibilities to carry out online coaching professionally:

- Communication via chat, audio and video,
- 2-D coaching tools, such as question sets, constellation figures, symbols and backgrounds, sociogram, inner team, image material, resource tree, whiteboard, presentation of documents
- 3-D world with avatars
- systemic solution-oriented coaching process with different coaching phases
- Individual and group settings with specific processes
- Client and session management (structured and revision-proof),
- Forum, knowledge and document pages,
- Evaluation instruments for coaching
- Competence assessments
- Skining possibilities (design of the website, own image material, configurable processes and questions, individualized content)
- Statistics and minute-precise billing options,
- Ethics guidelines

- Quality standards
- Barrier-free
- Support
- Scientific evaluation
- Training to become an online coach
- Coach database including Coach on Demand
- Availability via browser and on all devices (PCs, notebooks, tablets and smartphones)
- Multilingualism
- Self-coaching tools and apps.

The CAI® World is the subject of scientific research and is to be used as a reference platform for the following explanations of online coaching, as it allows synchronous and asynchronous work, online writing, reading, listening and watching in combination with the control of a professional coaching process and the use of corresponding tools. The continuous further development of this platform takes place in a close dialogue between practice and research. The development of competence in online coaching is described in various curricula and is carried out via the CAI® World.

The development of competence for online coaching must be based on professional coaching competence, whether as an additional qualification or as a basic qualification.

The available study material and the increasing academisation of coaching are helpful for this (Berninger-Schäfer & Webers, 2010; Strikker & Strikker, 2013).

The scientific foundation of coaching allows for verified effectiveness factors and their theoretical backgrounds to be incorporated into the competence development of coaching and online coaching. Therefore, the mechanisms of effectiveness that are empirically founded and allow statements about how coaching can be implemented in the understanding outlined above are described first. After the impact factors in online coaching are presented.

Success Factors in Coaching

Contents

E. Berninger-Schäfer, *Online Coaching*,
https://doi.org/10.1007/978-3-658-39133-1_7

The significantly increased coaching research in recent years has shown that coaching works (Theeboom et al., 2013; Geißler & Wegener, 2015; Greif, 2008; Greif et al., 2012; Greif, 2016; Grant, 2013; Künzli, 2009; Bozer & Sarros, 2012). This is often checked via a results evaluation (achievement of goals, satisfaction). The meta-analysis of the effectiveness of coaching interventions in an organizational context by Theeboom et al. (2013) should be mentioned as an example. The authors found that coaching has significant, positive effects on the following factors:

- Performance
- Well-being
- Coping behavior
- Work attitude
- Goal-oriented self-regulation.

Another result of their overview study is the finding that a larger number of sessions does not lead to better results, but rather to a stabilization of the results achieved. They explain this with the opportunity to actively test and reflect on the experiences made. This has implications for online coaching in that shorter units, especially for intensive implementation support, are also possible here.

In addition to the results evaluation, the question must also be addressed as to which criteria of a process and structure evaluation must be met in order to make qualitative statements about how these effects come about. Even if there are no uniformly accepted standards for this yet, some causal factors can be described that are empirically sound.

Effectiveness researchers in coaching, such as Greif (2008) or Künzli (2009), rely on the research of Grawe et al. (1994) and Grawe (2000), who identified nonspecific therapeutic factors in meta-analyses. His results are based on the Bern Therapy Comparison Study and the evaluation of a total of 897 studies with 2016 treatment groups (Grawe et al., 1994). The factors he identified are referred to as nonspecific because they are effective across different therapeutic schools, even though these schools have a different understanding of the role of therapists, the therapeutic approach, and the design of change processes. These nonspecific therapeutic factors are presented below and supplemented with results from coaching research.

7.1 Nonspecific Therapeutic Factors in Coaching

Grawe refers to the following perspectives as the most powerful nonspecific therapeutic factors in the therapeutic context.

■ Clarification Perspective

Clarification takes place when therapists help patients better understand their own experience and behavior, as well as their relationships with other people, to recognize their own motives and goals, and to see problems in new contexts. Grawe speaks in this context of motivational clarification, which could be identified as a highly effective variable, especially in conversation therapy.

▪ Problem-solving Perspective

Grawe emphasizes the importance of problem solving through concrete actions in everyday life, in which patients are supported in their goal-oriented implementation. The problem-solving perspective includes the implementation support by the therapists.

This includes the development of **self-efficacy** in the sense of Bandura (1977), i.e. the competence expectation to cope with the problem. The increase in self-efficacy is crucial when it comes to pursuing goals and changing behavior.

Self-efficacy is one of the best confirmed success factors in behavior therapy. With the problem-solving perspective, patients are supported in finding, implementing and mastering intrinsically motivated goals.

▪ Relationship Perspective

The design of the relationship between therapist and patient is the basis for openness and trust and, according to Grawe et al. (1994), the basis for the other perspectives and interventions to take place at all. These include:

- Intention realization
- Intention change
- Procedural activation
- Resource activation

Carl Rogers, pioneer of humanistic psychology and founder of client-centered conversation therapy, examined the behavior of psychotherapists using recordings. He then described the following three basic behaviors as decisive for the success of therapy:

1. Unconditional positive regard for clients
2. Empathy as an understanding of feelings
3. Authenticity and congruence as true presence and authentic involvement of one's own person

This attitude is fundamental for an effective relationship design and opens up a space of security and trust for patients/clients, in which they feel respected and accepted. This allows for the exploration and acceptance of one's own feelings, self-acceptance and resource activation. The consultant/therapist refrains from personal values, interpretations and explanations and does not give advice. Rather, it is this form of relationship design that causes the further development of patients/clients (Rogers, 1972).

According to Theeboom et al. (2013), it is also unspecific factors such as understanding, encouragement and listening that are better predictors of coaching success than the type of methods used. Likewise, the relationship between coaches and clients (working alliance).

The relationship begins with the first contact and is the prerequisite for a successful working relationship. This must be maintained throughout the coaching process, with appreciation and emotional support from the coach being the decisive relationship factors (Greif, 2008; Künzli & Seiger, 2011). The following quote from Edgar Schein corresponds to this:

> When I let "this stuff" pass before my eyes for the 40 years I've been practicing it, I realized that the key is contained in the word relationship. To be honest, I came to the conviction that the decisive factor in whether help takes place in interpersonal situations in which the personality of the participants, group dynamics and cultural factors play a role, is the relationship between the helper and the person, group or organization in need of help (Schein, 2003, p. 297).

Schermuly and Graßmann (2015) summarize the results of coaching research, according to which it is decisive for the relationship between coach and coachee that a coach is perceived as credible, which affects the satisfaction and performance of the coachees. Credibility, in turn, is related to the dimensions of trustworthiness and perceived expertise. The latter consists of methodological coaching competence and experience in the consulting field, that is, the field competence of the coaches.

Resource Perspective

A resource-oriented approach has the strongest positive effect on goal achievement and thus on the results of the process (Grawe, 2000). Grawe explains this as follows:

> Since the resource perspective is so important for the how of change, I have to ask myself why this perspective has been given so little attention in psychotherapy so far. ....Where does the neglect of this perspective, which is so important for therapy planning and therapy success, come from? (Grawe, 2000, p. 99).

Grawe explains this with the school-dependent and thus fixed methodological approach of the therapists and continues:

> The how of change must be determined by the conditions on the patient's side and not by the therapist's assumptions and preferences (Grawe, 2000, p. 99).

He therefore advocates orientation towards the principles of action instead of therapy methods. These effect factors were transferred to coaching, confirmed and further developed.

The biggest discrepancy here is in terms of problem updating and the role of the coach (pure process accompaniment and/or input-giving advice).

Problem Updating

The description of the problem situation activates negative emotions and directs attention to obstacles and limitations. In some schools, especially psychodynamic ones, the occupation with the personal and situational problem aspects, their interpretation and interpretation is considered to be decisive for the awareness and thus the change of the coachees.

However, according to Greif (2008), problem updating and resource activation are negatively correlated. The author refers to research by Kuhl, according to which negative affects make it more difficult for clients to cognitively explore themselves. Greif (2008) therefore speaks of affect calibration, i.e. of the need to give all the negative emotions that naturally go hand in hand with problem situations, space. This would have a relieving effect and would therefore reduce the negative affects in order to create the prerequisites for a results-oriented self-reflection, the actual goal of coaching and a condition for positive effects. This applies to both problem and self-reflection.

> When the coach guides the client through a state of reflection and analysis, the problem develops into concrete goal-oriented steps for the client to take (Greif, 2015, p. 55).

The classification of the importance of the problem analysis is very different depending on the school and reflects different paradigms.

Systemic-solution-oriented approaches assume that the problem analysis rather leads to a reinforcement of the problem patterns, since these are activated. In these concepts, the focus of attention on resources, goals and solutions is the decisive prerequisite for problem solving and behavioral change. Dealing with the problem is described as counterproductive (deShazer, 1989; Schmidt, 2004; Schmidt, 2014).

The position contrary to the analytical approaches mentioned at the beginning is expressed by Szabo as follows:

> From a solution-focused understanding of usefulness, it never makes sense to strengthen problem awareness. There is no connection whatsoever between the constructed problem and the constructed solution. Therefore it is also pointless to want to solve the problem. Instead of investing time in problem construction, a coach with a solution-focused understanding of usefulness would ask more details about solution construction (Szabo, 2015, p. 170).

The radicality of this view was somewhat softened in the differentiation of hypnotherapeutic approaches by Gunther Schmidt (2004), when he spoke of the appreciative balance between picking up and valuing clients where they are, namely in the problem pattern, and invitations to solution orientation. However, coaches can already use language interventions specifically when reflecting on and questioning the problem situation with clients, choosing words that trigger more positive connotations and thus initiate change in the problem pattern (Berninger-Schäfer, 2011; Prior, 2004). In a systemic-constructivist view, reality is constructed and co-constructed by clients and coaches in coaching. Coaches therefore have no interpretive authority over the reality experience of coachees and no better knowledge of right or wrong solutions.

▪ Solution Orientation

There is empirical evidence for the effect of solution-oriented approaches. For example, Grant (2012) was able to show that solution-focused questions have a significantly better effect on goal achievement, self-efficacy and positive affect in coaching than problem-focused questions.

The publications by Schmidt (2004, 2014) are a goldmine for research results and approaches in competence- and solution-oriented approaches. The focus is primarily on the effects of attention control on helpful experience processes that are present in every human being (potential hypothesis). Focusing on these is the task of the coaches, because this activates neural networks that allow clients to find competent, self-efficacious and goal-oriented solutions (see also the explanations of pattern and pattern state change in ► Sect. 7.2).

▪ Goal Focus

Grant (2014) examined four aspects of the coach-client relationship and their impact on coaching success in an exploratory, empirical study. These were the autonomy support of clients by coaches, the satisfaction of clients with the coach-client relationship, the extent to which this relationship approached an ideal relationship, and the goal-focused relationship design. The result of this study was that only the goal-focused relationship was a significant predictor of coaching success.

This result is corroborated by the study by Erik de Haan et al. (2016). The research team, consisting of de Haan (Ashridge Business School), Grant (University of Sidney), Burger (VU University Amsterdam) and Eriksson (Triolog, Stockholm, Sweden), interviewed 366 business coaches and 1985 clients in 22 countries between November 2011 and March 2013. The most effective variables for coaching success turned out to be the clarity of goals and tasks. This also had positive effects on the relationship between coach and coachee.

Custers and Arts (2005) showed that the unconscious activation of behavioral goals or goal states then has a motivating (in the sense of action support) effect on the participants if these states are associated with positive affect. This corresponds to the results of motivation research (Heckhausen & Heckhausen, 2010; Gigerenzer, 2007; Storch, 2005), according to which goals to be implemented must be emotionally anchored in a positive way. Reactions and action-guiding arousal patterns have their representation in neurological connections in the brain and thus associated with the whole body.

> The brain is not simply connected to the body by the neck, but brain and body form an inseparable functional unit (Hüther, 2010, p. 75).

The emotionally positive anchoring of goals seems to be an important switch in the change accompaniment of people if there is actually to be a change in behavior. Since the transfer of problem behavior into solution behavior is an explicit goal of coaching, this switch will be considered in more detail in the following chapter.

7.2 Patterns and Pattern State Changes

Neurological arousal patterns are associated with patterns of thought, experience, and behavior. These are referred to as a schema or pattern.

7.2.1 Schema

Migge (2013) refers to Jeffrey Young's schema therapy approach with his schema coaching approach. A schema represents a "conglomerate of thoughts, emotions, inner images, behavioral tendencies, and body sensations at the neuronal level …" (Migge, 2013, p. 73). A schema is a pattern that functions like a program. When it is triggered (triggered), internal processes begin that lead to external behavior. Schemata are implicit, organize what and how they are perceived, give the perception meaning, allow redundancies to be formed and new information to be sorted, represent knowledge that comes from different areas, and organize behavior.

Grawe (1994) refers to Piaget when describing schemata as basic organizational units of psychic processes that are based on interactions and develop as a result of interactions. Grawe distinguishes between the "motivational, energizing and directional component of psychic processes" and the action-controlling component, which he refers to as a plan (Grawe, 1994, p. 758). Since psychic activities are oriented in such a way that they organize perception in the sense of the schema activated at the time, references to self-organization of living systems in the concept of autopoiesis by Maturana and Varela can be made (Maturana & Varela, 2009). This also corresponds to the idea that schemata are formed, maintained and adapted by feedback processes, e.g. B. through assimilation and accommodation. They are accessed by cognition, emotion, and behavior. Since they are always also associated with neuronal activation patterns, but this was not the focus of the schema concept in earlier literature, the term pattern is used for holistically interconnected states in the following.

7.2.2 Pattern

Schreyögg (2015) also speaks of patterns when she states that coaches should ask coachees about their interpretation patterns, where their task is to expand or restructuring these (subjective, interpretive) patterns. These patterns have arisen in the course of family, cultural and subcultural socialization processes.

> These are partly firmly anchored, mostly unconscious categories of meaning that, as a stock of knowledge (cf. Bourdieu, 1987), belong to the basic equipment of every human being (Schreyögg, 2015, p. 151).

The author points out that it is particularly the early patterns that are difficult to change.

However, the term "pattern" does not only refer to knowledge and interpretation, but rather depicts a holistic state that also includes perception, thinking, emotion and behavior patterns that are mapped neuronally. A pattern in this comprehensive understanding, for example, in relation to a problem situation, means that certain thoughts (e.g. thoughts about the problem, searching, hopeless thoughts), certain emotions (e.g. helplessness, powerlessness, anger, anger, sadness), certain physical reactions (e.g. tension, slack posture, clenched teeth), fantasies and inner images (e.g. failure scenarios, threatening images, aggressive scenes) and matching behavior (e.g. authoritarian appearance, loud speaking, silence, withdrawal, escalation) go hand in hand. If someone is in a resourceful state in which solutions are possible, for example, clarifying and/or hopeful thoughts predominate, as well as relaxed or joyful emotions, as well as inner images and fantasies that are associated with solution scenarios. The corresponding physical reactions could, for example, be a straight posture, a smile or a spirited movement. The behavior associated with it could be shown in a appreciative and humorous conversation, in de-escalation or in a generally constructive and proactive approach.

7.2.3 Pattern States

When a certain neural network, a neural pattern is activated, thoughts, feelings, body reactions and behavior are connected to each other in a very specific way. This creates a holistic experience, hence the term pattern state.

The emotional evaluation of sensory information plays a decisive role in the formation of different pattern states. It is located in the limbic system, an older, unconscious part of the brain and, according to Damasio (1997) or Roth (2003), it functions according to the principle of "positive"/"negative" or "good"/"bad" or "approach"/"avoid". Basically, it is about creating physical well-being, which the organism is designed for. The feelings that are triggered via the limbic system have a warning function or a motivational function and are thus decisive for behavior control (Storch & Krause, 2007). The forwarding and networking of information within the organism takes place chemically via the bloodstream and electrochemically via the nerve cells. Thus, changes in the organism's state are always holistic changes in which feelings, thoughts and physical reactions are interrelated (Storch et al., 2011).

> The human brain and the rest of the body form an indissoluble organism, integrated by mutually interacting biochemical and neural feedback loops, including the hormone, immune and autonomic nervous systems. The organism as a whole is in interaction with its environment, in a process that is determined neither by the body alone nor by the brain alone (Damasio, 1997, p. 18).

7.2.4 Somatic Markers

Damasio uses the term somatic markers for the evaluation of a person's experiences. They refer to physical signals and feelings, where feelings also have a physical counterpart. They are considered decisive switches in the motivational process (see motivation and decision research, for example, by Heckhausen & Heckhausen, 2010; Gigerenzer, 2007; Storch & Krause, 2007; Grawe, 1994; Damasio, 1997). If the transition from desire (need, motivation) to intention (willingness) takes place, this happens through weighing and search processes. Somatic markers provide information about whether positive or negative evaluations are triggered in the emotional memory. They are thus decisive sources of information about whether an intention will lead to goal-oriented action. This means that goals must be developed from an emotionally positive state in order to actually be implemented. Goal formulations that begin with "maybe I should …," "it would be reasonable if I …," or "one could …," initially have no high implementation probability, as they arise cognitively. Only the emotionally positive marking goes hand in hand with intrinsic motivation and is decisive for the implementation of action and in the context of coaching for problem solving. This means that clients must come from a naturally negative problem state into a positive state of mind before implementation goals are defined. A problem pattern must be transferred to a solution pattern. A holistic pattern state change takes place.

7.2.5 Influencing Pattern States

A pattern state associated with certain experience qualities and their subjective evaluation thus consists of voluntary and involuntary events. Pattern states are produced, influenced and changed through attention processes.

This is what Gunther Schmidt (2014) has to say about it:

> The entire everyday life, even in the waking state, can be described as a permanently fluctuating and synchronously oscillating between more voluntary and more involuntary focus. Most people organize this in everyday life so that the conscious focus is often quite separated from the unconscious (which is then called unconscious), which only becomes a problem when these two levels act completely contrary to each other and interfere with each other (e.g. as with symptoms) (Schmidt, 2014, p. 40).

With targeted attention and focus, it is therefore possible to influence patterns. It is therefore the task of the coaches to specifically focus the attention on goal-oriented experience areas. Their behavior triggers associations for topics and experience processes that are comparable to indirect hypnotic induction, as is done in Erickson's hypnotherapy (Schmidt, 2014).

In her master's thesis at the Karlsruhe Institute of Technology (KIT), Carmen Wolf examined the physiological changes that accompany coaching interventions designed to bring a client from a problem to a solution state. It was to be found out whether the change in intended state pattern intended with the interventions carried out went hand in hand with changed physiological values. Various measuring instruments were used, such as the Multidimensional Mood Scale (MDBF) (pre- and post), further questionnaire instruments for the expectation of coaching (pre) and experienced change through coaching (post), behavior observation with a standardized observation sheet and video recordings. Physiological values for respiration, heart rate and electrodermal activity were recorded during coaching. This made it possible to derive a baseline before, during and after coaching or before, during and after certain interventions. The coach marked the interventions she made to change the state pattern with a previously agreed sign (stroking the hair over the ear), which was clearly visible in the video and thus made it possible to easily mark this time. Changes after interventions to change the state pattern could be seen particularly in the heart rate and electrodermal activity. In some cases there was an increase and in some cases a decrease in the values around the intervention to change the state pattern compared to the baseline of the clients. Some clients reacted to the change in state pattern with energization and activation, and some with relaxation and calming. What is a beneficial state pattern is therefore very different from individual to individual. In any case, the different physiological expression of different states (problem and solution states) could be physiologically traced back and associated with a specific intervention to change the state pattern (Berninger-Schäfer & Wolf, 2011).

Overall, it can be concluded that the empirically supported success factors in coaching include the design of a respectful, trusting and emotionally supportive relationship, the clarification of motivation, the activation of resources, the development of goals from a positive state pattern, and the problem-solving and action-oriented as well as the strengthening of self-efficacy.

From these effective factors, those steps of a coaching process can be derived which lead to a successful, results-oriented implementation of planned change measures. They are transferred into a phase sequence of a coaching process according to the concept of the "Karlsruhe School" in ▶ Chap. 8. However, before that, the effective factors in coaching so far described are supplemented by the specific effective factors in online coaching. Both together are important for the development of competence in online coaching (► Chap. 9).

7.3 Specific Effective Factors in Online Coaching

As described in ► Sect. 3.3. there are already some studies on interventions in the Internet in therapy, coaching and counseling. In the following, those effective factors of professional online applications are described which are mentioned several times.

7.3.1 Self-revelation

A frequently described characteristic of the media-based encounter is the greater self-revelation of the actors (Brunner, 2009). A paradoxical situation of proximity through distance arises, similar to the phenomenon described as "talk to a stranger" in the literature and often illustrated with the example of train passengers who do not know each other, but exchange deeply personal topics because they remain unknown and will get out again (Knatz, 2009; Brunner, 2009).

Six et al. (2007) describe channel reduction and filter theories. These are based on channel reduction (lack of expression on the non- and paraverbal level) with the reduction of social cues. They also name increased openness and honesty as positive effects of channel reduction, which Schütz and Rentzsch (2007) also explain as a phenomenon of self-disclosure. This refers to the disclosure of personal information, which occurs more frequently in computer-mediated communication. With visual anonymity, this self-disclosure is perceived as relatively risk-free and takes place quickly. The feeling of intimacy arises. The authors describe a study by Joinson (2001), according to which, in contrast to the control group, a project manager was described with many personal information (name, photo, CV, pets, etc.). In the experimental group, the test persons disclosed significantly more personal information than in the control group. The authors interpret this as a reciprocal process, according to which social interaction rules of direct communication are transferred to computer-mediated communication. If someone discloses something about themselves, then they can also be entrusted with information.

The willingness to self-disclosure is also explained by Schütz and Rentzsch (2007) that, due to the physical distance and visual anonymity, fewer negative feedback is expected. Status differences also play less of a role, as sociodemographic cues, such as clothing, are eliminated. The same applies to visible stigmata, such as overweight or disability.

Döring (2007) also points out that psychological contact barriers of certain groups of people can be compensated, which is rated very positively by the participants.

Self-disclosure has an effect on self-attention (focusing on one's own person), which is supported by this, as will be discussed in the next chapter.

7.3.2 Control, Self-reflection and Awareness of Identity

As an example of the compensation of limitations that exist in computer-mediated communication, Six et al (2007) mention the theory of hyperpersonal perspective by Walther (2002), according to which the control of what someone discloses about themselves, i.e. how self-presentation is designed, favors self-reflection.

The authors state in relation to SIDE (Social Identity Model of Deindividuation Effects) that in the case of chosen anonymity.

> personal or social identity becomes more conscious and possibly more salient than in face-to-face communication. This can lead to effects on self-attention, group polarization and stereotyping (Six et al., 2007, p. 43–44).

Boos and Jonas (2008) also refer to the SIDE model and the model of social identity. Social identity is characterized by belonging to groups, personal identity by individual properties. In computer-mediated communication, which allows anonymity, deindividuation takes place because the counterpart is not perceived as individualized. In groups this means that the group members perceive themselves more as a unit due to the assumed similarity and evaluate the communication partners more positively. This is particularly important to consider in online group coaching (▶ Sect. 10.4.1).

Reindl et al. (2016) also refer to the positive effect of the experienced higher control in online supervision.

In online applications, more self-control is also possible if, for example, people can decide when visibility or audibility is allowed, how long someone wants to be online, when and in what form (synchronous or asynchronous) or which tools are used. In this way, the feeling of control is also strengthened.

7.3.3 Relationship Formation and Emotional Closeness

Boos and Jonas (2008) also build on the aforementioned theory of Walther's hyperpersonal perspective and explain:

> According to this empirically well-documented approach, relationships of the same intensity and quality can develop on the Internet as face-to-face (Boos & Jonas, 2008, p. 214).

A frequently expressed question or concern in relation to online coaching relates to the elimination of physical signals that provide information about emotions and can thus provide valuable clues for relationship formation. Brunner (2009) writes on this:

> Even if the body is not on the net, the communication via the net affects the corporeality of the persons involved. Texts can, like online consultants who are confronted with very intense texts, confirm, annoy, touch, frighten, confuse, make laugh, create trust, generate understanding, produce knowledge, express experiences, cause love and also excite, as the phenomenon of cybersex shows (Brunner, 2009, p. 43).

Even if these feelings are conveyed through media communication channels,

> they do not take place on the net, but are experiences and states of the users (Brunner, 2009, p. 43).

The quality of the relationship (working alliance) is characterized by the emotional bond between coaches and clients and the resulting agreement of the clients with the coaches' approach (trust). Gieselmann and Pietrowsky (2016) quote studies that came to contradictory results. In part, the relationship between clients and counselors was compared in the face-to-face variant with the online variant as better, worse or described as the same. At least it was found in both variants.

Döring (2007) describes that the emotional proximity between communication partners who meet media can even increase. She explains this effect by the fact that

> that in copresence and multimodal perception, the counterpart is often taken for granted, while in absence it becomes the subject of intensified attention, perception, imagination and longing ("Romeo-Julia-Effect"; Döring, 2007, p. 306).

The lack of visual and auditory stimuli leaves room for construction processes.

In their study, Gieselmann and Pietrowsky (2016) examined the differences between chat communication and face-to-face interventions with regard to self-revelation and how the companions are perceived (as one aspect of relationship management). This was a randomized procrastination study in which 51 students participated until post-testing (one week after the intervention). One part received a face-to-face session of about 1.5 h and the other part was accompanied by chat in about 2.5 h. The interventions were carried out by the same companions (psychology students shortly before completing their master's degree in clinical psychology) according to the same process. The participants were given written material and an exploration, resource activation, goal formulation and behavior planning took place.

In both approaches, there was a significant reduction in procrastination, anxiety and uncertainty of the participants, a moderate reduction in aversion to study and also a, albeit smaller, reduction in depression symptoms. In these values, the face-to-face and the chat group did not differ. The conversations from the face-to-face setting were transcribed and analyzed in the same way as the chat protocols using LIWC (Linguistic Inquiry Word Count). In the chat group, self-disclosure was higher, as measured by the results of LIWC, which relate to the choice of actually used words, but not as measured by the self-assessment of the participants. The authors interpret this result as meaning that self-disclosure took place implicitly in the chat and therefore could not be reported. These participants were dependent on expressing their thoughts and feelings, which can also happen non-verbally in the face-to-face setting.

In the chat group, a clear connection could be established between self-disclosure and result.

The working relationship was equally good in both settings. However, the chat consultants were rated as stricter and less attractive.

In both the face-to-face and the online setting, there was a connection between achievement of results and the assessment of the consultant as humorous and attractive.

The clearest connection was between trustworthiness and result (symptom reduction), more in the chat group than in the face-to-face group.

In summary, this study points to the high importance of self-disclosure and the trustworthiness of the consultant as success factors in a successful online accompaniment.

7.3.4 Self-reflection

Poepsel conducted a study on the effectiveness measurement of an online evidence-based coaching program with regard to goal achievement, subjective well-being and hope (Poepsel, 2011) as part of his dissertation. This was a randomized controlled group design (experimental and waiting group) with post-tests. The eight-week intervention phase included structured exercises and open discussions. A professional coach controlled the proceedings. The participants had contact with the coach and with each other. The coach reinforced positive attitudes and behaviors, invited self-exploration, promoted a sense of responsibility and assertiveness, and reframed unfavorable attitudes. He promoted trust in the group, for example, by valuing personalization of participants (photo, short self-description). Significant differences could be shown for goal achievement and an increase in well-being, but not for hope.

The author interprets the effect of the online approach as supportive in that writing in the discussion forums triggered self-reflection processes. He refers to studies according to which written expression strengthens self-regulation and thus mental and physical health. Other effective variables were the exchange in the group with cathartic effect and the mutual support of the group members.

7.3.5 Transfer Support

A key success factor in coaching is the transfer security. It is gaining more and more attention, not least because of the online possibilities. The impact of a close transfer support by coaches on the coaching success describes Geißler (2011), Greif and Benning-Rohnke (2015) as well as Ribbers and Waringa (2015).

The transfer refers to the actual implementation of the goals and measures planned in coaching. Short contact periods between coaches and clients can clarify the status of implementation of the agreed measures, direct attention to it and support in case of emerging problems. These problems can lie in context variables that were not considered at first, in new situational challenges or in an insufficient fit of the goals or measures. While without the transfer support the clients might lose their implementation motivation in case of obstacles, the short-term adaptation of the goals and measures to the clients' real situations can be the basis for a successful achievement of the goals. Transfer coaching is described in detail in ▶ Sect. 10.4.4.

Coaching in 3-D worlds also promotes coaching transfer, as "trial and error" can take place in situations that can be modeled after the external or internal reality of the client. The inner reality refers to imaginations and emotions that can be represented with mood-related features in the 3-D world (e.g. by weather, light, landscape, symbols, etc.). The encounter in 3-D worlds challenges and strengthens the action orientation in coaching. This means that the 3-D world must be equipped so that coaching-relevant actions can also be carried out, which will also be addressed in the following chapter.

7.4 Specific Success Factors When Coaching with Avatars in 3-D Worlds

While in the world of gaming the use of avatars in 3-D environments is familiar, examples of professional approaches in 3-D environments are still rare in comparison to other formats of online communication.

Therefore, avatar research is still most closely associated with computer game studies, which are developing into their own branch of research that is multi-perspective, integrative, and internationally oriented. Here, as with coaching in general, various disciplines meet, such as media effects research, psychology, pedagogy, sociology, literary, film, and theater studies, communication and social sciences, ludology (rule-based game) and narratology (narrative structure of the game).

According to Pietschmann, the following factors are identified in the effect of computer games (Pietschmann, 2009, p. 39):

- Narrative aspects such as fantasy, suspense, and curiosity
- Self-efficacy (e.g. through competence acquisition)
- User experience, such as flow, immersion, and presence.

The following focuses on those factors that are specific to approaches in 3-D environments and also affect coaching in 3-D environments.

7.4.1 Presence

The presence research deals with the differences between the experience of virtual and real environments.

The term presence was coined by Steuer and describes the feeling of being present in an environment during media reception (Pietschmann, 2009). Presence can be divided into further subcategories.

- **Spatial Presence** refers to the illusion of being physically present in a space
- **Social Presence** is the feeling of being together with one or more people mediated by media
- **Self-Presence** is present when one's own representation is perceived in the virtual environment as if it were the real self (based on Tamborini and Skalski, quoted according to Pietschmann, 2009, p. 45).

Self-perception is formed according to Biocca and Harms (2002) from the sum of the real environment, the media and the imaginary.

The Stanford Virtual Human Interaction Lab, headed by Jeremy Bailenson, is also concerned with the impact of experiences in the virtual world on behavior in the real world. A study on this was carried out by Sun Joo Ahn in her dissertation. She showed that the experience of sawing a tree in a virtual world led to a greater awareness of the environment (lower consumption of paper towels) in the test subjects than if they had only read about deforestation (Ahn et al., 2014).

7.4.2 Immersion

Immersion is partly considered as an objective characteristic of a medial world, partly as a psychological state. With immersion, the feeling of immersion in a virtual world is described. This in turn depends on how strong the impression is that one is a real part of the virtual world. This feeling of being embedded is facilitated if continuous stimuli are offered that make subjective experiences possible (Pietschmann, 2009; Lehenbauer & Stetina, 2009). Interactivity and liveliness arise when several sense channels are activated by the medium at the same time. This is much easier to achieve in a 3-D world than with reduced-channel communication media, such as pure telephone or chat coaching. On the other hand, this world is also more vulnerable, insofar as it depends on the reliability and speed of the stimuli that represent a reaction to input.

Rosenberg, Baughman and Bailenson (2013) examined the effect of experiences in a virtual world on prosocial behavior in reality. They found that activity in virtual space, compared to a more passive stay in a 3-D world, allowed for a stronger feeling of immersion and led to more pronounced changes in behavior.

7.4.3 Involvement

Immersion is one aspect of involvement, which refers to the extent of self-involvement. It has motivational, as well as activity and attention components.

Involvement and immersion strengthen the extent of actual experience. Involvement is influenced by the content.

Weger and Loughnam (2013) were able to show that the insensitivity to one's own pain increased by an average of 18% by empathizing with an avatar in a virtual world. This can be considered as a phenomenon of involvement.

In coaching, involvement is given to the extent that clients themselves determine the content and this is strongly emotionally charged, as it is usually about problematic or conflictual situations for which a solution is sought. On the other hand, online coaches work specifically with emotions to develop congruent goals and appropriate solutions, which also promotes involvement.

7.4.4 Avatar Design

The avatar stands as a representative of one's own person. Avatars are familiar to many users from the gaming world and thus stand for both escapism and the ability to symbolize. In particular, children train the ability to stage symbols and role-plays, to live in imaginary worlds with imaginary companions and to express themselves, to compensate and to develop further. This fantasy activity is considered to be a link between inner and outer reality (Bredl & Bräutigam, 2012). When coaching with avatars, it is also about using the 3-D world as a place of development, of fantasized coping and of staging. Acting with avatars should be a link between the problem situation in real life and the future solution situation.

When choosing and designing avatars, the external appearance, character traits and abilities can partly be determined by the users. In their research project, Trepte and Reinecke (2013) investigate psychological processes that underlie the design of avatars. So far, correlations have been investigated between the gender of the users and the design of the avatars. The test persons of the study by Trepte & Reinecke designed their avatar according to their own gender and according to the gender role stereotypes required in the game.

Personalized avatars have an influence on the movement and eating behavior. In a dissertation at the Standford Virtual Human Interaktion Lab it could be proven that people who see an avatar with their own face on the treadmill subsequently exercise on average one hour more than people who see an avatar running that does not match them. A similar effect could also be observed on eating behavior (Blackman, 2010).

In a qualitative research survey, Nicole Steils (2013) has identified a typology of five avatar groups in virtual learning environments:

- Dislocated avatars
- Representative avatars
- Avatars as games and tools
- Avatars as extensions of the self
- Avatars as identity extensions

They represent different ways of constructing identity.

The question arises as to the interactions of identity in the virtual world and the real world.

Those who can design their own avatar experience it holistically. This is also supported by the results of a study conducted at the University of Michigan by Sangseok You. The participants (N = 121) were divided into four groups. Two groups were able to design their own avatar (e.g. by choosing gender, clothing, hairstyle) and two groups were already assigned designed avatars. All participants should climb three mountains in a virtual world and then assess how steep and how high they were. In the groups with the self-designed avatars, half of the participants were given a backpack and half were not. The same applied to the group with the foreign-designed avatars. The group that was able to create their own avatars and wore a backpack rated the mountains as significantly higher and steeper than the other three groups. So the virtual backpack changed the perception of the people if they could identify more with their avatar than other people (Vieweg, 2013).

The "embodiment" with avatars is therefore particularly helpful when action is used to enable and change experience. It is not meaningful if the setting of the face-to-face session is reproduced with avatars. This would mean that two avatars are sitting and talking to each other. Coaching with avatars in 3-D worlds is action-oriented and uses the possibilities of movement. By walking and running, specific places can be visited deliberately, e.g. threatening or beautiful landscapes, depending on whether it is a problem or solution representation. Flying allows the bird's eye view and the release (dissociation) from the problem or the problem location. The experiences made can be used directly for the further course of the coaching. 3-D worlds are particularly suitable for systemic constellations with symbols, animals, figures or other avatars. The client avatar can move around in the constellation and take different perspectives. Another special advantage is the trial action and the associated emotions, which can be used as valuable information for the coaching process. The transfer orientation of online coaching can be specifically supported in this way (Berninger-Schäfer, 2014b).

The influence of behavior in real life by experiences in 3-D worlds has implications for coaching also in so far as the ethical foundation of what happens in coaching in 3-D worlds is a basic prerequisite for the process control and avatar design, so that constructive, problem-solving behavior can result from coaching. If avatars act so strongly, their design is not arbitrary, but to be considered as an intervention tool.

The illustrated effective factors in coaching and online coaching can then unfold when they are taken into account in the control of coaching processes. However, the description of coaching processes is often very general in nature. The direct reference to empirically founded effective factors is rarely made, just as the meaningful sequence of individual phases. An exception is, for example, Greif (2008). Before some process models in coaching are presented, the general characteristics of the coaching conversation should first be addressed. The coaching processes are designed within this conversation (face-to-face or online).

Process Control in Coaching and Online Coaching

Contents

E. Berninger-Schäfer, *Online Coaching*,
https://doi.org/10.1007/978-3-658-39133-1_8

8.1 The Coaching Conversation

Coaching processes are controlled in coaching conversations or in an asynchronous online procedure also in a delayed interaction between coaches and clients.

Graf (2015) describes the coaching conversation from a linguistic point of view as a professional conversation in the sense of a helpful, goal-oriented interaction, which is co-constructed by the participants. She refers to Deppermann (2008), who characterizes conversations according to the following criteria:

- Constructivity (conversations are actively produced by the participants)
- Processuality (conversations as a temporal event with a sequence of events)
- Interactivity (the contributions of the participants are mutually related)
- Methodizität (construction and interpretation of the conversation contributions with culturally typical, recognizable contributions)
- Pragmatism (pursuit of goals and processing of topics)

The professional conversation is characterized by different participation requirements, responsibilities and knowledge of the participants and thus by asymmetry and different power relations (Graf, 2015). According to Graf, it is an institutionalized, structured interaction between representatives of a profession or institution and clients, where the orientation to a professional agenda determines the task and action logic of the conversation. The participants shape goal-oriented, socially constructed, delimitable, interactive events with specifications, e.g. also with regard to the permitted contributions. In doing so, they determine the activity type coaching.

Since the understanding of coaching as a standardized, professionalized consulting format is not uniform, Graf (2015) describes coaching with the help of four basic communicative activities:

1. **Define the situation:** The purpose of coaching, understanding, agreements (rules of the game, dates, fees, etc.) and evaluation are defined via metacommunication.
2. **Shape the relationship:** Roles and identities are discursively defined and the interaction is designed.
3. **Co-construct change:** A coaching agenda is worked on from the clarification of concerns to the finding and solution of goals.
4. **Evaluate coaching:** Contents, relationships and processes are evaluated

These activities do not take place linearly, but in constantly reciprocal shaping and in different time frames.

According to these explanations, coaching is characterized by metacommunication, relationship management, the control of a goal- and solution-oriented process in feedback loops, and its evaluation. In order to further concretize these generally formulated categories, process examples will be considered and a process model for online coaching will be developed.

8.2 Exemplary Process Models

In the coaching literature, different phase models for the control of coaching processes are described, which are based on different theoretical concepts. Even though the criteria for the evaluation of coaching processes are still not uniform (Geißler & Wegener, 2015), there is a great deal of agreement in the demand for a respectful and empathic attitude of the coaches, the relationship management as the basis of the coaching process, the voluntariness and self-determination of the coachees, the confidentiality of the coaches and the result orientation in coaching. Differences can be found in the idea of the role of the coach (pure process accompaniment versus advice and guidance or combinations thereof), in the design of the coaching process (targeted control of a defined process or situational courses, conceptual or empirically founded derivation of the process or arbitrariness) and in the way the encounter is concretely designed in the coaching conversation, or which interventions are used for this purpose.

The oldest model for controlling a coaching process is the GROW model by Graham Alexander, which has achieved great popularity through Whitmore (Whitmore, 2006). The questions of the coaches relate to the following coaching phases, which are symbolized by the GROW letters:

- G = Goal (goal)
- R = Reality (reality check/situation analysis in relation to the goal)
- O = Options (clarification of possible actions)
- W = Wrap up (implementation)

The GROW model is implemented by Bob Griffith in the CoachMaster software. This contains questions for the individual phases and can be used in addition to telephone or video coaching (► http://www.bobgriffiths.com/Coachmaster.html).

Loebbert (2015) describes the following coaching process in the process model of counseling action theory:

1. **Contact** (Establishment of the working relationship through empathic, respectful, appreciative, honest and supportive behavior of the coaches)
2. **Contract** (Clarification of coaching goals and working framework, including fee and setting, i.e. the formal agreement of the working relationship)
3. **Hypotheses/Diagnosis** (Exploration of resources and scope of action together with the client, if necessary diagnosis by the coach)
4. **Interventions** (Actions of the coach that lead to differentiation and change of patterns)
5. **Evaluation** (Clarification of possible and really positive results through coaching and responsibility)

Rauen (2002) outlines a process flow for a coaching process (◘ Table 8.1).

A similar description of a coaching process can be found in Bachmann (2012; ◘ Table 8.2).

In his generic model of goal-oriented self-regulation, Grant (2016) points to the effectiveness and importance of feedback loops in supporting goal achievement. He proposes the process described in ◘ Fig. 8.1.

Table 8.1 Flow chart for a coaching process according to Rauen

I	**Preliminary phase**
	Perception of the need for coaching
	First acquaintance (contact and first conversation)
	Contract formation (formal and psychological contract)
II	**Main phase**
	Clarification of the initial situation (actual and desired state)
	Goal setting (development of goals and solutions)
	Interventions (implementation of the found goals)
III	**Final phase**
	Evaluation of goal achievement
	Final session as the formal end of coaching

Table 8.2 Description of a coaching process according to Bachmann

I	**Kontrakt**
	Festlegung der formalen und sozialen Rahmenbedingungen aller Beteiligten
	Clarification of the task with realistic goals
	Agreement on the success control
I.I	Inquiry (first clarification of the match)
I.II	First meeting (getting to know each other, occasion and goals, procedure, roles, limits, dates, costs, duration, frequency, confidentiality, information, etc.)
II	**Situation analysis and clarification**
II.I	Analysis (diagnostics, definition of core issues, target justification with target hierarchy and sub-goals)
II.II	Flow chart (determination of a change strategy)
III	**Accompaniment**
III.I	Implementation (trial, transfer support, reflection)
III.II	Feedback (interim feedback, milestones, feedback loops)
IV	**Conclusion**
IV.I	Closing conversation (assessment of target achievement, mutual feedback, further steps, lessons learned, individual final reflection of the coaches, e.g. through supervision/intervision)
IV.II	Evaluation of structural, process and result quality by feedback or standardized evaluation instruments

Greif (2008) describes process steps that can be derived from Grawes' effective factors:

- Appreciation and emotional support
- Affect reflection and calibration
- Result-oriented problem reflection

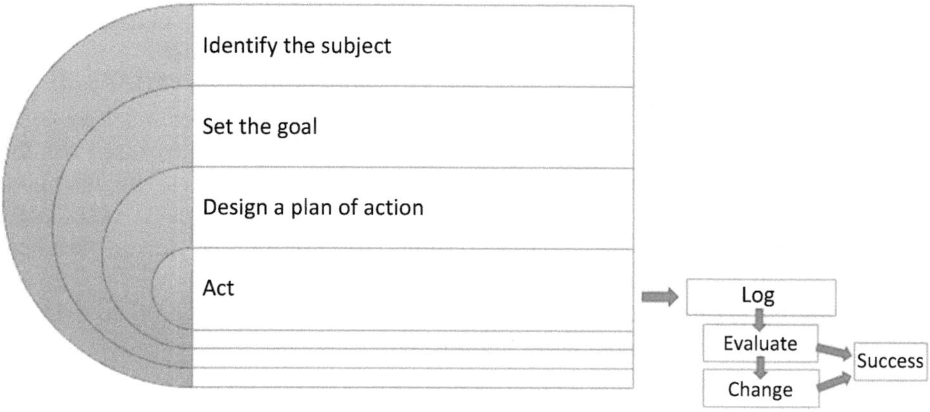

Fig. 8.1 Feedback loops according to Grant

- Result-oriented self-reflection
- Goal clarification
- Resource activation and implementation support
- Evaluation of progress during the course

These individual categories are assigned to behaviours of the coaches, with Greif (2008) pointing out that every methodological approach in coaching must be specific to the person and appropriate to the situation.

Greif and Benning-Rohnke (2015) also deal with transfer support in coaching. They focus on how the gap between goal and action (action intention gap) can be bridged. They refer to the Rubicon model by Gollwitzer, Kuhl and Heckhausen (1996), which describes the following phases in the process of motive formation up to the implementation of the action:

- Intention formation or pre-decisional phase (transition from need to motive, weighing of motives and selection of a goal)
- Volition or pre-action phase (conscious decision, will formation, planning and preparation of the action)
- Action or action phase (implementation of the action to achieve the goal)
- Evaluation or post-action phase (clarification of the relationship between action and successful achievement of the goal, possibly change of goal or action)

One success factor for the successful implementation of intentions is the explicit formulation of the implementation intention in If-Then-Sentences. Nevertheless, the implementation of many other context conditions depends, so that an implementation accompaniment of many cycles in which the attempted behavior in dependence on its interactions with environmental variables must be reflected, which may lead to a change or adaptation of goals and/or actions. Greif and Benning-Rohnke (2015) formulate an extended Rubicon model for this:

> In the Rubicon model, it would therefore be necessary to supplement that in uncertain implementation situations, additional observation-reflection-target clarification-implementation-action cycles are required to successfully cope with the situation (Greif & Benning-Rohnke, 2015, p. 4).

Even with the actional implementation, reflection loops begin to change motivation, to make quick adjustments and to strengthen self-efficacy beliefs.

Methodologically, this is done by Greif and Benning-Rohnke (2015) with telephone shadowing. In a face-to-face setting, target clarification, formulation of an implementation intention and planning of action and resources required for this take place. Then the implementation accompaniment takes place by telephone coaching. The post-action evaluation of the entire coaching process takes place again in a face-to-face setting, where it is about working out the "lessons learned" to strengthen for future challenges.

This approach can be effectively supported by online coaching of level IV far beyond the possibilities of telephone shadowing.

8.3 Process Model for Online Coaching According to Ribbers & Waringa

Ribbers and Waringa (2015) describe an online coaching process and first rely on Anthony Grant's six-stage model:

1. Definition of desired result
2. Goal setting
3. Increasing motivation through identification of strengths and building self-confidence
4. Finding available measures and developing an action plan
5. Result check in the target achievement phase
6. Adaptation of the action plan based on feedback

Ribbers and Waringa (2015) see advantages of online coaching in particular in phases three and four, since it would act here accelerating.

They conduct coaching completely writing-based via email and provision of text files (worksheets, notes) by their platform "ecoachpro". Thus communication runs exclusively asynchronous. They refer to the fact that this would by no means be a modern phenomenon, rather already communication by means of smoke signals, drums or fire signs had the same purpose, namely to send information over long distances. Also letters that were previously on the way with carrier pigeons or by sea, needed a certain time until they arrived at the receiver. The Internet now offers additional forms of time-delayed communication or different combination possibilities.

Ribbers and Waringa (2015) have developed the ABC model (Accelerated Behavioral Change). They aim for a rapid change in behavior.

In doing so, they try to take into account that there are both supporting conditions on the part of the clients, such as motivation and cognitive factors, but also hindering, such as beliefs, environmental conditions, time limitations, etc. They attach particular importance to the realization that a major limiting factor for coaching success is the planning of too large implementation steps. They refer to a study by Stanford University when they speak of the proven effectiveness of so-called "baby steps" (small implementation steps). The transfer problem of training interpersonal skills, according to which only 20% of what has been learned will be implemented later, they attribute to the fact that training takes place in artificial learning environments. Transferred to coaching, this would greatly increase the value of on-the-job coaching. However, this is rather a great challenge from an organizational and financial point of view in the face-to-face variant.

Ribbers and Waringa (2015) try to take these aspects into account in their ABC model. They describe with analysis, internalize (internalization) and sustain (result assurance) the three main phases of the model, which in turn are each divided into further phases.

8.3.1 Phase I: Analysis

- **Exploration**

Exploration takes place from different perspectives and information is collected and discussed. Methods used include, for example, writing a biography, answering target questions, filling out questionnaires, also in the sense of a 360° feedback.

- **Reality Check**

In this process step, the client's interpretations of the previously collected information are clarified, involving the distinction between assumptions, emotions and facts. The tool used is open questions. It is also about working out what advantages and disadvantages there would be if the problem did not change. Ribbers & Waringa point out that a breakthrough would occur if the "question behind the question" ("question behind the question", p. 48) could be found. Otherwise, coaching would only serve a "symptom cure".

- **Clarification of Possible Actions**

The desired situation and its advantages are worked out. An action plan is created to realize this wish. This scenario is developed with open questions, e.g. about the possibilities of realizing this change, what is needed for this (knowledge, skills, support, time, money), which persons are important for this, etc. It would be reinforcing if the clients were asked to imagine how they or someone else have already successfully coped with this situation.

- **Definition of Coaching Goals**

Several realistic and achievable coaching goals are defined. For this purpose, both the SMART rule (goal development according to the criteria: specific, measurable, attractive, realistic, timed) and scaling questions can be used.

8.3.2 Phase II: Internalization—the Client Circle and the Reinforcement Circle

This phase is described by Ribbers and Waringa (2015) as the one that is specifically for the ABC model and that distinguishes the model most from other phase sequences in coaching.

The client circle describes the frequent repetition of the following four steps:

- **Goals**

The previously defined goals are divided into sub-goals, for which the clients receive specific exercises or implementation suggestions to implement them in their home or work environment.

- **Action**

The previously agreed implementation steps are implemented in real-life situations. The more realistic the implementation scenario is and the more step-by-step the implementation is (baby-steps), the more often concrete results can be achieved.

- **Reflection**

The experience is interpreted in relation to the client and their environment. It is important that this can happen immediately and quickly, while the experiences are still present and questions can be answered, such as "What exactly happened?", "What happened afterwards?", "Which emotions were triggered?" (Ribbers & Waringa, 2015, p. 50, own translation). This should reinforce and internalize the new behavior in order to support the transfer of coaching results.

- **Evaluation**

The learning and implementation success of the client in achieving the goal is evaluated in very small steps with regard to effects in very different fields. There may be repetitions of the implementation steps or changes and new attempts. If the desired results are achieved, it is decided whether the same is done for another goal or whether the next phase of the coaching process is initiated.

The reinforcement circle accompanies the client circle permanently. Here, operant conditioning is to take place, according to which the reinforcement of behavior leads to the repetition of this behavior.

- **Reinforcement by the Environment**

Since the behavior of the client affects the people in their environment, a change in behavior will lead to reactions. If this is positive, the changed behavior of the client will be reinforced. If not, it must be taken into account in the reflection loops by the coach and, if necessary, lead to an adaptation of the goals or the implementation measures.

- **Reinforcement by the Coaches**

The coaches accompany and encourage the clients in the implementation of the planned behavior. They structure, evaluate the learning experiences with the clients and give positive feedback. This is done closely during phase II, so that successes are consolidated and helpful behavioral changes can be internalized.

8.3.3 Phase III: Result Assurance

This can be a short phase if the desired behavior has already occurred.

- **Validation**

Coaches and clients assess to what extent the desired target behavior has already been successfully internalized. For this purpose, the assessment of the clients, feedback from others or scales or questionnaires are used.

- **Sustainability**

In addition to internalization, the learning progress can be further reflected, for example by asking the clients to write down their learning experiences and successes. It is considered how these successes can be secured or transferred to other fields.

- **Future-Proofing**

The new behavior should also be shown in the future. Scenarios are described how this should happen. Coaches and clients can agree that they will contact each other on this topic at an agreed time.

When carrying out the coaching process according to the ABC model, the following three elements must be observed:

- **Awareness**
  The main focus is on strengthening clients' self-perception. This includes the ability to reflect on the relationship to the outside world (separation of perception, emotions, reflections and interactions), but also on one's own mental processes. Similarly, clients' awareness of their own values, strengths and personal learning challenges grows.
- **Feedback**
  One of the main tasks of the coach is to give feedback on the experiences and impressions made. This accelerates the process, especially in phase II.
- **Knowledge transfer**
  The coaches provide clients with information and knowledge in a structured way. This can, for example, be articles on certain topics, background knowledge, models, tests, videos, example situations or tasks.

Ribbers and Waringa (2015) point out that the ABC model is compatible with many other coaching models, but less so for coaching in a face-to-face setting. This is due to the close support of clients in the implementation phase (Phase II) and the implementation of baby-steps.

8.4 The Phases of the Karlsruhe School Face to Face and Online

In the "Karlsruhe school" a coaching process is implemented, taught and researched, which can be derived from the empirically founded success factors in coaching, as they are presented in ► Chap. 7. Behind this is a concept that describes the conditions and procedures by which a person (client) can be accompanied from an existing situation to a desired target situation. The current situation is often experienced by clients as problematic, in need of clarification, conflict-ridden or crisis-ridden or decision-making. For this, coaches need competence to design change paths of people depending on their respective contextual conditions. The phases of

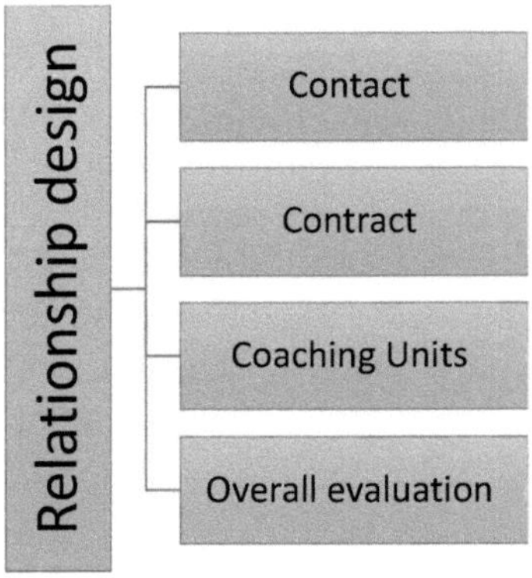

Fig. 8.2 Course of coaching from first contact to completion (level I)

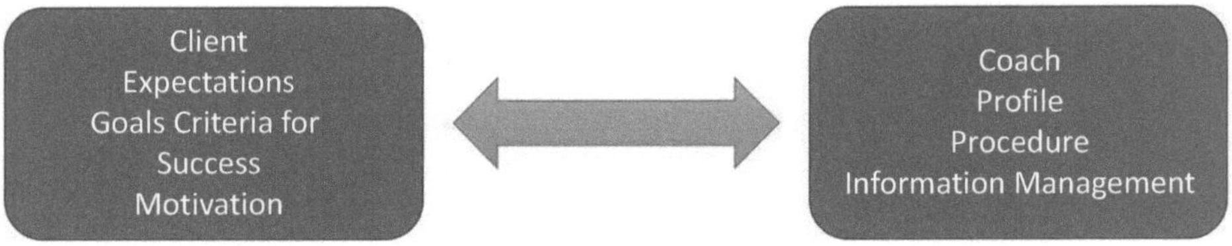

Fig. 8.3 Two-person contract between client and coach

the Karlsruhe school are theme-neutral and suitable for different coaching formats, which are dealt with in more detail in ► Chap. 10.

Process control in coaching is represented on two levels. On the one hand, it is the course of the entire coaching from the first contact, via the contract design (contract) to the target definition (level I). This process is first described with reference to online coaching. The design of the individual coaching units (level II) takes place on the basis of the coaching process of the "Karlsruhe School", in which the aforementioned success factors are implemented. Both the individual coaching units and the entire coaching process are evaluated. These evaluations also take place on two levels, which is illustrated after the description of the coaching unit.

Figure 8.2 shows the course on level I.

8.4.1 Contact

The first contact with the coach can be made directly by the clients or by other persons who commission the coaching (personnel development, executive, program responsible, etc.). This is usually done by telephone or via CAI® World. There is a first clarification of the wishes of the commissioning person or organization and the contract modalities, which can also be carried out in virtual rooms. The further course then depends on whether there is a contract between client and coach (Fig. 8.3), or whether an institution or third person is the client of the coaching. Here, triangular or quadrilateral contracts are conceivable (Figs. 8.4 and 8.5).

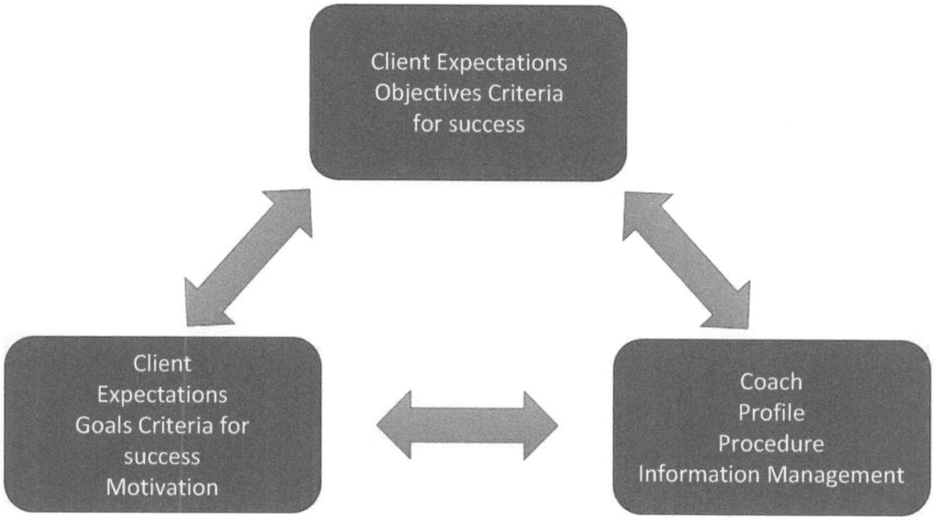

Fig. 8.4 Triangular contract with coach

Fig. 8.5 Quadrilateral contract with coach

It is particularly important in the case of a triangular or quadrilateral contract to clarify the expectations of the client and to find out whether there are already goals, e.g. based on an internal competence assessment, an assessment, a target agreement, etc. If necessary, these goals must be clarified and agreed. In this constellation, it is particularly about the question whether the clients are completely free to set the appropriate and important goals for the coaching directly with the coach, as is possible in the two-party contract. It may also be that the concretization of the goals for the entire coaching process is already part of the coaching and

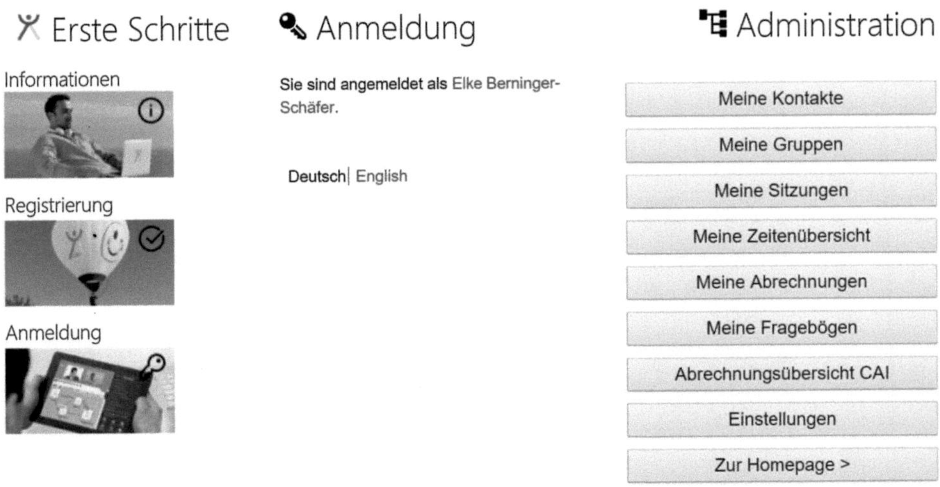

Fig. 8.6 Management view from the CAI® World

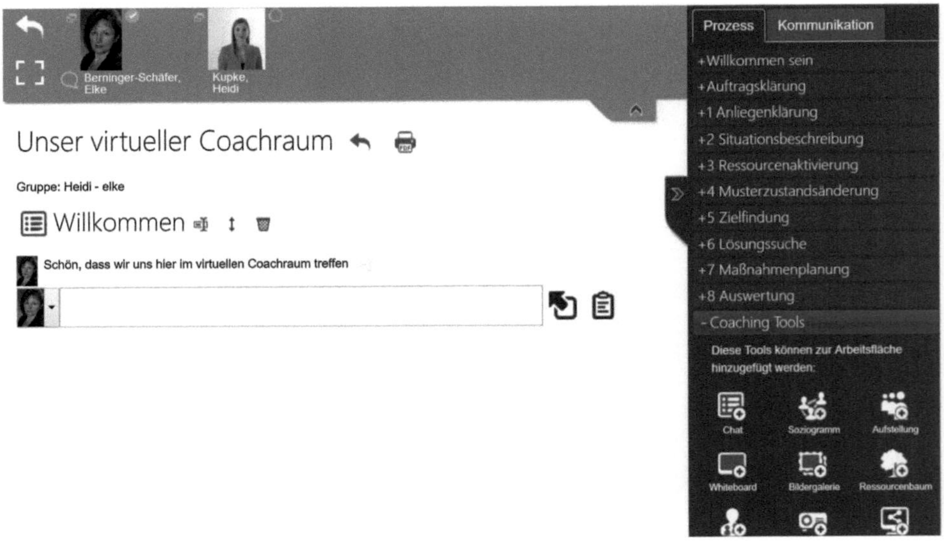

Fig. 8.7 The workspace in the CAI® coach room. (© CAI GmbH)

takes place in an initial conversation. In the online world, goal clarification can also take place asynchronously in writing.

In the CAI® World, the coaches first set up a coaching room. In Fig. 8.6 you can see the management view of the coaches.

The "My Sessions" button opens a virtual coachroom. Only the defined persons can communicate with each other in writing, acoustically and visually in this "room". The process flow and the online tools are available in this "room" (Fig. 8.7).

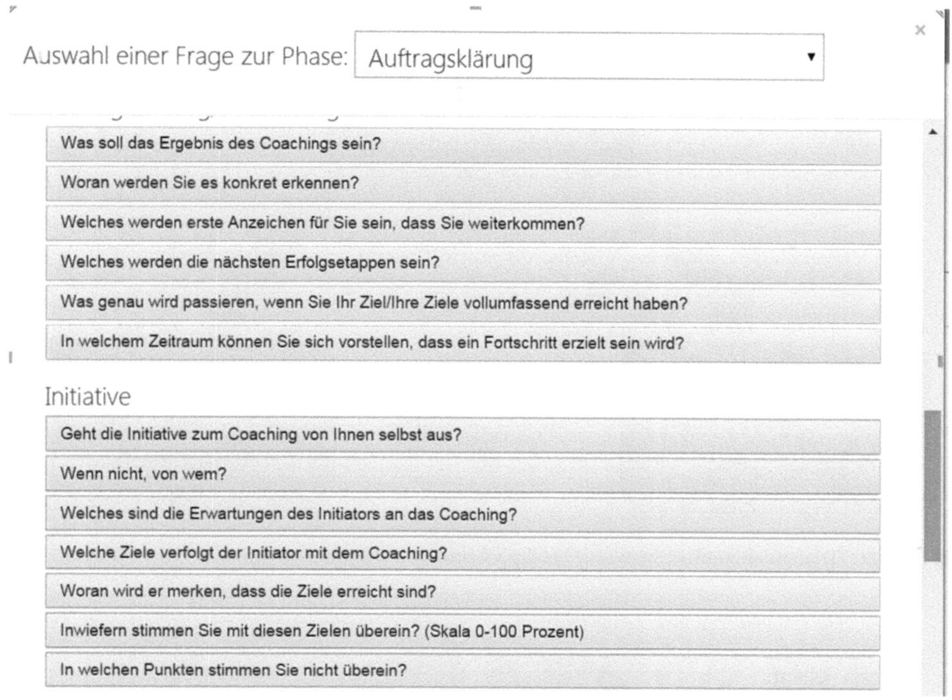

Fig. 8.8 Extract from the question catalogue for order clarification. (© CAI GmbH)

In a prepared chat window or on a whiteboard, questions can be stored that belong to the respective phases of the coaching process depicted. Coaches can click on the preformulated questions there and make them available to clients (in writing or verbally) or ask their own questions. In Fig. 8.8 an exemplary extract of such a set of questions can be seen:

The integrated, online available set of questions contains further questions, e.g. about expectations and resources (see also Prior, 2006) and is additionally freely configurable.

From the coaches' perspective, establishing contact is about clarifying the expectations, requirements and conditions of the person commissioning the coaching and making their own approach transparent. This includes the coaches' coaching concept, their focus areas, if they are not apparent from the stored coach profile, their approach and information management. This means that coaches cannot pass on any information about the coaching to the person commissioning the coaching or other context-relevant persons due to the duty of confidentiality (see Ethics Guidelines, ► Sect. 11.3). This is especially the case if it is a triangular or quadrilateral contract. The clients need the assurance that the content and course of the coaching process will be confidential in each coaching session.

This also applies if the contact with potential clients by Coachpool providers takes place, which represents a special form of an intermediate triangular or quadrangular contract (Figs. 8.9 and 8.10).

The task of Coachpool providers is to select coaches according to certain quality standards and profiles, to enter into a contractual relationship with them and to

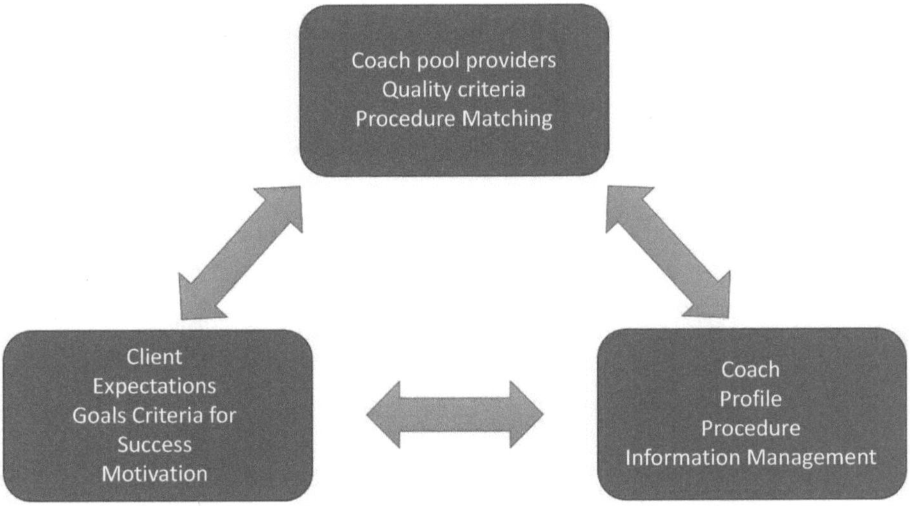

Fig. 8.9 Triangular contract between Coachpool provider, client and coach

Fig. 8.10 Quadrangular contract between Coachpool provider, client, coach and coach

ensure quality assurance. Another task is the so-called matching, i.e. the selection of those coaches from a pool who are best suited for the concerns of the clients. The initial contact between the pool provider and the client takes place here (usually by telephone or online). In a next step, the matching takes place, i.e. two to three selected coach profiles are sent to the clients or the future clients. This can be done online using an algorithm that also allows clients to find suitable coaches directly.

This is followed by the first meeting between coach and client, which is about building the relationship and, if not yet done, clarifying the procedure, the contract conditions and the goals for the coaching process.

The first contact is usually non-binding and the first 30-60 minutes are offered free of charge. This first contact gives the clients the opportunity to check and decide whether coaching should take place with a selected coach.

In order to keep the effort for coach and client as low as possible, this contact unit is also often carried out by telephone, otherwise online.

Coaches can offer their services on online platforms. Platforms differ in terms of whether they represent and check the quality of coaches or present everyone who calls themselves a coach for monetary reasons.

Furthermore, platforms differ in terms of whether they facilitate direct contact with coaches. Media communications enable "coach on demand", a requirement that is made in times of immediate availability of services, goods, knowledge and transactions of all kinds by customers.

"Coach on demand" means on the CAI® platform that the availability of the designated coaches is visible and that a contact can be made immediately. This can be done in writing (chat), by telephone/audio communication or directly via the virtual coaching room. There, individual process steps can already be partially automated and partially controlled by coaches. Automated means that coaches hold a virtual room in which they can welcome and invite potential clients, even in their absence, to first information. There they can leave information about their understanding of coaching and their approach, as well as their next availability in time, so that an appointment is already possible asynchronously.

8.4.2 Contract

As soon as there is an agreement between client and coach or client, pool provider, client and coach, a coaching contract is concluded. This is concluded formally and informally between the persons involved.

- **Two-Person Contract**
  - Offer (creation and acceptance), formal service contract (oral or written) and psychological contract between coach and client
  - Invoice from coach to client including performance proof
- **Three- and Four-Sided Contract**
  - Offer (creation and acceptance) and formal service contract between coach and the unit that places the order
  - Optional coaching goal agreement between client and executive or human resources
  - Psychological contract between coach and client
  - Billing to organization including proof of performance

■ **Coachpool Provider**

- Offer (creation and acceptance) and formal service contract between Coachpool provider and ordering organizational unit
- Formal service contract between Coachpool provider and coach
- Optional coaching goal agreement between client and executive or human resources
- Psychological contract between coach and client
- Invoice issued by coach to Coachpool provider including proof of performance
- Invoice issued to organization including proof of performance

After the selection of the coaches and the contract design have been completed and before the invoices are issued, the individual agreed coaching units take place.

The coaching contract results in the work assignment for the coaching. Goals are agreed, the achievement of which is evaluated at the (usually time-agreed) end of the coaching (level I).

To achieve these goals, individual coaching sessions are conducted (◘ Fig. 8.11).

There are thus goals on two levels. The goals of Level I are overarching goals that led to the commissioning of the coaching, were agreed at the beginning of the coaching and evaluated after its completion. The entire coaching process is designed in several units. The goals of Level II are developed within a coaching unit and concrete implementation measures for achieving the goals are planned.

■ Overarching Goals (Level I)

On the first level are goals that should be achieved with the entire coaching. The coach and client keep this level of goals in mind and align their topics, which they work on in the individual coaching sessions, accordingly. In each coaching session, the concern is clarified that is to be addressed in this coaching session. These concerns can be cross-cutting, e.g. improving conflict management skills or situationally conditioned, e.g. dealing with a conflict team. Within the agreed target corridor, several concerns can be addressed. Thus, each concern has its own coaching session.

▶ Example

The following goals (superordinate goals of the first level) are agreed upon for the coaching when contact is made:

- **Goal A:** Within one year, the client builds a new team structure in his work area. Success criteria:
  - Areas of responsibility, interfaces and process flows are defined and communicated.
  - The team members work successfully in the new structure.

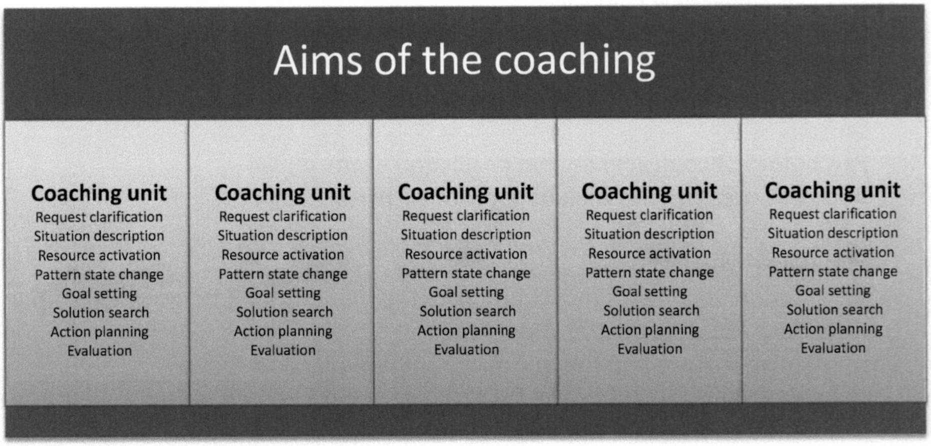

◘ Fig. 8.11 Coaching process in different coaching sessions, exemplarily five sessions

  - An employee survey is carried out for the review, as well as feedback from customers and colleagues.
- **Target B:** The client takes on strategic tasks and strengthens his assertiveness.
  Success criteria:
  - The client has an active role in the departmental and board meetings, agrees the goals of his department at this level and implements them.
  - The departmental goals contribute to the measurable success of the company. ◀

In order to achieve these overarching goals, against which the overall success of the coaching will be measured, many individual topics need to be addressed. These include, for example, role clarification, team diagnosis, process evaluation and process optimization, the processing of existing conflicts in the team, the topic of delegation when taking on additional strategic tasks, right up to the consequences of the new role requirements for personal work and time management.

For this purpose, the individual coaching units are carried out, partly synchronously and partly asynchronously. In each coaching unit, it is clarified which topic (which has something to do with the target horizon) is currently in the foreground for the client and which issue he would like to have clarified in this regard. Then the next steps are taken based on the process flow of the "Karlsruhe School".

Concrete Concern of the Coaching Unit (level II)

Within the coaching unit, it comes again to a goal definition, which however relates to the concrete concern of this coaching unit. For example, when it comes to the topic "new composition of the teams" the following goals were found:

- I develop a first plan about a strategically sensible competence profile of the team.
- I find a sensible solution for a competence assessment of the team members.
- I motivate the team members for an individual change process.

It is thus about goals of level II (within the coaching unit, related to a concretized concern) (◘ Fig. 8.12).

As seen in the figure above, A and B coaching goals are concrete steps that are planned out with the close supervision of the coach. When working with an online platform, there are options for creating divided (or small) steps that can be oriented around the clients work life. This makes it possible to carry out interim evaluations at regular intervals, which in turn make it possible to adapt the goals and measures sensibly via feedback loops (see also Grant, 2012; Ribbers & Waringa, 2015).

In order to achieve the higher-level goals (level I), an hourly contingent is usually agreed upon in the contract design. As a rule, this is an agreement of 10–20 h, which in the face-to-face variant is carried out as individual 90-min or 2–3 h sessions.

Half-day or day units are also agreed, e.g. B. in the face-to-face format "Coaching on the job" or when the meeting between coach and client is associated with a special time-consuming travel.

However, there are also coachings that consist of only one session, e.g. B. in acute decision-making situations.

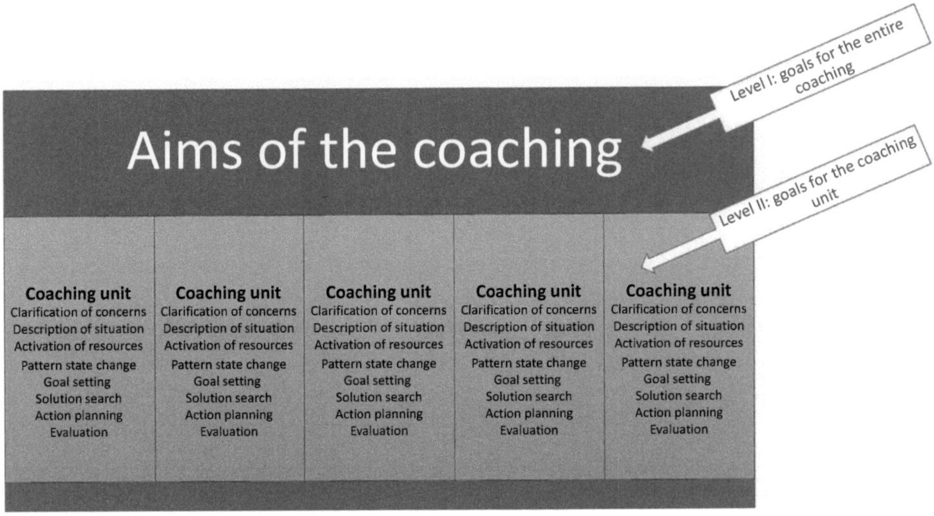

Fig. 8.12 Goal levels in coaching

Coaching can also take place as a continuous accompanying process without time limit, e.g. B. for people in high management responsibility.

Coaching is also increasingly becoming a fixed component of other personnel development measures (leadership training, trainee programs, etc.) and is also provided there with a defined time limit.

As a rule, coaches charge an hourly rate for their coaching services, sometimes also daily or half-day rates.

Just as in face-to-face coaching, the time spent by coaches in hourly contingents can be invoiced and commissioned accordingly in online coaching sequences. The time worked can relate to synchronous phases (video, telephony, chat plus tool use, if available on the platform) or to asynchronous phases. In the time-delayed phases, for example, the following work steps can be carried out by coaches:

- Review and feedback of topics processed asynchronously by clients
- Preparation of the next coaching steps
- Formulation of questions, appreciative feedback and reflections
- thematic preparation of whiteboards
- Instructions for working with coaching tools, e.g. constellation (► Sect. 9.3)
- Uploading of additional materials
- Processing of forum posts

The online session activities of the coaches are automatically recorded in the CAI® World, can be called up at any time to the minute and used as the basis for a transparent billing.

With the possibilities of online coaching, the variety of time management increases.

8.4.3 Process Design of a Coaching Unit

A coaching unit comprises a coaching process from the clarification of concerns to the planning and evaluation of measures and is embedded several times in the entire coaching process. In it, the factors of action described in ► Chap. 7 are implemented, which are listed once again in summary form here. In brackets are those phases of a coaching unit in which they are mainly realized.

- The type of relationship design (appreciation, empathy, authenticity, congruence, emotional support) is the prerequisite for the trusting cooperation during the entire coaching process (phase-independent, continuous basic behavior).
- The exploration and reflection of one's own experience and behavior, of motives, goals and relationships leads to a motivational clarification (phase 1: clarification of concerns and phase 2: description of the situation).
- Resource activation takes place in a holistic view, since problem and solution patterns consist of different neural networks, which are associated with certain cognitive, emotional and physiological activation (phase 3: resource activation). Similar to relationship management, attention to resources in addition to the phase of targeted resource activation is a phase-independent, continuous basic behavior.
- Coaching is goal- and solution-oriented. The probability of implementation of desired behavior increases if it is related to intrinsically motivated goals, i.e. goals that are emotionally anchored. This means that the definition of the goal should not take place from a problem state or problem pattern, but from a holistic positive state. For this, a change of a negatively colored state into a positive state of mind is necessary, i.e. before the goal finding a change of state pattern takes place. It can already arise through the resource activation or through targeted interventions of the coaches to transfer a problem state into a solution state (phase 4: change of state pattern and phase 5: goal finding).
- Problem solving is achieved by building self-efficacy and supporting the implementation of goals. Self-efficacy is promoted when clients can attribute solution ideas and implementation success to themselves (phase 6: solution finding and phase 7: action planning).
- Result-oriented self-reflection increases the ability to cope with problems when the coaching process is considered and evaluated in relation to one's own learning process on the meta-level (phase 8: evaluation).

A meaningful sequence of the depicted action factors is shown in ◘ Fig. 8.13.

In ► Chap. 7 it was made clear that somatic markers, interventions for psychophysical change and holistic states play an outstanding role in coaching. Therefore, these must also be able to be realized in an online application.

The concept of the "Karlsruhe School" is implemented in the CAI® World as the CAI® Coaching Concept (Berninger-Schäfer, 2016) and can be designed with various tools that are also available (► Sect. 9.3). The coaching process is mapped in the CAI® World with the individual phases. Each phase can be clicked by the coaches. Questions are stored for each phase, which the coaches can use in a chat window or for inspiration of their own questions, but do not have to. The set of

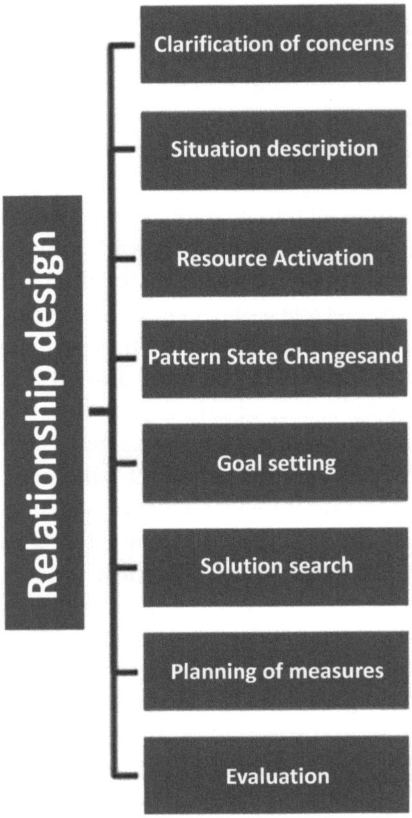

Fig. 8.13 Phase sequence of the "Karlsruhe School" in a coaching unit. (© Berninger-Schäfer)

questions can be optionally supplemented with own questions. This allows coaches to formulate own questions that are situation- and person-appropriate or to adapt the existing questions. Experiences in dealing with these questions, which are assigned to the coaching phases, show that they offer valuable orientation and support for coaches, even if they are not used in the same wording (Fig. 8.14).

In Fig. 8.15 a section of the question set for the phase of clarifying concerns is shown. One of the questions has already been selected and submitted. The questions can be asked in writing or orally (in the case of a synchronous meeting and the use of video and/or audio).

The responsibility for controlling the coaching process lies with the coaches, just as the transparency of the individual process steps towards the clients. The specific design of the individual process phases is based on the possibilities and needs of the clients. Thus, they are involved and the content-related decision-makers in the implementation of the coaching process. They are responsible for the implementation of the coaching goals. Other participants (commissioning organisation, manager, personnel development, pool provider) may contribute goals, shape the framework conditions for coaching and have the responsibility to support the clients in their further development, without gaining insight into the "black box" coaching.

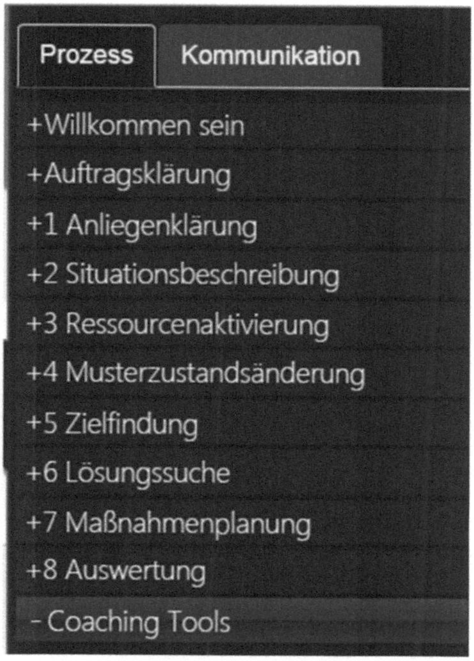

Fig. 8.14 Coaching process of the "Karlsruhe School" in the CAI® World. (© CAI GmbH)

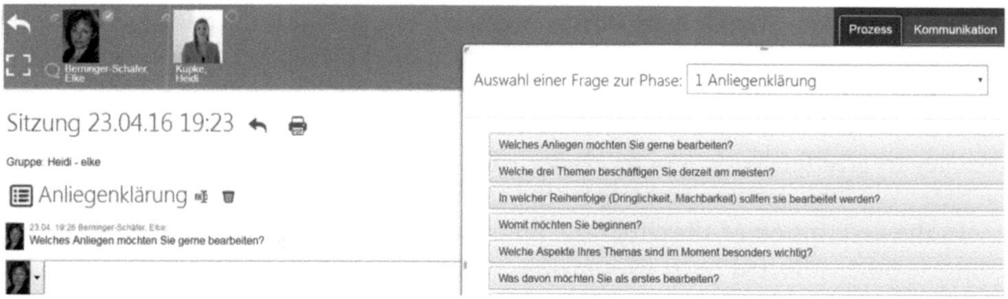

Fig. 8.15 Chat and question set in the phase of clarifying concerns. (© CAI GmbH)

As already mentioned several times, a major advantage of online coaching over face-to-face coaching is the intensive implementation support when carrying out previously planned measures to achieve goals. This is done in many feedback steps.

This makes it clear that it is not a linear coaching process and the linear mapping does not do justice to the actual event. Therefore, an alternative view is offered here as a process circle (Fig. 8.16).

Within the process circle shown, loops occur again and again. It may be that a resource state has already been developed holistically and the clients describe aspects of the problem situation again and thus fall back into the problem state. It is the task of the coaches to take this up empathically and to continue the process again. Loops can occur several times in each phase.

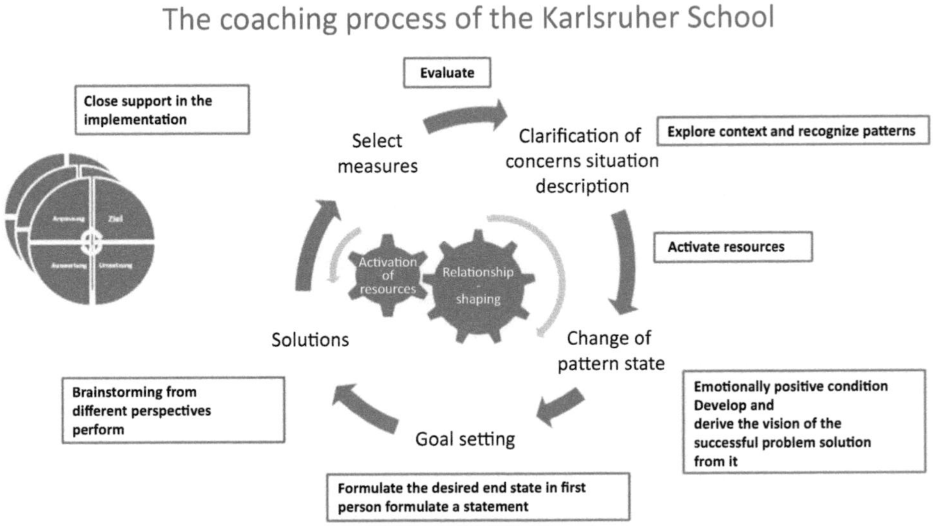

Fig. 8.16 Process circle of the "Karlsruhe School". (© Berninger-Schäfer)

8.4.4 Description of the Process Phases

The coaching unit begins with the clarification of concerns. This clarifies the topic and the question that the clients want to clarify in coaching. Sometimes the concern can be formulated directly or it is necessary to start with the description of the situation in order to identify the actual concern of the clients. In the course of the coaching unit carried out, the concern can change, for example, if additional aspects are added or a deeper underlying issue comes to the fore. It is the task of the coaches to give feedback and to clarify with the clients what the next steps should be based on. The decision is made by the clients.

In the description of the situation, information is provided about the person, the context, other affected persons, previous problem-solving and problem-solving attempts, opportunities and challenges. This is about the self-reflection of the clients, which is supported by encouraging, empathetic and appreciative suggestions from the coaches, by structuring and, if necessary, by visualization. Here, tools such as the whiteboard, drawing, work with inner and outer images, constellation, sociogram, inner team, etc. can be used for visualization (► Sect. 9.3).

In the phase of resource activation, the focus is on specifically strengthening the self-efficacy of clients and initiating a change in their state of mind. While dilemmas, problems and conflicts are in the foreground during the description of the situation, the clients are in a corresponding cognitive, emotional and physiological state. Through resource activation, another inner state is addressed. Resource activation can therefore already be used for a change in pattern state, for example when a previous solution behaviour is viewed differently. It can also be external resources, such as a pleasant landscape, the viewing of a work of art or other people. This can be easily implemented online. Resource activation is not only a phase in the coaching process, but a continuous attitude and perspective. Therefore, resource activation is in the middle of the process circle together with relationship management.

Appreciative feedback and the steering of attention to strengths, successes and helpful conditions are basic behaviours of coaches which carry through the entire process across all phases.

After the change in the reference state, the clients are in an emotionally positive state. Goals are derived from this. The justification for this approach is presented in ▶ Sect. 7.2. The goals are concretized and, if possible, formulated in "I-form" in present tense statements. This meets the requirement that the achievement of the goals lies within the clients' scope of action and can be realized in principle. For each goal, a solution brainstorming is carried out. Here it is the task of the coaches to open up a wide range of possibilities and to use many different perspectives. This is also supported by the use of certain tools in the online process (▶ Sect. 9.3). During brainstorming, no evaluation or decision should take place in order not to censor ideas too early. Online brainstorming has the advantage over face-to-face brainstorming that, due to the absence of non- and para-verbal communication, evaluations and decisions are not transmitted in the form as in face-to-face setting.

Only in a defined next step are implementation measures selected from the set of found ideas that are attractive to the client, terminable and feasible. Online coaches can support clients closely in the implementation of the planned measures. For this purpose, short contact units take place. The status of target achievement is reflected and helpful and hindering conditions are evaluated. This can quickly lead to necessary adjustments of the goals and measures to the current situation. These feedback loops can also be carried out asynchronously by the clients reflecting their status and sketching, whereupon coaches react supportively. Evaluations take place on this level permanently, once in terms of the evaluation of the implementation experiences and also by repeatedly considering the usefulness of the procedure in the coaching session to clarify the respective concern.

8.4.5 Evaluation

Evaluations usually relate to the satisfaction of the clients and the implementation of previously agreed goals. Since there are goals at different levels, the evaluation also takes place in different forms and at different times (◘ Fig. 8.17).

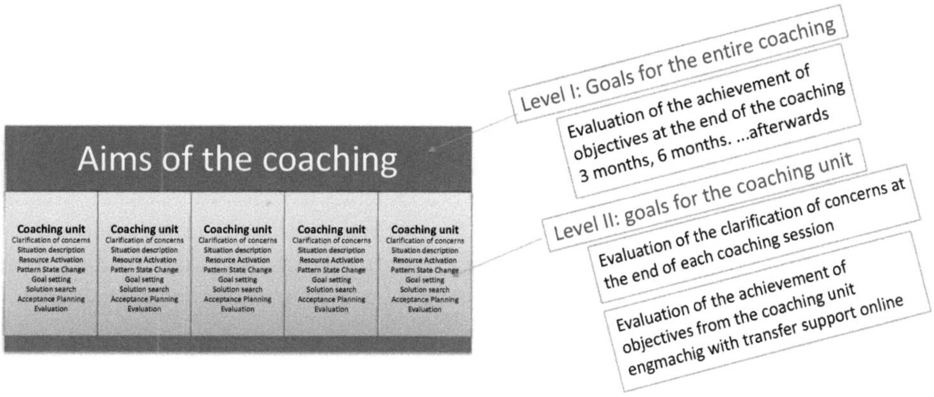

◘ **Fig. 8.17** Target and evaluation levels in coaching

As the goals are, the evaluations are also located on two different levels throughout the coaching process.

Level I

The goals of Level I are agreed upon for the entire coaching process at the beginning and evaluated at the end.

The end or duration of coaching is usually specified in the coaching contract in the form of desired or approved hours. Coaching as a continuous accompaniment process is an exception.

In online coaching, the possibility of asynchronous further work can optimally use a given contingent.

A coaching is finished when the agreed number of sessions is used up, or when the goals of coaching are achieved. In the final discussion, coaches and clients evaluate their experiences in shaping their relationship, the process and the results. In addition, a standardized evaluation instrument should be used. The result of this evaluation is received by all participants. For coaches, this is an important feedback instrument for their own development and thus quality assurance in coaching. Ideally, the effectiveness of coaching should be evaluated again in a certain period after the coaching has ended, e.g. after 3, 6, or "x" months, in order to obtain information about its long-term effect.

At the Zurich University of Applied Sciences (ZHAW), an evaluation instrument for coaching was developed by Prof. Künzli, which is to be used on a large scale with many test subjects in order to create a broad basis for scientific research and benchmarking in coaching. This evaluation tool is implemented in the CAI® World, so that it is available to online coaches who work with the CAI® World. They can use the instrument for their own evaluations and at the same time contribute to the large-scale coaching evaluation research of the ZHAW (◘ Fig. 8.18).

Level II

The goals of Level II are developed within the individual coaching units for the respective topics and issues to be addressed in these units. They also serve to achieve the goals of Level I. The evaluation at Level II refers to the respective coaching unit and thus to the satisfaction and progress of the clients in the processing of the issue of this coaching unit.

◘ Figure 8.19 shows an excerpt from phase 8 (evaluation) from the CAI® World as an example of evaluation questions.

Thus, the evaluation ends both each coaching unit and an entire coaching process.

In order for the illustrated coaching process to be successfully carried out, in addition to a concept-based approach to the control of individual and interactive change processes, further methodological competence is required, especially in the use of online media. These competence fields concern media competence, media communication and methodological competence in the use of online tools. These are particularly helpful for emotional, associative and physiological work in the coaching process. The following chapter is dedicated to these competencies.

4 Perspektiven und Zielklarheit

Wenn ich an mein Anliegen / Thema denke, ...

	trifft nicht zu					trifft voll zu
... bin ich mir im Klaren, war für ein Umfeld ich brauche, damit ich meine Stärken am besten entfalten kann.	○	○	○	○	○	○
... kann ich deutlich zwischen für mich passenden und nicht passenden Lösungen unterscheiden.	○	○	○	○	○	○
... sehe ich vielversprechende Spuren in meine Zukunft.	○	○	○	○	○	○

Wenn ich an mein Anliegen / Thema denke, ...

	trifft nicht zu					trifft voll zu
... tappe ich bei der Zielformulierung noch im Dunkeln.	○	○	○	○	○	○
... habe ich konkrete Vorstellungen davon, was ich will.	○	○	○	○	○	○
... habe ich nur unbestimmte Ideen, in welche Richtung es gehen könnte.	○	○	○	○	○	○
... habe ich (immer noch) keine Ahnung, wie es weitergehen könnte.	○	○	○	○	○	○
... sehe ich die Lösung(en) nun völlig klar.	○	○	○	○	○	○

Fig. 8.18 Extract from the coaching evaluation form. (© CAI GmbH)

Auswahl einer Frage zur Phase: 8 Auswertung

Wie zufrieden sind Sie mit dem durchgeführten Coaching?

Welchen Wert würden Sie auf einer Skala von 0 bis 10 vergeben (10: sehr gut)?

Was ist an diesem Problemlöseweg für Sie besonders wertvoll?

Was hat Ihnen dabei am besten gefallen?

Wann haben Sie sich dabei am wohlsten gefühlt?

Was hätte besser sein können?

Welche Ihrer persönlichen Ressourcen wird durch die Problemlösung besonders gestärkt?

Fig. 8.19 Excerpt of questions for the evaluation of a coaching unit. (© CAI GmbH)

Competencies for Online Coaching

Contents

E. Berninger-Schäfer, *Online Coaching*,
https://doi.org/10.1007/978-3-658-39133-1_9

Many authors agree (e.g. Döring, 2007; Geißler, 2012; Ribbers & Waringa, 2015) that the simple transfer of familiar coaching practices to an online variant does not work well and may be one of the reasons why coaches give up quickly after initial attempts. Online coaching requires specific competencies, which will be addressed in the following.

Six and Gimmler (2007) define competencies as follows:

> We define competencies as stocks of knowledge, skills and abilities that, together with motivational conditions, enable an individual to behave in a competent manner in a given context—in the present context, communication and media behaviour—functional and creative, self-determined and self-regulated, but also socially and personally appropriate and compatible. Competencies are therefore essential, but by no means the only, influencing factors for individual behaviour and action (Six & Gimmler, 2007, p. 272).

The following competence fields for professional online coaching can be derived from the effect factors presented in ► Chap. 7 :

- Media or multimedia competence (► Sect. 9.1)
- Media communication (► Sect. 9.2 "Media Communication" with a special focus on reading, writing and listening competence)
- Process competence (as described in ► Chap. 8 "Process Control in Coaching and Online Coaching")
- Method competence (► Sect. 9.3 "Method Competence")
- Format and design competence (► Chap. 10 "Coaching Formats" and ► Chap. 12 "Media Concept for Virtual Coaching Settings").

Since process control has already been described in detail in coaching and online coaching (► Chap. 8), the following subchapters will deal with media competence (► Sect. 9.1), media communication (► Sect. 9.2) and methodological competence (► Sect. 9.3). The format competence is dealt with in a separate chapter (► Chap. 10) because, especially in the case of online applications, this field of knowledge is much wider, so that basic knowledge and many examples can be conveyed. The content-related design competence also results from the online competence for coaching described up to this point. It is supplemented and requires a media design competence, which is described in detail in ► Chap. 12 when it comes to criteria for media conception in professional online coaching.

9.1 Media Competence

Media literacy, according to Süss (2008), refers to the following skills:

- Media criticism as the ability to reflect on media
- Media literacy as the ability to know production conditions
- Media use as the ability to use media appropriately for different needs
- Media design as the ability to create own messages through media

> Media literacy is usually understood to mean the ability to deal with media in a critical, self-determined, creative and responsible way (usually involving both the role of the recipient and the role of the communicator) (Six & Gimmler, 2007, p. 281).

The authors distinguish between the view that communication competence is the basis of media competence and the view that media competence is a subfield of modern communication competence.

According to Six and Gimmler (2007), media literacy includes the following aspects:

1. Media knowledge and technical competence
2. Reflection and evaluation skills
3. Usage and processing skills
4. Special communication skills

Online coaching as technology-supported coaching communication requires the ability to use computer-related technologies and programs in such a way that their professional use is possible. According to Seel and Ifenthaler (2009), this competence has been introduced into the literature as computer literacy since the 1970s. The authors quote Culbertson et al. (1986), who distinguishes the following levels of computer literacy.

1. Operational skills: knowledge of hardware and software in order to be able to work effectively with a computer (see also point 1 by Six and Grimmler).
2. Instrumental skills: being able to work on specific tasks with the computer (see point 3 by Six and Grimmler)
3. Algorithmic skills: being able to do programming.
4. Understanding alternative roles: versatile use of computers and its consequences, e.g. in a professional context, for playing, for shopping, etc.

When working with computers in a professional coaching context, points 2 and 4 are of particular professional importance to coaches. Point 1 is important for the assessment and selection of the appropriate technological requirements for coaching applications that enable safe handling and facilitate and ensure professional conduct. Point 3 requires IT competence that the software developers (point 1) must have so that the coaches can use the software as intuitively as possible. This is about the interplay of coaching know-how with IT know-how in order to create professionally usable methods and tools. This is only possible from levels III and IV onwards if online coaching really takes place. Otherwise, it is the implementation of face-to-face coaching via media, without necessarily taking into account the particularities of the online setting.

Similarly to point 1, for practically active coaches, the ability to assess how useful and professionally useful a program offered on the market is or what form of support they may need to secure for themselves. Six and Grimmler (2007) also point out the need to build up usage, processing and communication skills in this context.

In addition to computer literacy, multimedia literacy refers to the active and intelligent use of constantly evolving information and communication technologies (Seel & Ifenthaler, 2009).

According to Köhler et al. (2008), multimedia means that four technical aspects of media must be integrated in media applications.

1. Linking of time-dependent and -independent media
2. Multitasking as simultaneous execution of multiple processes
3. Parallelism as simultaneous presentation of individual media
4. Interactivity with the possibilities offered by the media

In online coaching, the technical operation of the media must be intuitive and in accordance with standards, as the coaching process is in the foreground and the presence and attention of those affected is decisive for the interaction and design of a helpful coaching process. Therefore, the media used should make this possible and favourable. They should be easy to use and supportive, and equip coaches with the tools, processes, formats and management systems that showcase and further develop their professionalism. It is the responsibility of the coaches to choose the technically feasible solution and acquire the necessary skills, as has been mentioned several times, because mediated communication has special characteristics.

9.2 Media Communication

Boos and Jonas (2008) describe communication as a social act in which the communication partners relate to each other to convey meaning through messages. These messages have content and formal characteristics, are intentional and make use of different media. These include language, non- and paraverbal behaviour, the use of technical devices and communication via the Internet. Encoding and decoding processes take place at the semantic, syntactic and pragmatic level (Boos & Jonas, 2008). The content of communication can differ on the way of encoding and decoding.

Six et al. (2007) speak of different media that are always in play in communication. They distinguished between the following means of communication:

1. Direct or face-to-face communication (personal media) consists of
   - verbal expression (language)
   - paraverbal signals (tone, rate of speech, speech pauses, articulation, clearing of throat, etc.)
   - nonverbal signals (gestures, facial expressions, eye contact, body language, etc.)
2. material communication means
   - individual communication via letters, boards, photos, stickers
   - public communication via symbols (e.g. flags) or in print media
3. Communication about technology
   - Classical media, such as telephone, loudspeaker, microphone, etc.
   - Classical mass media, such as television
   - Computer technology for individual and mass communication (new media)

Döring (2007) still speaks of "quartary media" or "computer, online or net media" in the latter case.

The effects of these different categories are dealt with by various scientific disciplines, such as communication, journalism and media studies, linguistics, social psychology, computer science, engineering, psycho-informatics and communication psychology. The latter has the focus on experience and behaviour in the context of communication processes, i.e. their conditions and influencing factors on cognition, emotion and action.

The task of media psychology is defined by Six et al. (2007) as follows:

> The focus is on the cognition, experience, behavior and action of individuals in their media communication environment, including the relevant conditions and influencing variables on the part of the individuals, the situation, the micro- and macro-social context, the non-social environment and not least the media themselves (Six et al., 2007, p. 37).

Media-mediated communication has many features that require special skills, such as dealing with misunderstandings. According to Schwan and Buder (2007), senders and receivers have a very active role in a communication process in that they have to continuously signal how a message is understood in negotiation processes. This is done non-verbally in face-to-face communication, e.g. by nodding or paraverbal signals, e.g. "hm, hm", or also linguistically by a further meaningful question or statement. Therefore, it is particularly important to formulate very carefully and to secure the common understanding through feedback loops in medial communication. In the following, therefore, special communication skills will be explained which have to be considered in professional online communication.

9.2.1 Reading and Writing Competence

In addition to the purely writing-based approaches, such as with e-mails or chats, reading and writing competence is also an essential part of a professional approach with multimedia platforms that combine various media (audio, video, chat). This is especially true for the asynchronous phases of the coaching process.

Advantages of the Written Language

According to Döring (2007), written language has certain advantages over spoken language. The sender can formulate and revise texts more carefully. The receiver can read, archive and further process them several times. They can decide when and how to react. The social presence experience (linguistic presence) can be stronger than in telephone communication.

Written communication can go hand in hand with a high degree of social anonymity. Feelings and thoughts can be presented more openly than in immediate social situations. Ribbers and Waringa (2015) refer to a study by James Pennebaker, in which very positive effects were found in traumatized patients when they wrote about their trauma. All participants were asked to write for 20–30 min. for three days. While the control group wrote about any topic, the experimental group was asked to write about their trauma and the thoughts and feelings associated with it. They were able to report on their trauma more openly than other patients, they smiled and laughed more and changed their circle of friends. This is attributed to a cognitive restructuring favored by writing and the associated behavioral changes. Significant differences were found between the control and experimental groups, which were accompanied by improved physiological values regarding stress level and susceptibility to illness in the experimental group.

Writing increases the motivation to deal with problems and has a relieving effect, simply because the stressful aspects are recorded and do not have to remain constantly present in memory. Writing is associated with an increased reflection of one's own person and context factors. It strengthens self-confidence and independence, insofar as suppressed emotions can be expressed and understood, and thoughts clarified. This increases self-awareness and self-regulation, which also explains the therapeutic effect of writing.

The great advantages of text-based communication include the increased sense of control of clients, the greater self-reflection and the elimination of socially desirable behaviors that play a greater role in face-to-face contact. Both coaches and clients have a greater decision-making space as to which information they want to share and which not. They also have a greater decision-making space as to how they want to react to an utterance of the other, as more time is available for this. Written messages can be changed, overwritten or sent immediately. Since the post-correction is not possible with most chat functions, it was introduced at the request of the users in the CAI® World. In particular, in writing-based phases of coaching, the careful formulation is of great importance. This can lift the restrictions of face-to-face communication. According to Ribbers and Waringa (2015), the feeling of intimacy and sympathy is stronger because clients attribute positive qualities to coaches, at least as long as the coaches do not destroy this illusion directly.

In our own practice, the following advantages of written communication are reported back by our online coaches:
- Concentrated silence is helpful for reflection and formulation.
- You can't interrupt the other person.
- You yourself are not interrupted and can stay in your flow.
- You can think and exchange at the same time.

The act of writing itself creates a certain distance for the writers to the described event and thus already has a relieving, structuring, clarifying and self-reflective effect. Ribbers and Waringa (2015) also point out that writing is associated with gaining insight, improving self-reflection, optimism, self-esteem and above all a sense of control.

Knatz (2009) reports from studies from the practice of online counseling that those seeking advice report that it was possible for them to address issues that they would not have expressed themselves on the phone due to the written communication.

▪ Special Features of the Media-Supported Written Language

There are already evaluations of experiences with media-supported encounters, as for example Ploil (2009) describes when evaluating the experiences of online counselors of the telephone counseling, or as Brunner (2009) and Knatz (2009) present. These include the following findings:

Users
- write something less polite,
- express themselves more emotional (honest?),
- get to the point faster,
- are more open in exchange.

In order to achieve this effect, however, the use of language in the media-supported encounter must be considered very carefully, as it has changed greatly. It rather corresponds to a globalized communication.

This includes, for example:
- Computer language,
- Anglicisms,
- Sign language,
- Emoticons,
- Abbreviations,
- Neologisms.

Speed often takes precedence over correct language in media-based communication, which leads to partial changes in familiar communication patterns.

Carefully formulated texts are possible in time-delayed procedures, but no vague, verbose or confusing formulations, because there can be no immediate questions. The message must be conveyed clearly, briefly and positively (Ribbers & Waringa, 2015).

Here is a counter-example in three stages:

► Text 1

Dear Mr. Müller,
Thank you very much for your explanations. They touched me very much. I notice that you are struggling very much with the experiences you have had in your work context in the last 4 years and also more often before. It must be very strenuous for you to fulfill your daily duties in this way. I understand your fear of the future and also what worries you. We could also look at the topic of work-life balance. The conflicts you describe in your team, especially the aversion that has grown over the years in at least three people, are a great challenge for leadership. It would be good to reflect here on which measures might be useful. I am happy to be there for you. In the description of the situation that you sent me, maybe the one thing or the other is still missing. For example, I would find it exciting to know how your predecessor managed to lead the team. How is the leadership culture in general? Since writing is always helpful, you could maybe continue on these points. I am already very curious about your further explanations and will get back to you immediately.
Many greetings
Coach ◄

► Text 2

Hello Mr. Müller,
Thank you for the text. I see the following topics:
- *Problem solving*
- *Work-Life-Balance*
- *Conflict management*

I suggest we work through the points one by one. Please send me a concrete example for each point.

LG
Coach ◄

► Text 3

Hi,
that doesn't sound ok.

Everyone would be down.

What is your greatest strength?
If you use it, what changes?
Hello, I'm glad to hear from you.

Coach

 ◄

However, in simultaneous text-based communication, speed is very important, because otherwise the interlocutor will say goodbye or be distracted, for example by processing e-mails and no longer concentrating on the topic. Nevertheless, it should be ensured that communication is respectful, clear and understandable, and not just via emoticons and abbreviations (see also the chat editing function mentioned before).

■ **Chatiquette**

In order to provide a certain degree of orientation and assistance for appropriate written communication on the Internet, the Chatiquette (etiquette for chatting) or the Netiquette (etiquette on the net) has become established.

In netiquette, the following is specified:
- Behavioral rules
- Character set, line length (prevention of "mutilation" depending on the used terminal)
- Readability (sentence structure and spelling, formatting, uppercase, lowercase, abbreviations and emoticons)
- Security (who is allowed to see the message?)
- Real names, code names, pseudonyms?
- Familiarize/formalize, address

Communication rules on the Internet such as netiquette or chatiquette can be found, for example, under ▶ www.netplanet.org.

Companies formulate their own netiquette and thus convey their values. They determine the desired spelling, capitalization, use of abbreviations and emoticons, the desired style (factual or emotional), and the desired attitude, e.g. friendly tone, tolerance and respect for other opinions. (e.g. ▶ http://web.archive.org/web/20120418205344/http://www.knigge-rat.de/themen.html).

▪ Effect of the Use of Media-Supported Language

Ploil quotes Döring and Hinterberger when it comes to the positive effects of the changed language use and lists the following aspects (Ploil, 2009, p. 21):

- Reduction of the overload of stimuli
- Increased production of own images and thoughts (increased feeling)
- Positive attitudes and expectations towards the communication partner (advance sympathies)
- Productive tensions: “physical absence—sensory presence” as well as “physical distance—psychological closeness”

In the psychosocial sector (social counseling), there exists expertise in the practice of using purely written coaching mostly via e-mails or chats. Valuable findings resulting from this can be found in Ploil (2009). Overall, writing is not a new phenomenon in professional accompaniment processes, but can look back on a long tradition, such as in bibliotherapy, creative or therapeutic writing (Petzold & Orth, 2005). Nevertheless, the written language is subject to great changes due to the new media.

▪ Net Jargon or the New Language on the Net

Therefore, the ability to read and write also includes the knowledge of an emerging and rapidly changing language usage when communicating over the Internet (net jargon).

The lack of nonverbal communication is met with other tools that have the function of paralinguistic elements (Hinterberger, 2009; Ribbers & Waringa, 2015). As Vogel points out (2007), new expressive language means and symbols are emerging that can compensate for the lack of non- and paraverbal indications of emotions to a certain extent. These include, for example, emoticons, sound words or action words.

Emoticons Emoticons communicate emotions as paralinguistic information. Hinterberger (2009) refers to Schubert & Ernst, who were able to show that the real mimicry of chatters corresponds to emoticons used to a high degree. However, there are intercultural differences to be considered here.

For example, a smile is represented by :-) in Western cultures, by ^-^ in Eastern cultures. This corresponds to cultural norms according to which emotions are expressed more openly through the corners of the mouth in Western countries, while the eyes are used more for the interpretation of emotions in Eastern countries (Ribbers & Waringa, 2015).

Sounds Sounds, for example, are expressed by “hmm”, “uh” or similar to indicate an emotional state or to give an indication that something is still being thought about.

Emotional Comments Emotional reactions are set behind certain statements, e.g. "beautiful", "joyful", "ha, ha" "thumbs down", etc.

Acronyms New short words are formed from the initial letters of several words.

Examples:
- Lol: laughing out loud
- Omg: oh my god
- Mfg: with friendly greetings
- Tbd: to be defined
- Fyi: for your information

Inflective Constructions Parallel actions or further nonverbal information are composed so that they replace whole sentences.

Examples: "red-feeling-speaking", "shield-meeting"

Typeface The attention can be drawn to certain words or sentence parts by changing the typeface, italics or boldface, and characters, e.g. "I don't want ***that***!!!!!!".

The repetition of individual letters also emphasizes certain words, e.g. "This is my Visioooooooon!!".

Uppercase letters symbolize loud speaking or shouting.

Symbols In order to avoid overlaps as much as possible when writing and still keep it short so as not to lose the attention of the other person, sections of text are already sent even if the sentence or message is not yet finished. This is symbolized, for example, with three points and, if necessary, the end with "E". This is even more important in a group context than in a single setting, as different strands of discussion can intersect and the discussion can thus become confusing and difficult to moderate. It is important that all participants know the symbols.

There are various symbols that can be used for different purposes in the CAI® World. In addition to personal identification (image, video), there are symbols that can express a mood, for example. Likewise, signs can be given here, e.g. message, pause, faster, slower, etc. which are particularly important in group work. It is also very important in groups that roles are symbolically identified, e.g. moderator, interviewer, group member (◘ Fig. 9.1).

A small moving pen indicates when another person is currently writing in a chat.

Further symbols with which associative and visual work can be carried out are described in detail elsewhere (▶ Sect. 9.3 and ▶ Chap. 10).

▪ Active Reading

In order to create a trusting, open and purposeful relationship it is important to deal with every textual information from clients with care and to actively use resources. Similar to Active Listening, "Active Reading" means reflecting the effect of the written on the person reading it, and responding in a way that shows appreciation, respect, empathy and genuineness. Schwan and Buder (2007) explain that

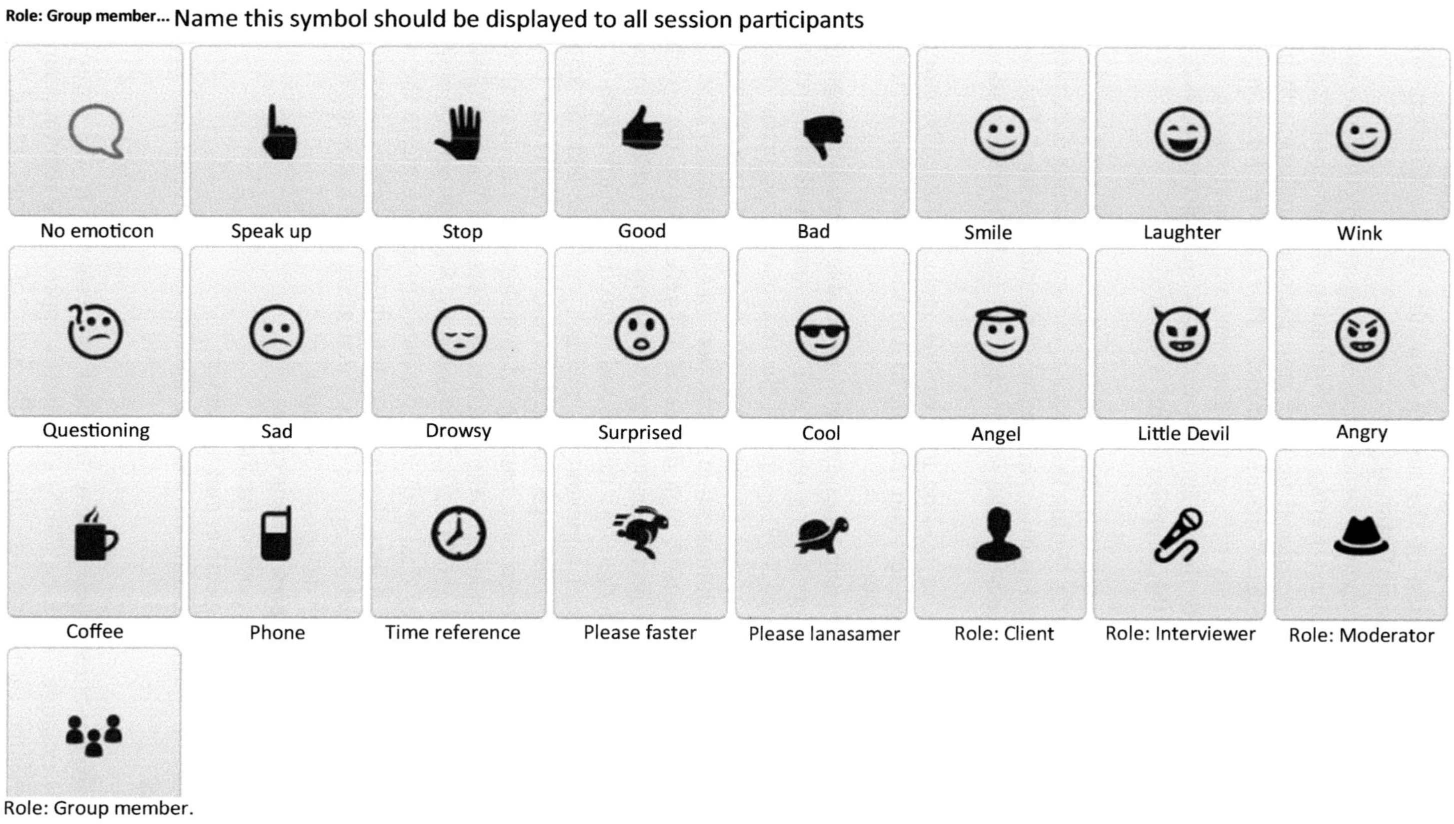

■ **Fig. 9.1** Symbols for emotions, roles and informative messages in the CAI® World. (© CAI GmbH)

while reading a text, a mental representation of the intended meaning of the text is developed. This process goes through several stages which include:
- Short-term representation of the surface structure of a text (letter, word and sentence analysis, syntactic features)
- Representation of the semantic structure of a text (text structure into individual propositions with argument overlaps) and formation of a propositional network
- Translation of the propositional network into pictorial-analogous mental representations, which creates a "situation model". This includes, for example, a described sequence of events with spatial and temporal causal chains, as well as the people involved with their intentions and goals and relevant objects. Whenever there are changes, this situation model is updated.

Reading a text is therefore an active-constructive process and not a passive reception (Schwan & Buder, 2007). Within this process, the text meaning is extracted, it is decided what can be omitted as irrelevant and what should be added. This has to do with the construction processes of the readers and not with the transmission of objective information.

Therefore, competence in reading and writing includes formally, emotionally and meaningfully grasping a text and reacting to it in such a way that certain effects can be achieved (Knatz, 2009).

It is important to understand messages and to be able to read between the lines without labeling and understanding one's own perceptions and interpretations as those of the other. Brunner (2009) speaks of the imaginative asceticism that is particularly important because, due to the limitation of sensory perceptions, for example in purely written communication, projection and imagination arise from the available written information. A high degree of self-reflection of the coaches and knowledge of their own projection patterns are very helpful in order to do justice to clients and to meet them in their own images and subjective constructions of reality.

When reading, the social anonymity (sometimes even the lack of knowledge about name, profession, gender, age, appearance and life context) can be a great challenge for the development of a trusting relationship and the dealing with the interpretations and inner images of the coaches. Ribbers and Waringa (2015) have developed the eCoachPro (eCP) method specifically for text-based communication (see ▶ Sect. 8.3). They deal with how coaches can communicate the message they want to send and which they should have thought about before, structured and clear, without being too verbose, using short e-mail texts. The following factors are decisive for the relationship design, for example:
- Attention to clients, represent their needs
- Give only appreciative, positive feedback
- Establish common perspectives and agreement
- Transport an optimistic attitude towards the clients\1'\2 topics and humorous remarks

The exclusively appreciative, positive feedback corresponds to the approach described, for example, by Szabo (2015) as radically appreciative reinforcement in his solution-oriented short-term coaching. In the sense of a feed-forward for future solutions, useful, functional and impressive aspects are reinforced. In this way, the effectiveness factor of resource activation (see ▶ Chap. 7) is used specifically.

The exclusively positive feedback must be authentic. This requires coaches to take a perspective when reading that enables them to look for positive information. For this purpose, coaches can be guided by questions such as, for example.

> What speaks to me, what surprises me in a good way, what triggers astonishment and joy in me, what is remarkable?

Ploil (2009) describes the processing of an e-mail in 14 steps, which can be adapted for text processing in coaching.

It may be that clients have a lot to communicate. The task of coaches is then to keep the coaching goals in focus and to understand which need of clients is expressed. It is not about reacting to all aspects of the text, but rather about considering which the core message in the answer should be. This includes an empathic response to the perceived need and the feelings of clients as well as a focus on resources and goals (positive feedback, feed-forward). The use of tools, such as a whiteboard on which keywords can be noted, is also helpful here. A protocol function in the virtual space also simplifies this process (checklist for coaches for text-based communication).

Checklist for Processing Text-Based Expressions of Clients According to Ploil

- Which facts are described?
- Which topics are represented with which emotions?
- Which words, metaphors, images are repeated?
- Which evaluations are visible in the text (self-foreign and situational evaluation)?
- Which ambivalences and tensions are hidden in the representation?
- What does this trigger in me?
- What resources are there hints?
- Which appreciative feedback is appropriate?
- Which interventions bring the process further?

Recommendations for Dialogic Writing

Dialogic instead of monologic writing is achieved by addressing the clients by name and asking more questions, such as: "Is that right? How do you see that?" Social proximity is created by aligning the writing style, as explained above. A match is achieved when coaches keep referring back to the words used by the clients and repeating them. This is especially important in an anonymous setting.

The written greeting begins the relationship between coaches and clients. Here it is important to pay attention to the fact that the way the greeting is formulated, the salutation and the writing style convey a relationship offer in which clients feel welcome and accepted.

▶ Example

- Client: "Dear coach, it would be great if I could get a solution to my problem here."
- Client: "Hi, this is GM2fu. Can someone help me?"
- Client: "Dear Mrs. Berninger-Schäfer, I hope you will read these lines soon, because I am already very curious about your reaction." ◀

With the first reaction of the coaches, be it an initiative to welcome or in response to the client's contact, communication rules are already transported, e.g. whether an emotional language is possible or not.
- Coach: "Dear Mrs. Müller, I'm glad you're taking coaching for your topic."
- Coach: "Hi, great, if we can do it together."
- Coach: "Dear Mr. Meier, I am very pleased that you have contacted me."

Since the relationship design is decisive for coaching in both the face-to-face and virtual environment, the following basic behavior applies to both settings:
- go into contact,
- design atmosphere,
- adequately mirror and question.

A written answer should be structured (based on Ribbers & Waringa, 2015) as follows.
- Introduction, heading, address (depending on the chosen medium, e.g. mail, chat, text on a platform)
- Positive feedback (e.g. on the perceived progress)
- Core message (e.g. the introduction of the next coaching phase, the assignment of homework, etc.)
- Motivating conclusion (e.g. by expressing confidence and hope for the successful achievement of the next steps)

These recommendations can be integrated into the general framework of a writing process, which Schwan and Buder (2007) describe with reference to the psychological model of the writing process developed by Hayes and Flower. According to this, working memory is occupied with the following three process steps during a writing process:
1. **Planning:**
   In this phase, the writing person considers which goals and statements should be conveyed with the text and how the text can be structured for this purpose. For this purpose, the long-term memory is used, specifically the knowledge stored there about the topic, the addressed person and about text forms.
2. **Translation:**
   The writing plan is gradually transferred into text elements, which then form larger paragraphs.
3. **Revision:**
   The text is read and possibly adjusted.

Recommendations for text-based communication in online coaching are summarized in the following overview.

Recommendations for Text-based Communication in Online Coaching
- Targeted planning of the writing style, core message and motivating conclusion appropriate for the recipients and context
- Careful formulation, corrections are usually not possible[1]

1 Exception: in the chat of the CAI® World, corrections can be made subsequently using the editing function.

- correct spelling
- short sentences, preferably no subordinate clauses
- small units, structure with paragraphs
- sorting, using punctuation marks to structure
- Clear, direct questions, avoid ambiguity
- Ask fewer instead of more
- Short instead of long answers
- Focus (always only one aspect)
- Mirror instead of interpret
- Separate factual information from evaluations and interpretations when reading
- Exclusively positive, appreciative feedback
- Give positive feedback on behavior, write in present tense
- Do not react to everything, select and formulate core messages based on a resource, on goals and solutions
- Connote words positively (instead of "that's bad", better: "that doesn't feel so good")
- Note that word meanings are different
- It is important to work with the meaning-making of the clients and not to try to convince them of their own (in the context of meaning, in the inner system of the other person)
- Take your time when (re)reading your own text and make corrections if necessary
- When writing at the same time: Wait, because the sense of time is different when writing than when speaking
- Focus on resources, goals and solutions
- The positive feedback leads to the fact that clients look forward to the answer of their coach, which promotes the coaching process and the implementation motivation of the clients (Ribbers and Waringa 2015).

9.2.2 Hearing: Acoustically Mediated Communication

Schmidt-Tanger (2014) describes the voice and body language as the "most important carriers of process information—the relationship offer" (Schmit-Tanger, 2014, p. 445). The quality of the voice ideally conveys warmth, confidence, openness and optimism. The author therefore describes the coach as a living relationship offer.

> The eye leads the person into the world,
> The ear leads the world into the person.

This quote by Lorenz Oken, among others, begins the book by J. E. Berendt "The Third Ear. From the Hearing of the World." Berendt (2008) describes the sense of hearing as the richest and most differentiated of the human senses. It is the first and last functioning sense in human life.

Even when making a phone call, you have to realize that the greatest possible proximity arises. The voice of the other is directly at your own ear. You usually don't get that close in professional face-to-face contact. This is especially true for pure communication via audio transmission.

▪ Procedure in Coaching Based on Audio Transmission

As with all other forms of communication, certain basic procedures must be observed via the "audio" medium. They also apply to the face-to-face or purely written approach, but there are more correction possibilities there than with the purely spoken word without eye contact.

Report
To establish a good rapport, for example, the following questions can be asked, which express interest and appreciation:

- What is the external framework in which the conversation takes place (location, time of day, room)?
- What is the state of mind of the clientele?
- What is the desired time and content framework for the conversation?

9

Questions of this kind can be helpful in establishing a connection. However, if the pressure on the clientele is so great that they want to get involved immediately, these procedures or small talk would be contraindicated. In addition to what is said, the pressure is also evident in the voice, e.g. in the tempo and the tone. For example, if someone speaks very quickly, words are "swallowed", sentences are not finished, this indicates high pressure. If someone speaks very slowly and quietly, this may be an indication of a depressed mood, of insecurity or helplessness. To feel aware means to adapt one's own language (voice position, modulation) in such a way that the feeling of resonance arises. This is the prerequisite for building a sustainable relationship.

Relationship Quality The relationship quality is built up and maintained by permanent tuning in to the counterpart (see also Pacing) as well as by appreciative and empathic statements. At the same time, the conversation is steered towards resources, solutions and helpful states of mind for the counterpart (balance between picking up and attention guidance on positive experiences).

Pacing Pacing is done by picking up people in their subjective view of things and their very personal experience in a appreciative and accepting way. Schmidt (2014) writes about this:

> » For example, you can choose similar language patterns as the client (sometimes it is enough to simply repeat empathically what they said), speak at the same rhythm, take similar body positions or tune your own language to the breathing rhythm of the client, etc. (Schmidt, 2014, p. 86).

Give Security A framework, for example, on time, procedure and uninterruptedness, gives orientation, as well as, if desired, information about the person and the environment of the coach. It is important to have a technical check or a fallback solution, i.e. an agreement on how to proceed in the event of a connection break or distortion of the transmission.

Transparency of Process Steps Coaches should explain their approach very transparently. This includes information on individual process steps, summaries and feedback (for clarification). This approach increases trust and strengthens the security and sense of control of clients.

Vocal Expression

In addition to these features of good communication, it is important in purely vocal encounters that attention is constantly focused on the language and voice of the client. This is important in order to recognize the baseline (the normal speech behavior of the person) and to identify deviations that represent markings, e.g. for special emotional states or thinking events. Thinking events include thinking pauses or special insights. Particular attention should be paid to:

- Breathing (intensity and frequency, sighing, holding breath)
- Dynamics
- Volume
- Tempo
- Emphasis on individual words
- Unintentional non-articulated expressions
- Pauses
- Articulation security/insecurity
- Pitch

In addition to the perception of the language and voice of the client, it is just as important to perceive and control one's own voice and language. Training of one's own voice and the hearing of moods and/or the being in tune, e.g. tension, fear, openness, security, smile, laugh, regret, sadness, desire, hope, etc. increases professionalism.

Recommendations for Audio-Based Communication in Online Coaching

The following guidelines provide coaches with orientation for their conversation behavior:

Conversation Behavior of Coaches via the Audio Medium

- Utilize metaphors by listening to the client's self-talk and preferred linguistic images, and using them consciously
- Provide frequent feedback and verification of meaning
- Maintain a sense of tension (concentration), and sensitively steer the conversation
- When using certain interventions (e.g., tools), pay attention to clear descriptions and instructions, without being too directive
- Ask more questions about colors, smell, somatic markers, and inner images
- When using imagination, involve all senses, and focus on positive patterns
- Focus on resources, goals, and solutions, and only update the problem to the extent that it contributes to the emotional relief of the client and provides context information
- Speak with a positive connotation

Finally, a quote from a client is included (digression from a case documentation by B. Pfisterer, 2016).

> As a client in the context of a virtual collegial coaching conference® I have experienced that it is easier for me to work on the description of the situation and the clarification of the concerns on the phone than in a "real" KCK. The conversation and the conversation topic at hand begin quickly and without preliminary small talk. The consultation takes place exclusively on the channel of hearing. I can concentrate on the voice of the coach and his language. I find this reduction to be a helpful limitation, as distractions are avoided by visual stimuli. This apparent reduction is very helpful to me when working concentrated on a topic.

Reading, writing and listening skills are basic skills in online coaching. They are supplemented by the methodological competence for the meaningful use of online tools.

9.3 Methodological Competence

The specific media communication skills already presented form the basis for active listening, question and feedback techniques. These run through the entire coaching process. In addition, other intervention methods can be used. These serve to visualize, stimulate associative and dissociative work and creative brainstorming, targeted resource activation and perspective change. When using tools, it is important to note that they only gain in importance when they are used sensibly and effectively to control the coaching process. This is particularly about directing attention to resources and desirable, holistic experience patterns. The goal is to increase the self-regulation ability of clients. Schmidt describes self-regulation ability as the ability to trigger helpful patterns even in their involuntary parts (Schmidt, 2014). These involuntary parts are, for example, shown through somatic markers (► Sect. 7.2). Strengthening this ability of clients increases their sense of self-efficacy and, as a result, the success of coaching.

By directing attention, coaches can facilitate dissociation and association phenomena. Clients who are in a problem state usually feel highly associated with the problem, the suffering and their helplessness, so that no other perspectives can be taken. Here, dissociation is helpful in creating a space of possibility that allows for different perspectives. Schmidt (2014, p. 36) writes on this:

> The central active ingredient is always the position from which I perceive the phenomena (which also includes my attitude towards them), and the proximity or distance that I establish to the observed phenomena. If we keep this in our field of vision, we can develop many liberating intervention opportunities…

Schmidt recommends the installation of a protected observer position (dissociation from the problem), which creates options and makes it easier to focus on desired experience patterns. These are activated by directing attention to them. In online action, invitations for dissociation and association are partly easier and more targeted than in face-to-face procedures. Just sitting at the PC with the gaze directed at the screen promotes "looking at". If work is done in interactive 2-D worlds, e.g. with the arrangement tool, the clients look at the image from the outside with a certain distance. They can design and change it. They experiment with what happens when they make the symbol that represents themselves or other people bigger or smaller, move it or redesign it. However, in 3-D worlds, association phenomena are much more strongly given by presence, involvement and immersion (▶ Sect. 7.3). Therefore, it makes sense to use the feeling of the current experience in 3-D worlds for helpful experience patterns and to proceed less problem-updating.

The linguistic expression promotes dissociation, as the use of language activates explicit, narrative brain areas. However, the purely cognitive approach is not sufficient, as the areas responsible for decision-making and implementation are located in a part of the brain that is developmentally older. They are rather reached via images, metaphors, imaginations and somatic markers. The targeted use of coaching tools makes it possible to interact with both areas and ideally forms a bridge between them.

The following describes the function of online tools that can be used in coaching. Examples of the use of the tools are described in more detail in the coaching formats (▶ Chap. 10). While chat, whiteboard and presentation are tools that are part of the standard offering of many online services, tools such as sociogram, image gallery, arrangement, resource tree and inner team have been specifically developed for online coaching in the CAI® World as online tools. Together they enable a tailor-made approach for different concerns, people, situations and formats.

Recommendations are given for the preferred phase of use of each tool. There are tools that can be used across phases and tools that are more suitable for certain coaching phases. In addition, statements are made about the function and effect of the tools. In the online world, it is particularly exciting to have tools available that provide access to associative and involuntary phenomena, so that pattern state changes can be made holistically (7.2).

Confidentiality is the top priority in coaching. Regardless of the tool, it must be ensured in particular in the online world that no unauthorized persons have access to the documented results and spoken words. Technically, this means that both the transmitted data including audio and video data must be transmitted encrypted and access to the online rooms is only possible for the coach and his client or in the group or team setting for his clients. The coach is responsible for this, as in face-to-face coaching.

In the CAI® World, virtual group rooms are created. It is determined who has access to this respective room. Only these persons can communicate with each other via audio, video and chat.

If a tool is suitable for both the current situation and the desired situation (target situation), then an existing copy function supports this by copying the result with the tool. By asking what would have to change, the clients can interactively design and experience how the current situation changes step by step. Whether the desired situation is built up step by step, by copying and changing, or rather on the "green meadow" by calling and creating a tool, the coach decides depending on the situation.

9.3.1 Chat

In a chat, in contrast to a verbal conversation, the conversation contributions are typed. The chat between two or more people can take place synchronously or asynchronously. Even in the case of synchronous events, work can be done based on writing, whether communication takes place exclusively in writing or what is spoken is noted down in the form of keywords. The chat can be used for this.

In the CAI® World there are three chat platforms:

A. **Chat as a communication tool:**
   The chat symbol is located in the tool overview. If it is opened, the following chat history is built up chronologically one below the other. Its content is freely designed by the chatters. It is possible to provide the chat with a timestamp (optional; ■ Fig. 9.2a).
   If the chat is used for documentation, the protocol symbol is selected instead of the own image (■ Fig. 9.2b). Coach and client agree on who writes.
B. **Chat with integrated question set:**
   If you click on a phase in the process menu, a chat can be triggered. Here is a box with an attached question set, which includes typical, systemic, solution-oriented questions that fit the respective phase (Kindl-Beilfuß, 2008; Patrzek, 2015). By clicking on a single question, it is transferred to the chat window. The question can be changed individually if necessary. This chat can also be used freely, i.e. the offered questions are an option and not a compulsion for the coaches (■ Fig. 9.3).
C. **Chat within an online tool:**
   If one of the other online tools that are listed in the tool overview is used, a chat appears to the right of the tool. This means that the tool area does not have to be left when the chat is used for communication or as a protocol in parallel (■ Fig. 9.4).

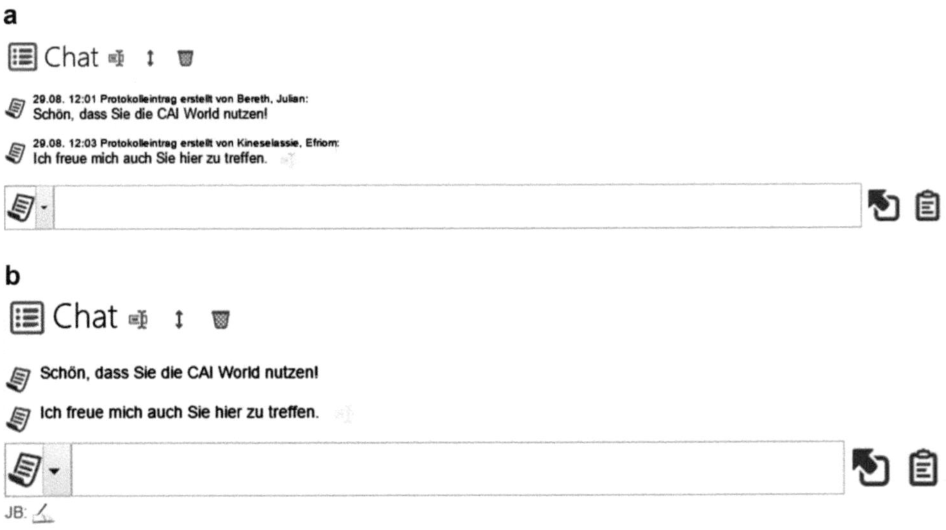

■ **Fig. 9.2** **a, b** Chat window. (© CAI GmbH)

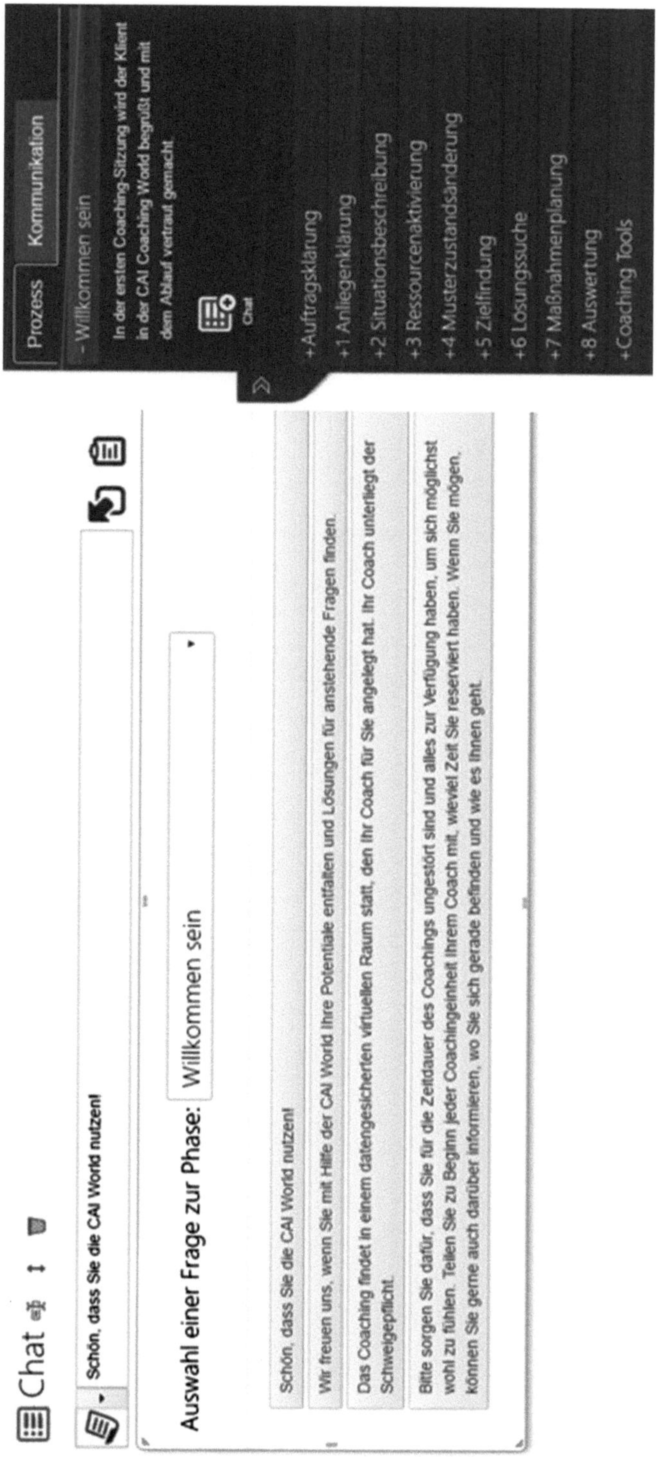

Fig. 9.3 Chat with open question box. (© CAI GmbH)

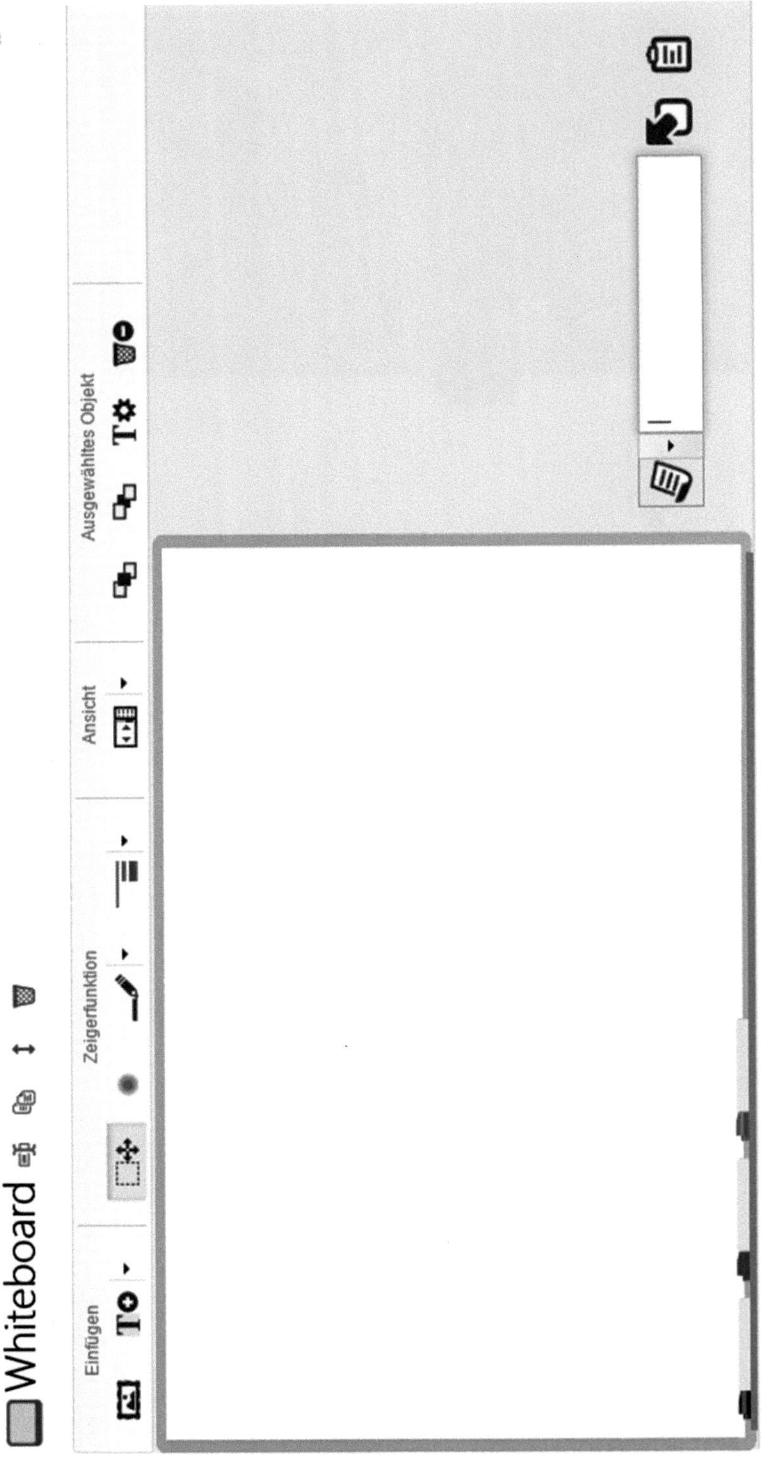

Fig. 9.4 Whiteboard with chat function. (© CAI GmbH)

In all chat variants, a small pen symbol is displayed when another person is writing. In the course of coaching, it is important to know whether the counterpart needs time to write or is waiting for a reaction from the coaches in case of breaks.

An editing function also allows corrections (e.g. spelling) to be made subsequently, i.e. after chats have already been sent. It is essential in coaching, on the one hand, to rectify misunderstandings (e.g. "We are talking today about your dismissal as a board member" or "We are talking today about your relief as a board member") and, on the other hand, to enable appreciative communication (e.g. "How are you today, Mrs. Meier?" or "How are you today, Mrs. Mayer?"). It should be noted that each person may only correct the words written by him/her and this is also indicated.

The professional behaviour when chatting is described in ► Sect. 9.2.1 (reading and writing competence).

▪ Use in the Following Coaching Phases

Chat is a phase-spanning tool. It can be used to design each coaching phase exclusively and it can accompany all other tools.

▪▪ Function

Process design, documentation, feedback.

Chat is also used mainly for process design when the phase transitions are initiated and tools are announced or described. Chat has an important documentation function, especially if it is not the only communication medium. If audio and video are used, a keyword-like protocol can run in the chat. In this respect, the chat also has the function of immediate feedback and serves to ensure understanding, which is particularly important in online events.

▪▪ Effect

cognitive, reflexive, emotionally relieving, dissociative.

9.3.2 Whiteboard

Coaches usually have flip charts and/or Metaplan walls in their coaching rooms to capture facts. In the online world, the so-called whiteboard is available for this purpose. It serves the purpose of joint writing, drawing and sorting. For this, freehand lines or shapes (line, circle, triangle, rectangle) are used.

Expansion options are useful for the whiteboard as an online tool in coaching. First, a background can be selected, e.g. for a SWOT analysis, coordinate systems, etc. Alternatively, a white background or the look of a corkboard can be selected. Various colored cards can be clicked, described and positioned on the wall. Unlike Metaplan cards made of paper, their size, shape and color can be changed. A pen function allows drawing and further design (e.g. marking, relating, clustering). The further design is supported in particular by the copy function. This way, a whiteboard already created can be inserted again in the further course of a coaching process. This makes it possible to carry out evaluations or make changes that document the progress of the process.

For example, a stakeholder analysis can be carried out following King and Vollmer (2014). This is usually used in strategy processes in organizations and can relate to different groups of people (e.g. external and internal customers, committees, etc.). In coaching, King & Vollmer use the stakeholder analysis in relation to system-relevant persons. This can be easily mapped and carried out on the whiteboard (◘ Fig. 9.5).

Similarly, visualizations of feedback loops, topic collections and much more can be made.

▪ Use in the Following Coaching Phases

The whiteboard can basically be used in any phase. It is particularly suitable for describing the situation, for example when it comes to sorting topics, collecting important context information and creating an overview. Furthermore, the whiteboard can be used for resource activation (in the sense of a collection), for the clear formulation of goals, for solution brainstorming and the measures assigned to them.

▪▪ Function

Visualization, sorting, clustering, overview.

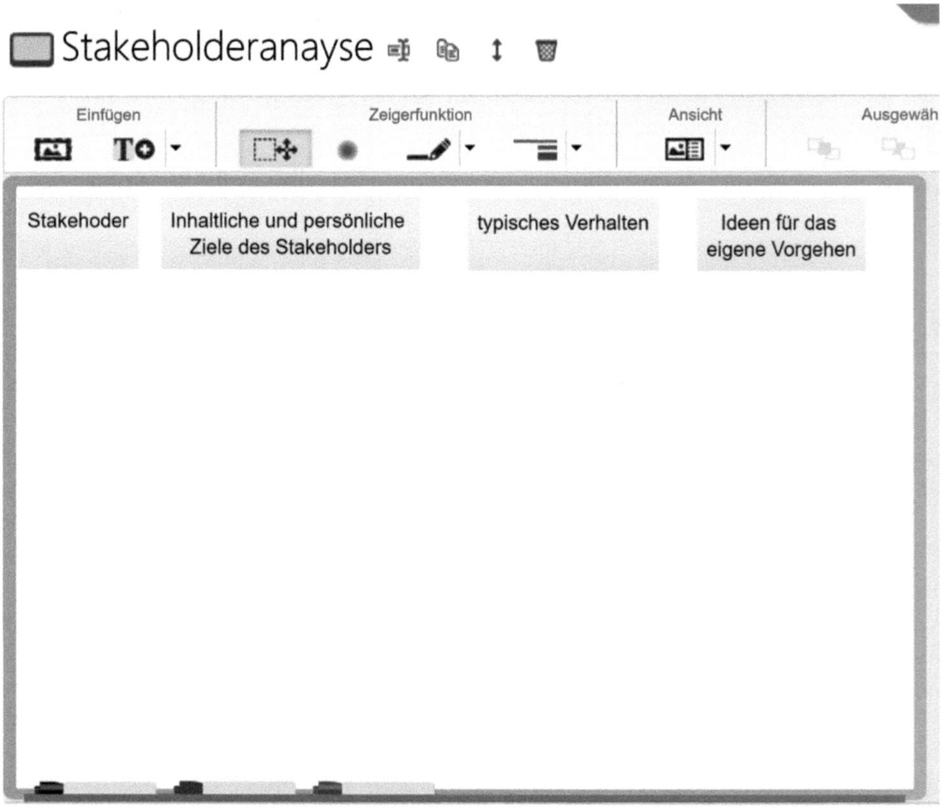

◘ **Fig. 9.5** Stakeholder analysis according to König and Vollmer (2014). (© CAI GmbH)

▪▪ Effect

cognitive, reflexive, dissociative; if the sign function is used creatively (e.g. for drawing a body schema, from bodily signals, etc.), also creative and associative.

9.3.3 Presentation

The presentation tool can be used to upload any documents, e.g. Word, Power Point, Excell or image files, and view them in the coaching session. This way, information can be provided that can be evaluated and used with coaching methods. This enriches the coaching process content-wise without coaches taking on the role of input providers. The presentation tool can also be used, for example, to jointly evaluate results of potential assessments, 360° feedback, target agreements, evaluations, etc., especially if these were the starting point for coaching (◘ Fig. 9.6).

▪ Use in the following coaching phases

The presentation tool is particularly suitable in the phases of contract and issue clarification, description of the situation and evaluation.

- Function: Information, evaluation
- Effect: cognitive, reflective, dissociative.

9.3.4 Sociogram

The sociogram is a graphical representation of relationships in a group. Moreno developed this technique and used it with different target groups, e.g. with nursing teams (Moreno, 2008). He identified different people with a letter or initials and represented relationships between them with arrows. Minuchin used a similar approach in his structural family constellation with the system drawing (Minuchin, 1997). Hauser and Schlömer (2014) describe the application in leadership coaching. First, the system to be considered is determined. Then the relevant persons are symbolized, e.g. by cards or signs (square for man, circle for woman). They are positioned next to each other as the clients perceive them. Connection lines represent the type of relationship between the persons. In the creation of the image and the subsequent reflection on it, aspects become conscious to the clients which they might not have perceived before. Here too, an IST image (current situation) and a Wunsch image (target situation) can be worked with (◘ Fig. 9.7).

The "Soziogramm" online tool can be used to schematically represent and annotate people. These person schemata can be changed in size and arrangement on the surface. A drawing tool and relationship arrows are available.

◘ Figure 9.8 shows a sociogram with relationship arrows. In addition, conflict-prone relationship hotspots were marked with red arrows.

▪ Use in the Following Coaching Phases

The sociogram is particularly well suited to visualize relationship structures in the phase of situation description. This first represents an actual situation. The sociogram can also be used to create a target image.

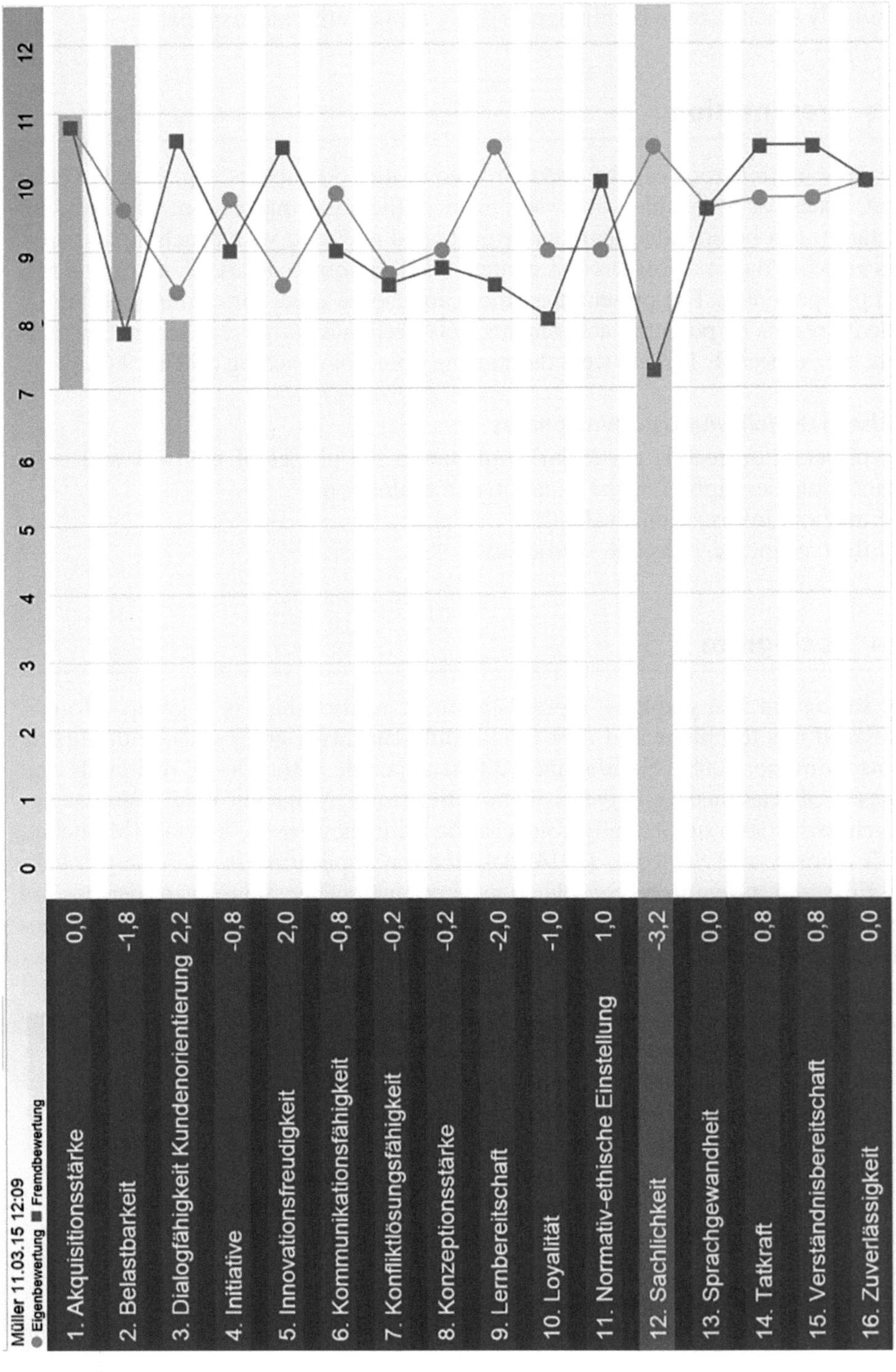

Fig. 9.6 Competence assessment displayed in presentation tool. (© CAI GmbH)

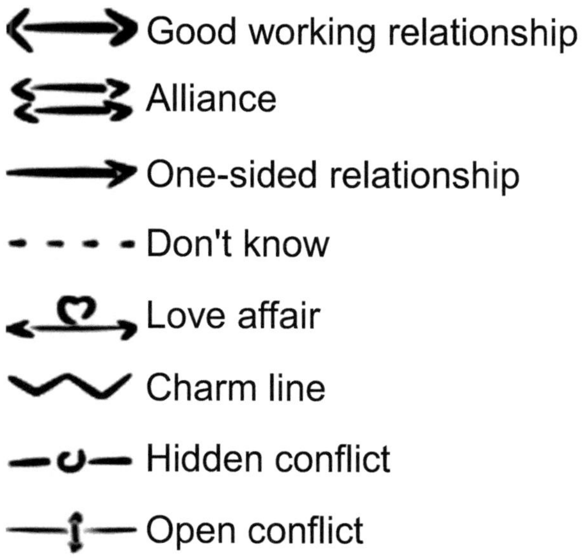

Fig. 9.7 Relationship arrows in the sociogram. (© CAI GmbH)

- Function: Visualization of relationship structures
- Effect: cognitive, reflexive, dissociative, associative (if the clients are part of the sociogram *are*)

9.3.5 Picture Gallery

The spoken language is connected with the explicit information and memory system and characterized by logic, linearity and consciousness. It creates distance to one's own experience and is helpful for reflection and integration processes, but not complete. The language of images is useful for the reflection and integration of unconscious parts, as it is connected with the implicit memory and the emotional center, i.e. with preverbal brain areas, which, as already mentioned (see ▶ Sect. 7.2) are essential for decision-making and behavior change. Especially in online coaching, where the question of access to emotions and physiological processes arises, the work with image material is of great importance. Messerschmidt (2015) lists the following characteristics/advantages that can be achieved through pictorial communication (e.g. through pictures, scenic representations, metaphors as linguistic images, imagined images):

- Images are perceived and processed more easily and effectively than texts
- Images are perceived not in fragments, but as a whole
- They reduce complex situations to the essentials
- They allow distance from one's own experience and support self-reflection
- Images are a mirror of the inner constitution

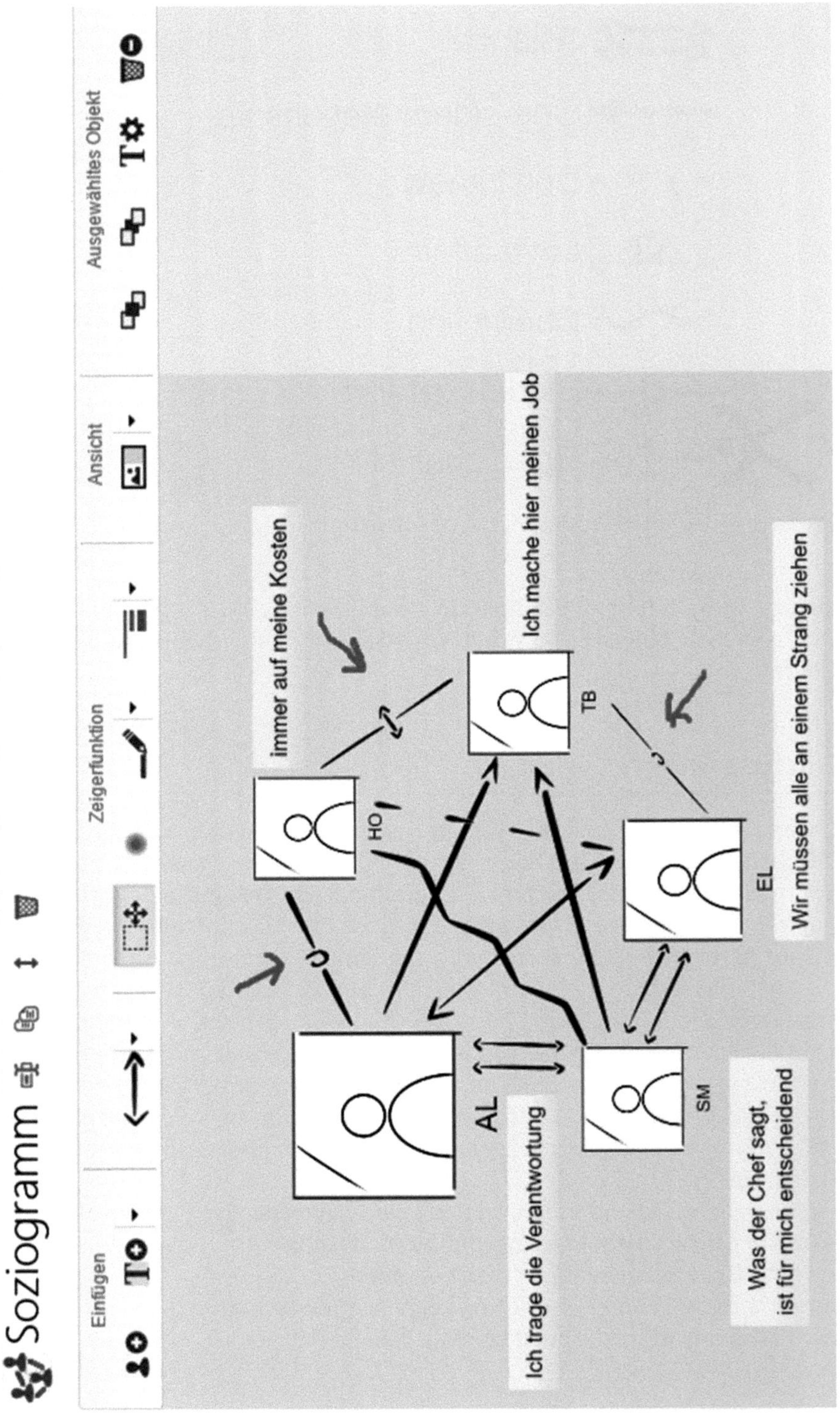

Fig. 9.8 Sociogram. (© CAI GmbH)

- They enable communication about difficult-to-communicate experiences and ambivalences
- Images connect cognitive and affective dimensions
- They convey "felt meaning"

Storch (2014) uses picture cards when it comes to aligning unconscious needs and conscious motives. The image material is used to activate resources via an associative level that are evaluated via somatic markers. If images are decoded, "unconscious components can be made accessible to consciousness and understanding through language" (Storch, 2014, p. 343). The decoding takes place for Storch via self- and foreign associations and is used for the formulation of so-called motto goals.

"The motto goal also meets the three criteria of action-effective goals: It is formulated as an approach goal, is under its own control and has a resource-activating affect balance" (Storch, 2014, p. 345).

Messerschmidt (2015) was able to show in her empirical study on the use of image material to promote self-reflection and self-change processes in individual coaching that images can take on an appropriate mediating role between mind and unconscious components. They support the finding of self-congruent development goals, as well as awareness processes and holistic change processes. However, this strong effectiveness also means that image material must be handled very professionally. In online coaching, this means even more than in face-to-face coaching that it should not be worked on in a problem-deepening, but in a resource-, goal- and solution-oriented way. Coaches should pay particular attention to positive formulations and the constructive use of image material. The following result from the study by Messerschmidt (2015) speaks in favor of this:

"It was shown that expressive, colorful, large-format and multi-interpretable image collections have the greatest effect on clients" (Messerschmidt, 2015, p. 380).

The multi-interpretability supports the attitude that it is not the coaches who should make a pre-selection of certain image cards, as they would orient themselves on their own interpretations. The clients are the only evaluative and interpretive instance.

In the CAI® World, therefore, clients are also offered very different images in the categories of buildings, landscape, trees, art and single-color background, so that they can choose the image that is right for them. The coaches make no preselection (◘ Fig. 9.9).

In the chat next to the image gallery, the associations of the clients to the images they have selected can be noted down in the form of keywords (◘ Figs. 9.10 and 9.11). With the drawing function, it is possible to draw or mark within the image.

▪ Use in the Following Coaching Phases

The image gallery can be used in the situation analysis if it is important to change the level. So it may be that at first with a whiteboard or the sociogram is worked, so rather cognitive and reflexive and the emotional level is initially left out. In addition, then image material can be used, which directly addresses the associative, emotional level. Furthermore, the work with image materials is suitable for resource activation and in particular for pattern state change, as this can never be done purely cognitively.

Fig. 9.9 Example of image selection in the “landscape” category. (© CAI GmbH)

■ **Fig. 9.10** Image association problem situation. (© CAI GmbH)

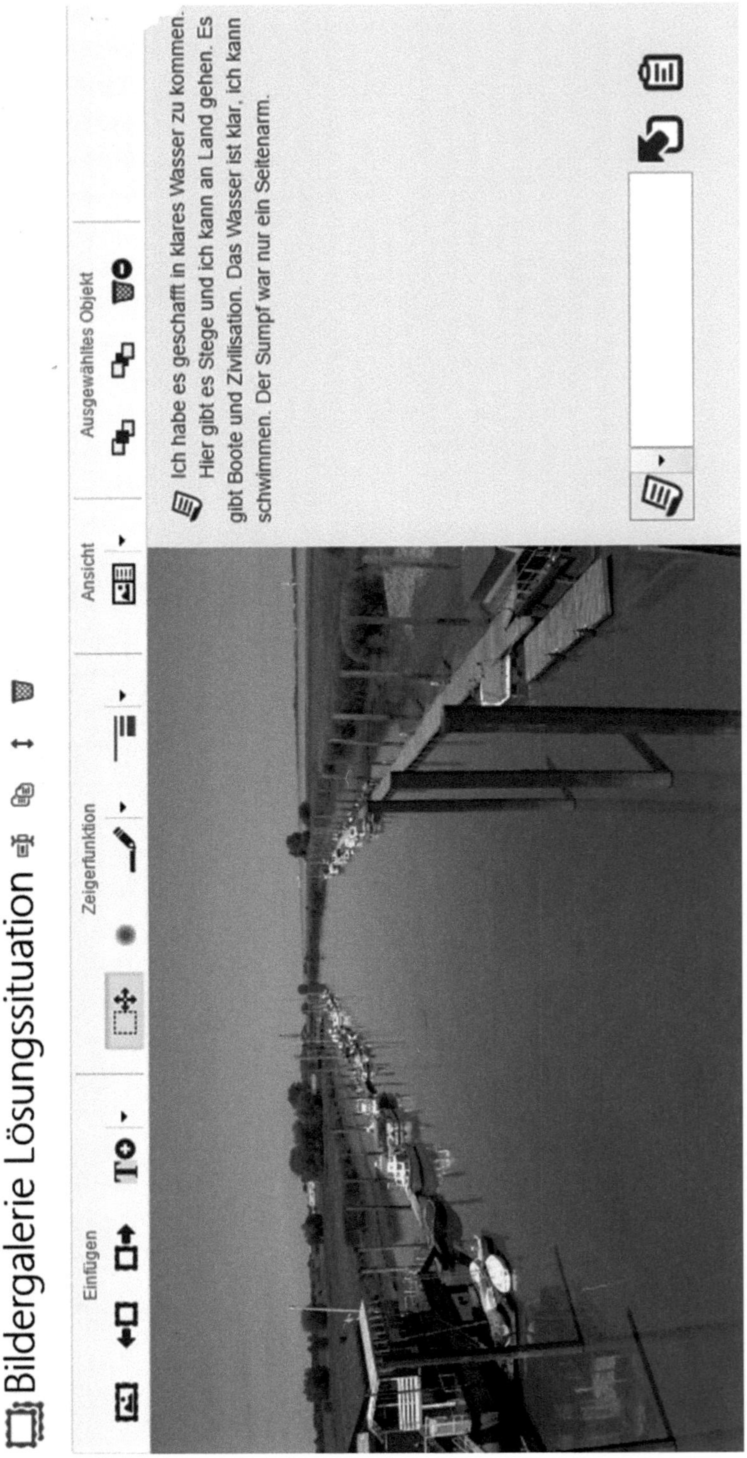

Fig. 9.11 Image association solution situation. (© CAI GmbH)

- Function: emotional expression, association, integration, perspective change
- Effect: emotional, associative, dissociation arises from the observation and linguistic evaluation, then also reflexively

9.3.6 Constellation

The "family constellation" originally stemming from family therapy was transferred to organizational systems (Weber, 2002; Varga von Kibéd & Sparrer, 2009). Organizational constellations can be used to represent teams and groups. Here too, the focal system is first defined. The constellation itself requires a group of people external to the system. These are chosen by the constellation leader (client) as so-called representatives and positioned in the room. This procedure is based on the assumption that these representatives will have perceptions that correspond to those of the actual team or group members, or that they will grasp the dynamics of the system through their position in the room. They thus provide valuable insights for the client's concerns, especially when it comes to making desired changes to the system.

If no group is available from which personal representatives can be drawn for a systemic constellation, work is done in analogy to the family board or system board used in coaching, which also stems from family therapy. For this purpose, the constellation is carried out with figures. It is a visualization of systemic relationships. The constellation process carried out by the client and the view of the board make it possible to gain insights into relationship dynamics, subsystems or important topics, to try out redesigns and to take different perspectives in finding solutions.

In online action, some of the possibilities subsumed under the term "constellation" are shifting and expanding.

Constellation in 2-D worlds means that figures can be arranged on a flat background (similar to a system board). In principle, an inexhaustible supply of figures can be selected, although it is recommended to limit the number offered so that the client is not overwhelmed and the selection process does not take too much time. In the CAI® World, current and historical figures, children's pictures, playing figures, chess figures, mythical figures, etc. are offered. There are also various symbols, stones and relationship arrows (◘ Figs. 9.12, 9.13 and 9.14).

Furthermore, it is possible to select a background image in the online process. This leads to a combination of the possibilities offered by the image gallery with the possibilities of the arrangement tool. The emotional "coloring" of a scene to be set up can be conveyed more strongly than on a given board or table (◘ Fig. 9.15).

The figures/symbols set up can be changed in size and direction of view. In addition, markings and symbolizations can be made using the drawing function. With insertable cards, additional information is recorded or the figures represented are given a "voice". The accompanying chat also allows for a keyword-like logging, or an associative and reflexive evaluation (9.16).

In group situations, the group members present can represent themselves or be assigned a symbol/person by the respective clients. They react from the perspective of this person or this symbol. This can happen when setting up the problem and solution situation and in particular during the solution brainstorming. This approach is particularly suitable when encountering intercultural contexts.

■ **Fig. 9.12** Extract from the selection of people in the CAI® arrangement. (© CAI GmbH)

■ **Fig. 9.13** Extract from the selection of animals in the CAI® arrangement. (© CAI GmbH)

The pictorial language represents a bridge that facilitates joint work and makes it possible to express or address topics that are not directly verbalized due to cultural reasons. This is supported by the possibility of anonymity, for example, in a group situation someone can choose a figure for themselves without revealing their name.

Further variants and, if necessary, deepenings arise if the same procedure takes place in 3-D worlds (► Sect. 9.3.9).

Fig. 9.14 Extract from the selection of symbols in the CAI® arrangement. (© CAI GmbH)

■ **Use in the Following Coaching Phases**

The arrangement is a phase-spanning tool. It is usually introduced in the phase of situation description and used for pattern state change and target finding by creating a situation image and a solution image. If the goals are defined, the arranged figures and symbols can also be used as a source for a solution brainstorming.

- Function: emotional, associative information and its integration, perspective change
- Effect: emotional, associative, creative-forming, dissociation arises through observation and linguistic evaluation, then also reflexively

9.3.7 Resource Tree

The design of a "resource tree" leads to an intensive resource focus throughout the use of this tool.

However, under the label "resource tree" different approaches are understood, as the following examples illustrate.

Beushausen (2010) describes a tree exercise called "resource tree" in which a tree is painted and it is about becoming aware of what feeds this tree. The food metaphor is then used to find out with the affected what they would need in a transferred sense for "food".

Reddemann (2004) also uses the food metaphor when she suggests to clients an imagination exercise in which they see a tree in a landscape that they associate with well-being. They are guided to lean on the tree, to identify with it, and to imagine that they are "nourished" from the ground and through the crown like the tree.

At the Lower Saxony Institute for Early Childhood Education and Development, Research Unit for Talent Promotion, the image of a resource tree can be

■ **Fig. 9.15** Extract background images arrangement. (© CAI GmbH)

found, in whose trunk and branches resources from the following areas are entered: performance areas, environmental resources, personal resources, talents and self-competence (► https://www.nifbe.de/das-institut/forschung/begabung/materialien-downloads/materialien-ressourcenorientierung/183-ressourcenbaum/file).

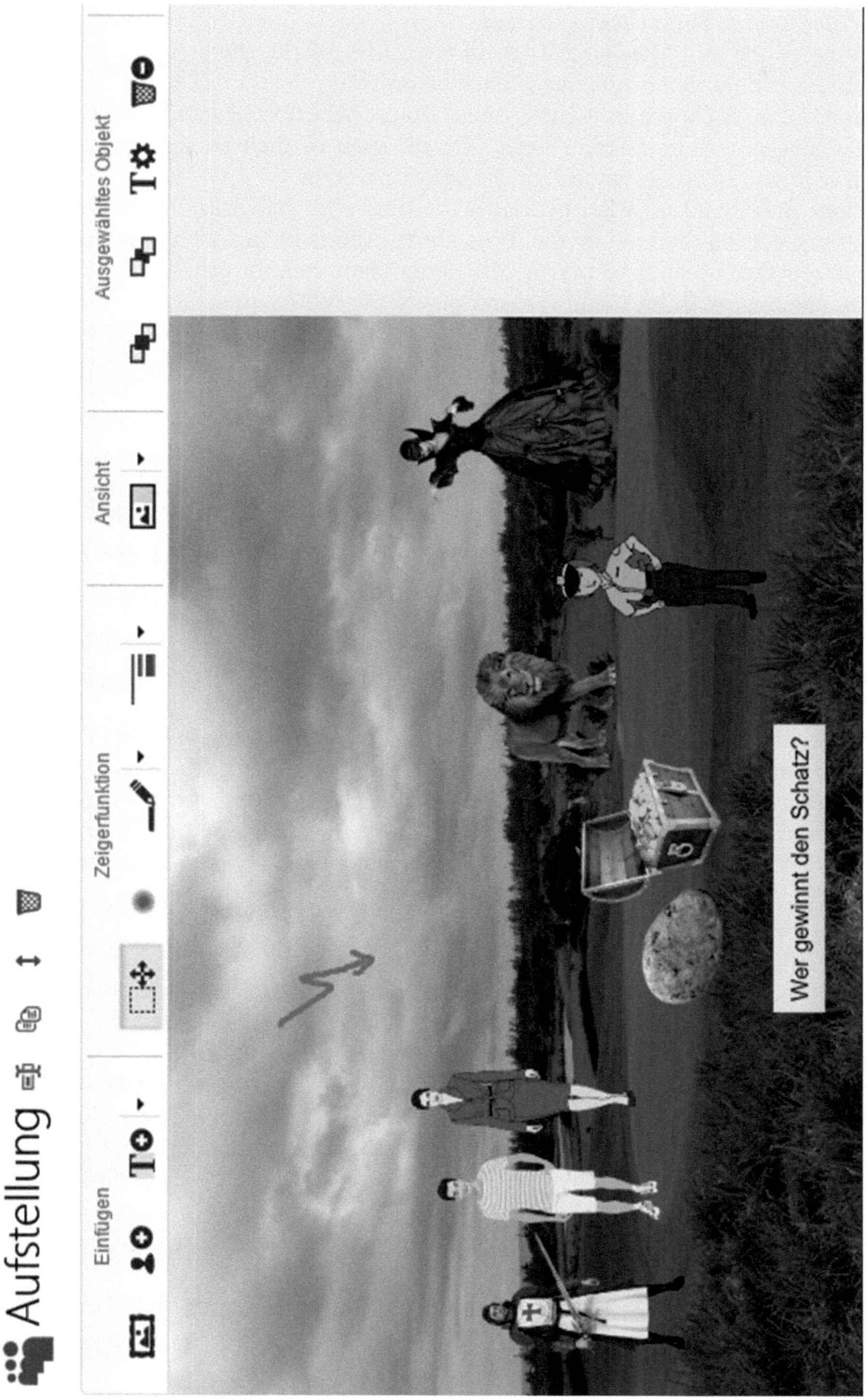

Fig. 9.16 Arrangement in the 2-D world. (© CAI GmbH)

Kaster (2014) proceeds similarly when working with the resource tree. In his description, the client paints a tree and lists all resources that come to mind and that she relates to in the branches of the tree.

In the online tool “Resource Tree” in the CAI® World, the process can be carried out according to the integrated coaching process.

First, a tree is chosen as a background from a selection of templates. Then the process is continued in different steps, with the roots of the tree, the trunk and the crown each representing symbols for the individual steps.

A. **Roots:** they stand for what nourishes the tree, what stabilizes and locates it. In this respect, on the level of the roots, those aspects of the client’s life are gathered together which have exactly this value. These can, for example, include values, personality traits, social systems, places, etc. With cards, these mentions are arranged on the level of the roots.
B. **Trunk:** in analogy to the formation of annual rings, on the level of the trunk all those abilities, skills and positive experiences are gathered together which the client has built up.
C. **Crown:** The crown is worked from top to bottom. The upper edge of the crown is adorned with the characteristics of a successful life. For this, questions from the question set of the phase of pattern state change can be used. From this “vision of life” the branches are stocked. They stand for already achieved and still to be achieved goals. After that, measures can be derived based on the current topic.

In ◘ Fig. 9.17 the online tool “Resource Tree” can be seen with the individual processing steps as a coach’s guide.

A resource tree that has been carried out is shown in ► Sect. 10.4.5 in individual coaching and in ► Sect. 10.4.2 in team coaching.

According to the procedure described, the term “Life Tree” would also be appropriate, as it is a resource-oriented view of the whole life. However, the term “Life Tree” is historically and mythologically documented (e.g. the Tree of Life in the Bible, Yggdrasil or Irminsul among the Germans, etc.), so it is not used.

▪ Use in the Following Coaching Phases

The resource tree is a tool that can be used across phases. It can be used to design a complete coaching unit. But it can also be introduced specifically in the phase of resource activation. By using it, a positive experience pattern is already prepared so that the pattern state change takes place smoothly, at the latest when developing a successful life vision. This is followed by the phases of goal finding and action planning. The clarification of concerns and evaluation are not actually part of the tool, but rather frame its use and are carried out with other tools (e.g. question tool in chat).

- **Function:** resource activation and continuous resource focus, decision-making in the holistic life context
- **Effect:** emotional, associative, imaginative, reflexive and cognitive by verbalization, then also dissociative

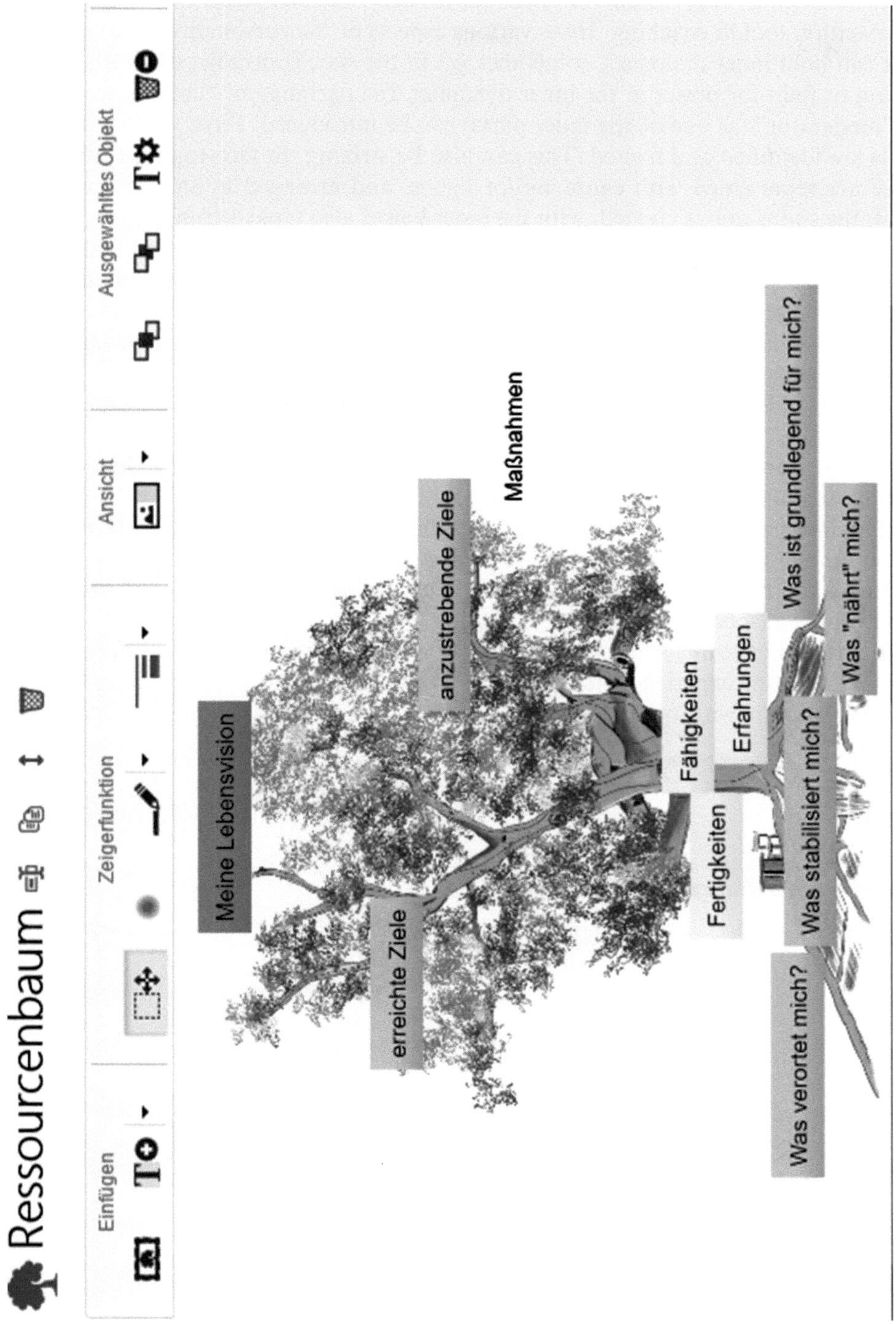

Fig. 9.17 Resource tree. (© CAI GmbH)

9.3.8 Inner Team

The "inner team" that Schulz von Thun (2013) describes has become a very popular intervention tool in coaching. Here, various aspects of the personality are identified that can hold inner dialogues, sometimes get in the way, contradict each other, coalition or fight for power in the inner dynamics. In coaching, an "inner/inner boss" or "moderator" (as one of the inner parts) can be introduced. First, inner voices or parts are identified and named. This can also be striking. In face-to-face coaching, these are represented with cards and/or figures and arranged in an arrangement. First, the status quo is created, with the inner voices also typical sentences or words can be assigned. When changing to the desired image, it should be noted that none of the "inner parts" "flies out" of the arrangement. All "voices" are part of the personality of the clientele, for example, needs, values, drivers, attitudes or beliefs. The arrangement is changed when creating the desired image. From this, goals and action options can be derived.

Küster (2014) describes the ability of clients to deepen self-awareness and self-reflection as a prerequisite for working with the inner team.

In the "Inner Team" online tool, clients first select a silhouette (◘ Fig. 9.18). Various templates are offered for this purpose.

The inner parts can be represented in different colors and arranged in the selected silhouette (◘ Fig. 9.19).

Cards can be used to make further labels, e.g. typical sentences that are to be assigned to the respective shares.

If the "inner team" is carried out in 3-D worlds, there are even more possibilities for activating experiences (◘ Fig. 9.20). It is possible to arrange the inner shares with symbols or with other people or their avatars if a group context is available (► Sect. 9.3.9).

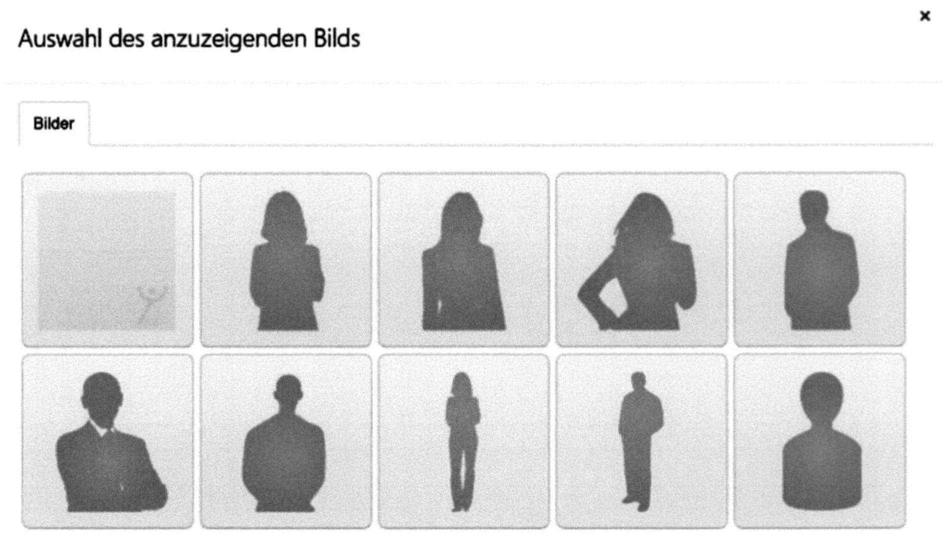

◘ **Fig. 9.18** Silhouettes for the Inner Team. (© CAI GmbH)

Fig. 9.19 Selection of inner parts in the inner team. (© CAI GmbH)

- **Use in the Following Coaching Phases**

The inner team can be used in the situational analysis, for changing the pattern state and for finding the goal. An actual image and a solution image are created in doing so.

- **Function:** emotional, associative information and their integration, perspective change
- **Effect:** reflective (at the beginning through the tool instruction of the coaches, which is somewhat more extensive here than with other tools), associative and shaping (by the selection of colors and by the placement of the small symbols in the silhouette), dissociation occurs through the observation and linguistic evaluation, then also reflective.

9.3.9 3-D world

In 3-D worlds, many possibilities for activating experiences and changing perspectives can be used. If they are designed (see ► Chap. 12) in such a way that factors such as presence, involvement and immersion (see ► Sect. 7.3) can have an impact, the emotional and physiological level is addressed directly. Whole states can be activated and changed through landscapes, light, seasons, weather, avatar design and colors. The clients experience the change directly. This happens, for example, through systemic arrangements of actual and solution situations with figures, symbols and avatars, similar to face-to-face coaching (Varga von Kibéd & Sparrer, 2009). A special feature is that the clients can look through the eyes of their avatars and thus create the impression that they are facing another figure directly. They can make themselves and other figures or symbols larger or smaller, fly high and look down from a bird's eye view, and make slight changes easily. This creates a clear advantage compared to system visualization, in which people are represented by cards or symbols and placed on the floor or on a table. König and Vollmer (2014) describe this method in the face-to-face variant and use it to make use of the clients\1'\2 implicit knowledge or their emotional intelligence for the coaching process. Based on the fact that systems change when the position of a system member

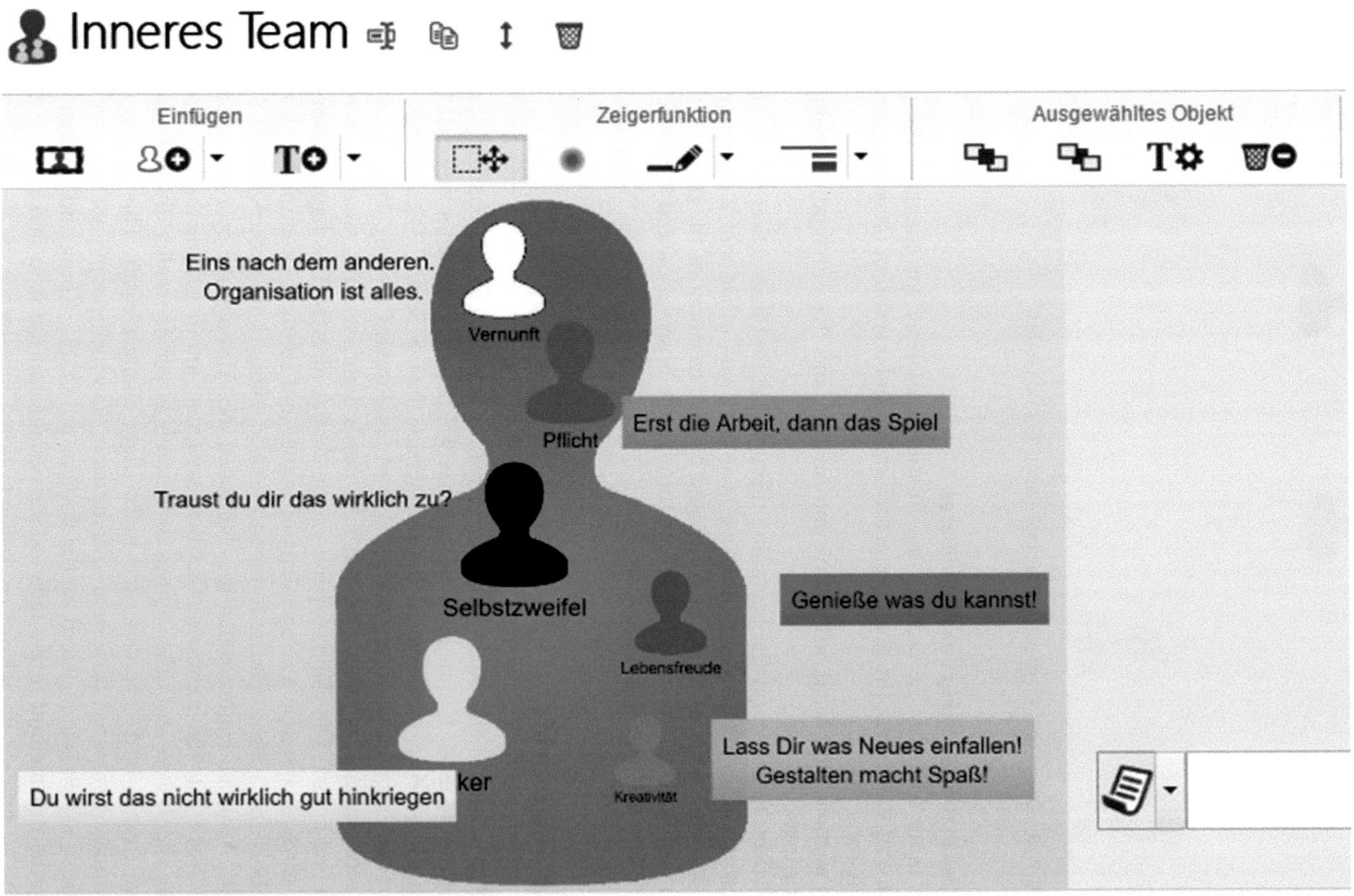

Fig. 9.20 Das Innere Team. (© CAI GmbH)

changes, the clients can change their own position in the three-dimensional system and thus experience directly which further changes this entails.

Since immersion in 3D worlds promotes holistic experience to a great extent, it is particularly important here to focus attention on resource activation and solution focus (Schmidt, 2014). Problem updating by shaping and deepening the problem situation and the problem context should only take place to the extent that it is necessary to understand the situational variables, or as a helpful starting point for shaping solution scenarios.

If inner parts are set up in 3D worlds, immediate communication with them is possible.

In contrast to 2-D worlds, 3-D worlds also allow the experience of movement. To come or be in motion is the metaphor for change par excellence. It is the special feature of 3-D worlds that movement takes place in them. While an arrangement in the 2-D world is static and the clientele looks at it, they move in the three-dimensional arrangement in the middle of it. It would be rather strange if two avatars sat and talked to each other while coaching (see ▶ Sect. 7.4). It is the experience and design of actual and target situations, the concretely experienced changes and the trial action, which makes the advantage of the 3-D world in coaching. The coaches do not leave their clients alone in the world, but move with them, accompany them, talk to them, as they would do if they used movement as an intervention strategy in face-to-face procedures. They can go for a walk together, or work with floor anchors or a timeline. With the timeline, a change of perspective in time is possible (Resch & Tomaschek, 2014; James & Woodsmall, 1998). A time axis is created on which today, the past and the future are marked. In face-to-face contact, this is usually done with cards that are laid out on the floor. Clientele stand or sit on these cards and can perceive what this respective place triggers in them. They can walk the distances in between and gain insights from it. Avatars can also do this in 3-D worlds.

Coaching in 3-D worlds fulfills the effect factors of action-oriented methods, which Ameln and Kramer (2007) represent. The physical representation of social and innerpsychic themes, as they are carried out, for example, in psychodrama, leads to emotional confrontations, cathartic experiences and creative redesigns. For this purpose, the creation of a surplus reality (Moreno, 2008) is used, which leaves room for projections and changes. An action and a reflection space can also be defined and used.

The arrangement in 3-D worlds can be carried out both in individual and group coaching (◘ Fig. 9.21). In individual coaching, it has the value of visualization with deepened experience activation and action possibility; in group coaching, other people can be present and arranged as avatars. They can feed their perceptions and experiences into the process as valuable information, similar to what happens with systemic arrangement and representatives.

■ Use in the Following Coaching Phases

Coaching in 3-D worlds can take place across phases. It is particularly helpful to symbolically recreate situations three-dimensionally in the phase of situation description, resource activation, and change in the pattern state.

Fig. 9.21 Arrangement 3-D world. (© CAI GmbH)

- **Function:** Experience activation, trial action, perspective change
- **Effect:** Involved, emotional, associative, creative-designing, Dissociation arises from the observation and linguistic evaluation, then also reflexively.

9.3.10 Example Case

The following example case refers to a coaching that was carried out exclusively online.

The first coaching session took place online with the client, here called Michael Hübner. Therefore, the target framework for coaching (level I, ► Sect. 8.4.2) was first delineated and some observable success criteria for a later evaluation were defined. The client took on the new role of head of a main department and wanted to get involved in coaching at this first contact. His concern for this unit was the reflection of the situation in his new team in order to identify possible conflict or problem areas early on. After some information about the situation had been gathered (situation description), the constellation tool was used. The constellation tool was used twice, once to illustrate the actual situation and once to work out the desired situation after the change of the pattern state. For the dissociation from the problem state, the client was asked after a positive experience in relation to "new beginning". Spontaneously, the birth of the first child came to his mind. He could easily recall and experience this phase of his life. From this emotional state of mind, he designed the desired image in relation to his team in the phase of reorientation. The desired image formed the starting point to develop goals in the next step. These

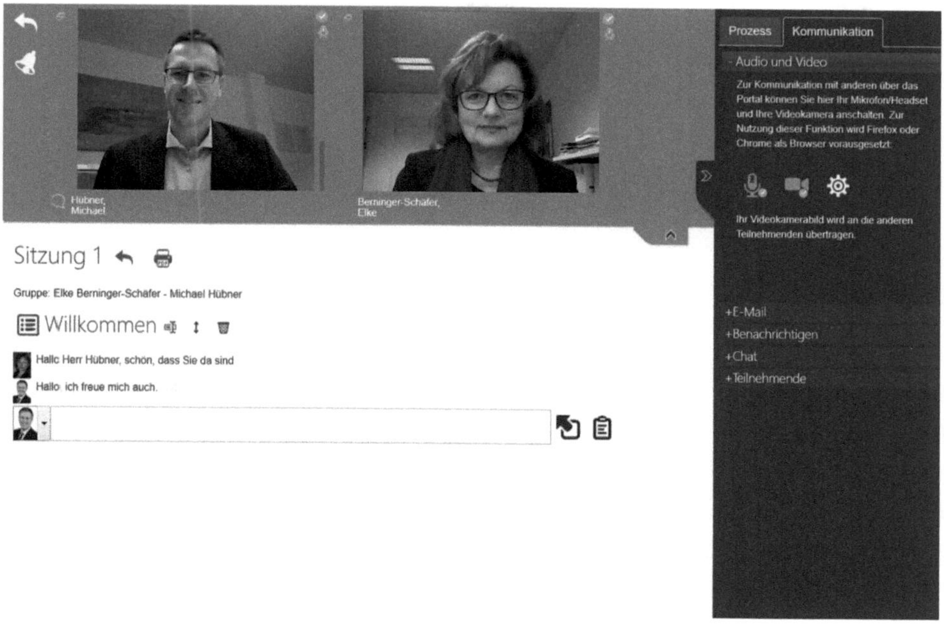

Fig. 9.22 View from the coaching session. (© CAI GmbH)

were arranged on a whiteboard. The "figures" from the constellation were asked for "advice" when it came to carrying out a solution brainstorming to find concrete measures for achieving the goals. From these measures, first steps were selected and their implementation was concretized and scheduled. A feedback on the coaching unit ended this sequence.

The communication took place via video and audio (Fig.9.22). In addition, both the coach and the client have written down the questions and answers that are essential to them. This makes it possible to trace the course of the session well. The client anyway intended to look at this course again and evaluate it. For him it was also about deepening those aspects that he had not chosen for the immediate implementation. The scrollbar was used again and again to scroll back to the whiteboard with the goals and solutions in order to make additions.

Coach		Elke Berninger-Schäfer	EBS

Client		Michael Hübner	MH

- **First Steps**

EBS: – Have you ever had any experience with coaching?

MH: – No, not yet. This is my first time!

EBS: – Does the coaching initiative come from you?

MH: – Yes, it came from me. Because of my new position, I expressed the desire!

EBS: – What expectations do you have of the coaching?

MH: – I would like to better define my new role as head of department and expect your support.

EBS: – What will you notice at the end of our coaching journey together that you have achieved your goal?

MH: – I will then be more confident in dealing with my employees and colleagues and will be perceived by them as a leader.

EBS: – What will you notice in everyday life that you have more confidence in your new role?

MH: – I get positive feedback and my employees recognize that I, although I was on the same level before, am now a valuable leader.

EBS: – What makes the value of a leader for you?

MH: – My professional competence is respected as well as my social competence and I can help my employees on both levels. The value is therefore not only in the professional, but also in the general dealings.

EBS: – How will your superiors react if you achieve your goals?

MH: – My work is also recognized and appreciated there and the career ladder is not over.

EBS: – If we take the perspective of the customer, how will this affect you when you achieve your goals?

MH: – I will also have a more confident appearance there and the contact with the customer will be closer and more familiar, and thus more successful.

EBS: – That means that in coaching it is about role clarification, how can I receive security and appreciation for both my professional and social skills and make further progress in my career?

MH: – Yes, exactly!

EBS: – In what time frame would it be important for you to achieve these goals?

MH: – Three to six months.

EBS: – What first events will you notice that you have already progressed?

MH: – My deputy, who is currently planning a new release, already involves me in the concrete farewell of the content in advance and asks for my opinion.

A colleague in the board is temporarily out of action and the chairman of the board temporarily entrusted me with the tasks of the colleague.

EBS: – Very nice, that are clearly observable signs.

To achieve these goals, we can carry out several coaching sessions. Do we want to start today?

MH: – Yes, very gladly

- **Issue Clarification**

EBS: – So that we can deal with your topic well, we will take up individual focal points.

With which concrete situation would you like to start today?

MH: – I would like to analyze and understand my closest environment in the team, and how the connections are there.

EBS: – What is it about for you?

MH: – I would like to recognize whether there are conflict issues and problem areas.

EBS: – This means that your concern is to identify the relationship structures within the team in order to identify any potential conflicts and problems.

MH: – Right. And if there are any, how do I deal with them?

EBS: – O. K. Then let's look at the team situation.

- **Situation Description**

EBS: – How long have you known the team?

MH: – I have known one part for several years, another part of the team comes through a merger of departments. I do not know these people. They have only been in my environment for two weeks.

EBS: – What has been the atmosphere in the new, large team so far?

MH: – Mixed! Some see it as a great opportunity, others see more risks.

EBS: – How would you briefly describe the team's task?

MH: – The new department is active in project business. Parts of the team work at the customer and in support, others are closely linked to the development department and coordinate the deliveries.

EBS: – What are the current challenges for the team?

MH: – New processes and new structures have to be created, which of course means that existing processes and structures have to be changed. This creates potential for conflict.

EBS: – To understand this challenging and complex situation well, it is helpful to carry out a systemic set-up.

MH: – Systemic set-up means that we symbolize the people in your team and position them to each other.

EBS: – Please first select a background image for this arrangement, which expresses the current mood in the team.

Very nice. What does this image mean to you?

MH: – Soberness, unknown territory, non-visible angles

EBS: – You can now symbolize people using the second button from the left. If you click on them, they appear in the image.

You can change the size of the figures and position them relative to each other as you perceive their relationship.

In the next step you can identify the people with an abbreviation

With relationship arrows between the people we get an impression of the system

Aufstellung der IST-Situation im Fallbeispiel. (© CAI GmbH)

- **Image Description and Resource Activation**

MH: – The relationship between M. S. and R. A. is not clear to me: I was told that they sometimes agree, sometimes argue about trivialities. K. L. is often in the background, but manipulates the others very skillfully, which I have also been able to observe.

I have the feeling that I am in the middle. S. W. should actually support me, but we also have noticeable communication problems.

EBS: – What do you perceive there exactly?

MH: – We interpret the same situations differently, even when we talk about them, I have the impression that we still have two perspectives afterwards.

EBS: – What does the wall stand for?

MH: – I see almost insurmountable differences in the perception of situations.

EBS: – What is the relationship between M. S. and you?

MH: – He is not honest and tries to pursue his own interests, often to the detriment of the team.

EBS: – Who else in the team supports you the most?

MH: – Definitely R. A.—he and I are on the same wavelength and value things similarly. K. L. is generally on my side as well.

EBS: – What other positive aspects are there for you?

MH: – It's positive that I actually see myself in the position to improve the situation with S. W. In addition, the situation is new for everyone, I assume that over time there will be a mutual approach.

EBS: – I notice that everyone is looking in the same direction and is quite friendly, except for the snake.

MH: – Yes, that is also correct, I think we all have the same goal in mind.

EBS: – That is, the conflict field is still most likely at the snake and the manipulation strategies of K. L. and a problem is the communication with S. W.

MH: – Yes, I have now become clear.

- **Change of Desired State**

EBS: – I assume you've had a restart before. Which was the most positive in your biography so far?

MH: – The most far-reaching, positive event was certainly the birth of my child.

EBS: – What was so great about it for you?

MH: – To see new life that is so dependent on oneself is impressive. Also, the fact that one suddenly has a multiple of responsibility is imposing.

- **Wish Situation**

Aufstellung der Wunsch-Situation im Fallbeispiel. (© CAI GmbH)

EBS: – Responsibility for others seems to be something very positive for you. How does that feel?

MH: – Taking responsibility for others is a good feeling. It gives you the feeling of being needed, but you can also achieve a lot more together with and through others than alone.

EBS: – Assuming you experience this great feeling of positive responsibility and shared goal achievement in your new team …

how do you feel then?

MH: – Very good. This is my motivation for my work.

EBS: – I would now like to invite you to make a systemic setting based on this feeling. Perhaps you would like to start with a new background image that fits this positive mood better.

The procedure is the same as before, only based on a desired state.

You have chosen a different background image than before. What does this image mean to you?

MH: – Summer, warmth, relaxation, nature

Open, clear view

EBS: – Please symbolize the important people again and position them so that it feels good to you.

I see that everyone is here, only the snake has changed. A sun and a treasure chest have been added. The wall is gone. What does that mean to you?

MH: – For me it is important that we all stand in a circle and are together. The treasure chest is our common goal. The snake behaves as a team player and the sun seems to be shining for all of us.

EBS: – S. W. and M. S. have swapped places.

MH: – That's not so important, what's important to me is that they're standing at the same distance from me.

- **Goal Finding**

EBS: – How will you recognize in everyday life that everyone is standing in a circle? What is different then?

MH: – Open words, mutual support, e.g. for clarification in case of different opinions, trusting approach in everyday life.

EBS: – How do you recognize the trusting approach concretely?

MH: – By, for example, openly expressing one's own opinion, but also a change of opinion in the group is no longer a loss of face.

EBS: – What will you notice when the snake has become a team player?

MH: – The snake orders its personal interests under the interest of the team and is also willing to compromise if necessary.

EBS: – Does that mean that the team interests are placed before the personal interests for you?

MH: – No, that means that the personal interests and the interest of the team grow together over time. So there can be no conflicts in the future.

EBS: – What do you think is necessary for this?

MH: – The team's interests should be jointly defined.

EBS: – I have the goals we just worked out clustered on cards in the whiteboard in color. Is that right? Are there any other goals from your point of view?

MH: – Yes, that's exactly right!

EBS: – Then our next step would be a solution brainstorming, i.e. we bring together what measures there can be at all to achieve these goals.

Do you have any ideas about this? Then we can take them to the whiteboard.

MH: – Yes, I already have ideas. I add them to the whiteboard.

EBS: – We can enrich the solution brainstorming with further perspectives.

What would A. R. advise, what should you do to achieve your goals?

What would K. L. advise?

What solution idea would M. S. offer?

What solution tip would S. W. have?

to S. W.: What do you have to do concretely to give S. W. more trust?

Zielfindung und Lösungsbrainstorming auf dem Whiteboard im Fallbeispiel. (© CAI GmbH)

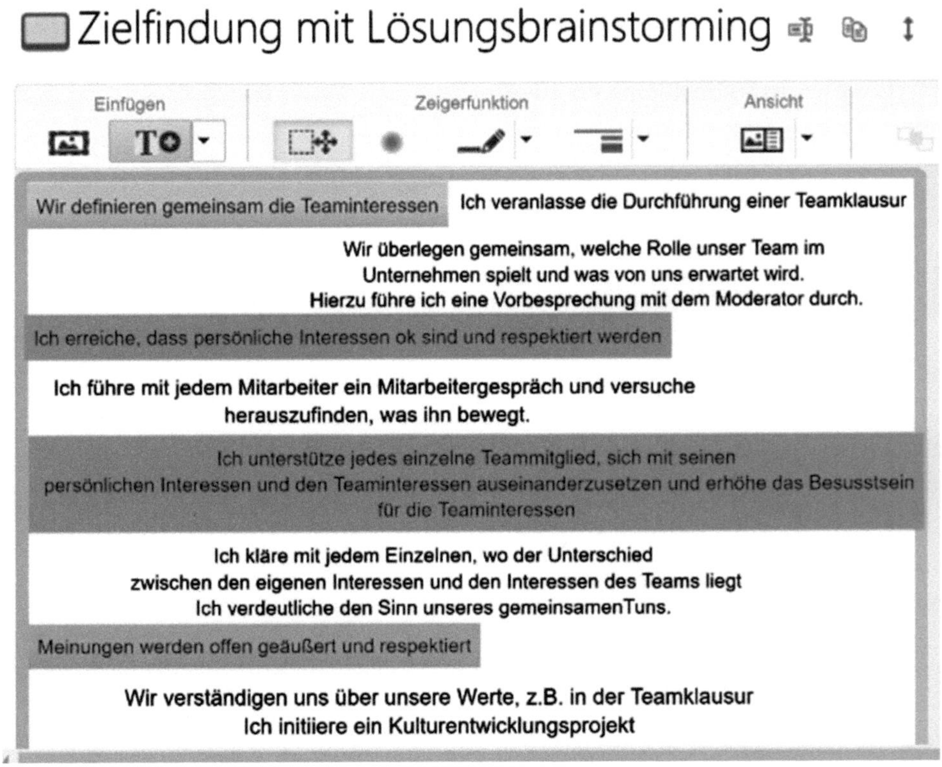

- **Planning of Measures**

Aufstellung Wunsch-Situation und Lösungsbrainstorming im Fallbeispiel. (© CAI GmbH)

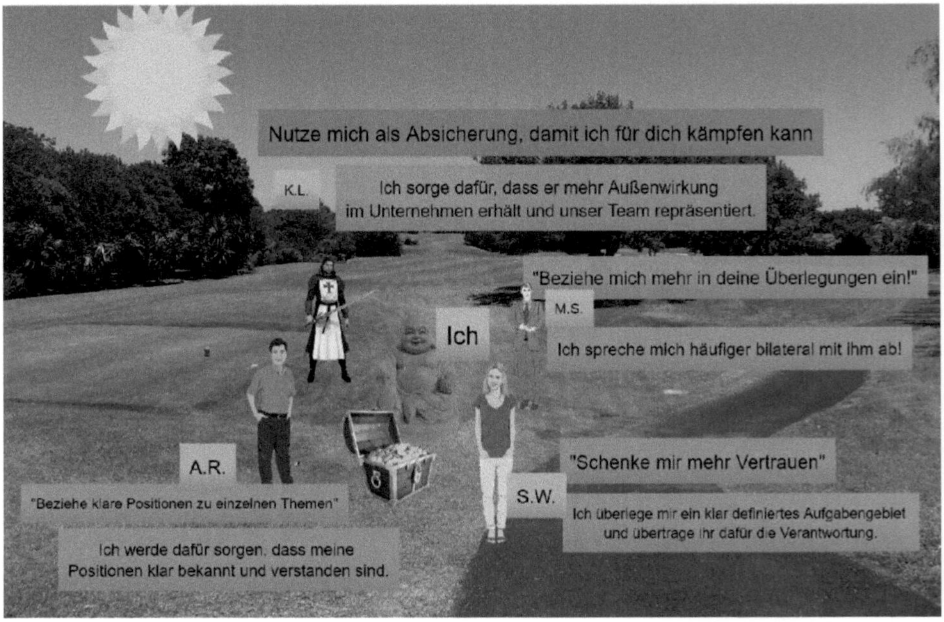

EBS: – We have collected some possible solutions on the whiteboard and in the minutes. If you look at them again, which do you think are appropriate and feasible?

MH: – I think the individual employee conversations are urgent and appropriate. The team seminar is very important and can be carried out very quickly. All other ideas are also valuable, I would like to check again in four weeks what I have already achieved and what still needs to be done on the basis of this protocol.

EBS: – Very nice. What are you going to start with specifically?

MH: – I will set dates for the employee meetings.

EBS: – That would be a first step. What would be the second?

MH: – I will prepare the team retreat.

EBS: – When will the preparation be completed?

MH: – I think in three weeks at the latest.

EBS: – This sounds good and very concrete.

- **Evaluation**

EBS: – Your concern was to identify the relationship structures within the team in order to identify any potential conflicts and problems.

Have you made progress in addressing this issue?

MH: – I have the impression that I have made a great deal of progress with the knowledge I have gained.

EBS: – On a scale of 0 to 10 (10: very good), how would you rate this coaching session?

MH: – This is a 10 for me because the relationship dynamics were very clear to me and I also have concrete points of reference on how to proceed.

EBS: – Thank you very much, I'm very pleased.

MH: – I have to thank you!

EBS: – How do we want to proceed?

MH: – I have to go through all this again and will make another appointment with you in about two weeks.

EBS: – I am looking forward to it and I am already curious which issue we will then deal with.

I say goodbye for today, until next time.

MH: – I am also looking forward to it. Goodbye!

In this case study, the coaching process of the "Karlsruhe School" was carried out in a coaching unit. It lasted 70 min. Methodically, questions were asked, reflections were made, and visualization was done on the whiteboard and Aufstellungstool. This was the format of business coaching in a two-person setting, which was carried out synchronously via the CAI® World. Video, audio, chat, and visualization tools were used as communication media.

The coaching process of the "Karlsruhe School" presented can be applied to different topics, settings and formats. The following chapter is therefore dedicated to the coaching formats, some of which are described and illustrated with examples.

Coaching Formats

Contents

E. Berninger-Schäfer, *Online Coaching*,
https://doi.org/10.1007/978-3-658-39133-1_10

The development of coaching formats is linked to the historical development of coaching as a professional discipline, as described in ► Sect. 4.2. Phase 10 in the development of coaching, "Digital Coaching, Online Professionalism", is described there, among other things, with the topics of format extension and differentiation of topics, settings and target groups. This makes a great variety of coaching products possible. In turn, this means that coaches need to know and implement the diverse design options for coaching, i.e. they need a format or design competence in order to be able to specialize. Gross and Stephan (2015) also come to the conclusion in their market study that it will be this specialization that makes coaches future-proof.

> The marking for specialization corresponds to the results of the first Marburg Coaching Study, according to which coaches who specialize can realize significantly higher order and sales figures than coaches who do not specialize (Gross & Stephan, 2015, p. 24).

This specialization requires format competence.

10.1 Explanation of Terms Format and Setting

The formats emerge in the course of the differentiation and specification of coaching and, in particular, through the possibilities offered by new media. There is very little to be found in the existing coaching literature about coaching formats. An exception is the book "E-Coaching and Online Counselling. Formats, Concepts, Discussions" edited by Geißler and Metz (2012), which focuses specifically on modern media. In the compendium of the German Coaching Association "Coaching as a Profession", Dietz and Müller (2012) name individual, group and team coaching as different settings. They speak of organisational coaching and of coaching as a form of consultation within other formats, e.g. training, workshops or crisis management.

Due to this situation, a clarification of the terminology format and setting should take place before format criteria are presented in the following.

The term Setting is not found in the German etymological dictionary by Döbler (1995) nor is the term Format. The definition of "Form" closest to that found in Döbler is "sinnlich wahrnehmbare Gestalt eines Gegenstandes oder einer Vorstellung" which translates to "the sensually perceivable shape of an object or an idea". This also corresponds to part of the definition of "Format" as found in DWDS, the German language dictionary of current usage (a compilation of various lexicons, including the etymological dictionary and the dictionary of current usage): [1]

> **Format** n. 'Größe, Gestalt, Maß, Bedeutung, stark ausgeprägtes Persönlichkeitsbild', entlehnt aus dem substantivierten Neutrum des Part. Perf. lat. *formātum* von lat. *formāre* 'formen, gestalten' (s. Form). Seit dem 16. Jh. in der Buchdruckersprache 'Papiergröße, Höhe und Breite eines Bogens, eines Buches', danach allgemein 'Größe, Geformtes, Ausgeprägtes, Bedeutendes'.—**Formation** f. 'Gestaltung', militärisch

1 ► www.dwds.de.

'Aufstellung, Gliederung, Einheit', im 16. Jh. aus lat. *formātio* (Gen. *formātiōnis*) 'Gestaltung, Bildung' (Verbalabstraktum zu lat. *formāre*) entlehnt; seit dem 18. Jh. geologischer Terminus für 'Zeitabschnitt der Erdgeschichte mit charakteristischer Schichtenbildung' (▶ http://www.dwds.de/?qu=Format, eingesehen am 15.08.2016).

However, format is described in the Duden as "(standardized) size ratio of an object according to … 2a. strongly pronounced personality; extraordinary rank … 2b. special level, great importance" (▶ http://www.duden.de/suchen/dudenonline/Format, accessed on August 15, 2016).

There is also no entry for setting in the DWDS.

In the Duden, setting is described as frame or environment. Something happens in this frame or environment (▶ http://www.duden.de/suchen/dudenonline/Setting, accessed on August 15, 2016).

Transferred to coaching, format refers to the form of implementation (in the sense of the perceivable shape) and setting refers to frame or environment variables. The factors that influence the coaching process in the sense of a frame setting are described in the following chapter as setting factors.

10.2 Setting Factors

The following list of setting factors does not claim to be complete. Rather, it should represent a first systematic collection, which is brought into an optical form at the end of the chapter. The setting factors can be flexibly combined in different coaching processes.

- **Connection of the Coaches—Internal and External Coaching, Internal and External Coach Pools**

The employment relationship of the coaches usually has no influence on the form of coaching carried out, but is a variable that characterizes and influences coaching (◘ Table 10.1).

We speak of **internal** coaching when coaches are employed in the organization for which they work as coaches. This is a relevant setting variable as it affects the possibilities of use of the coaches. Internal coaches cannot coach at a higher hierarchical level than they themselves hold and should also not coach in their own work unit. The applicable coaching formats remain unaffected.

◘ **Table 10.1** Overview of coach connections

Internal coaches	External, freelance coaches	Internal coach pool	External coach pool
Employed in the organization where the coaching takes place	Offer individual coaching services, independently	External and internal coaches are subject to the same quality standards and quality assurance criteria and are used for employees of the organization	Offers individual coaching services to different clients, which are carried out by different coaches

External coaches offer their coaching services in a freelance or employed capacity at an external provider. They can be members of coach pools, as some organisations set up coach pools or work with external pool providers for their internal needs. They usually define the admission criteria for the pool, the commissioning and implementation processes of coaching, as well as the quality assurance of the coaches and the coaching units carried out. This also applies to coach pool providers who offer coaching services on the market and use coaches from their pool for this purpose.

▪ Commissioning Form

Another setting factor is the type of contract design in coaching. This is usually a two-person contract or a triangular or quadrilateral contract. This was explained in ► Sect. 8.4.2.

▪ Selection of Coaches

The connection of the coaches and the order form often influence the selection of the coaches. Thus it can happen that with an order of a coaching by the personnel development or the respective executive the selection possibility of a coach by the clients is restricted. The potential clients receive a preselection, which is ideally linked to quality standards.

When coaches are sought on the free market, the situation is very unclear.

Coaches are recommended by word of mouth, may be listed with associations or platforms, or found on the Internet under certain search terms "somehow". For potential clients who seek professional coaching, the question of quality and competence is paramount. Whether clients "land" with self-proclaimed coaches, with certified, professional coaches or with coaches selected in advance according to certain criteria, influences the way coaching takes place, how it works and what side effects it has.

▪ Personal Reference—Anonymous, Known

A particularly specific feature of online coaching is the possibility of anonymity for clients. For some people, anonymity is a condition for professional accompaniment at all. Anonymity can also mean that in a company it is not known who uses coaching, although the company finances this. There are organizations that equip the management level with a certain number of vouchers per year, which they can redeem for coaching with coaches of a coach pool defined by the company. Online spaces also offer the possibility of not revealing one's true identity, e.g. because they do not have to be visible online, do not have to give their name or can give themselves a chosen identity, e.g. in the form of avatars, nicknames, etc. Coaches can also make use of this possibility. Clients can also design the coach's person if both agree. Here many facets of the design of the encounter open up.

▪ Initiating Contact—Appointment or Coach-on-Demand

The time and the type of contact between clients and coaches arise from the different commissioning forms, which in turn are associated with different commissioning processes. Regardless of whether there are intermediate bodies (e.g. the personnel development or the management), at some point there is always a first personal

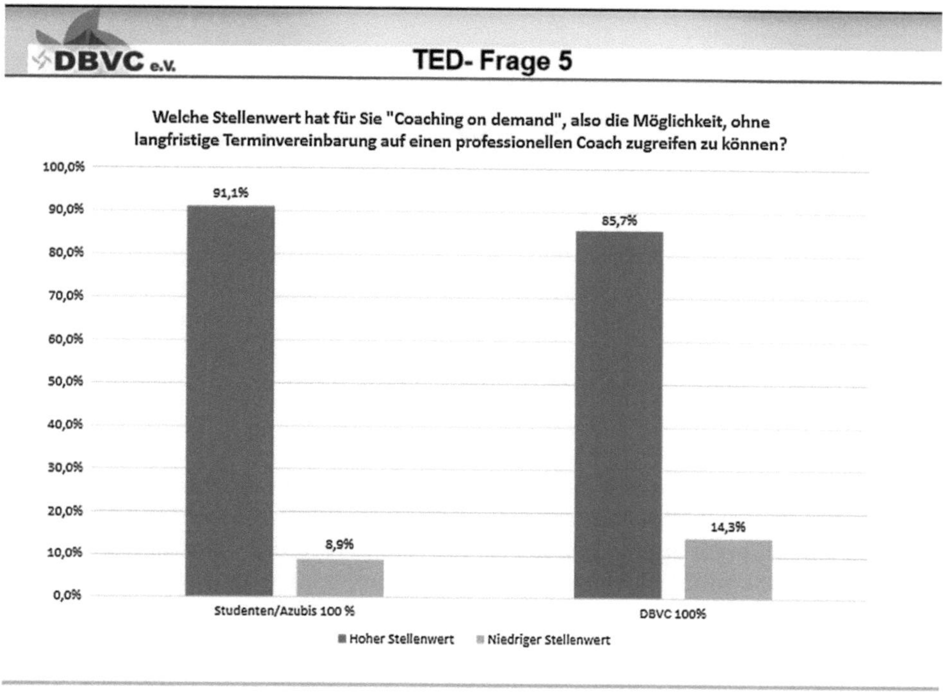

Fig. 10.1 Extract from the TED survey by Radl (2016), TED question 5

contact between the client and the coach. This can take place in the form of a first face-to-face meeting, or mediated. Often, the first direct contact is made by telephone or in writing by e-mail or chat. Recent developments take into account a generally changed customer behavior. The digitalization of life and work has led to an expectation that knowledge acquisition, product information, services and encounters take place ad hoc. The usual procedure in the coaching industry of making an appointment for a contact conversation (face-to-face or by telephone) and the scheduling of coaching sessions with a long lead time requires a change here in order to meet market requirements. In a project, which was carried out by a working group of the "Expert Coaches for Organizations" (FCIO) pillar of the German Coaching Association (DBVC), a survey of students and trainees as well as members of the DBVC was carried out, among other things, on their expectations of coaching. One of the most impressive results was the topic of "Coaching on demand". The respondents expect to be able to contact potential coaches ad hoc (Radl, 2016; Fig. 10.1).

Platforms should support coaches in identifying their status, e.g. as immediately available or available within a certain period of time. They should also offer the possibility that clients can enter a virtual coach room directly, be welcomed there and guided through the first steps. The first contact is therefore made without prior appointment, but ad hoc. Here, the competence of the coaches in online relationship design is already required. They are challenged to design a virtual meeting space in such a way that appreciation and trust-building are supported, especially with an asynchronous start.

- **Context**

As already explained in ▶ Sect. 4.3. the categories of profit and non-profit sector are context factors of coaching. Within these contexts, which differ in terms of their strategic orientation, structures and values, a great variety of different industries and types of organizations branch out. They are important influencing variables on the experience and behavior of people in organizations from a systemic point of view and therefore play an important role in coaching. Another reference point is given by more personal issues, e.g. by the private life or by the type of self-organization. Within these different application fields, similar topics can be located. For example, topics such as decision-making, health, time management, career planning or conflicts could be coaching issues in both the profit and non-profit sector, in every industry and also in the personal environment.

- **Relevance to the Topic**

The topics dealt with in coaching were outlined in the application areas in coaching (▶ Sect. 4.1). Coaching formats are usually open to different topics and can be implemented in different application areas. The relevance to the topic has rather consequences for the profile formation of the coaches, as it goes hand in hand with field competence and target group sharpness. So a coaching in the top management of a chemical company needs a different background of experience than a coaching in the student or educational environment.

Career coaching requires different content-related competencies than health coaching. A format competence is equally important for all content-related topics.

- **Cultural Background**

The cultural background of the persons coached requires the language competence and the intercultural knowledge of the coaches. If it is a group or team coaching, it is of great importance to know whether there is an intercultural composition of the members or not. This has an impact on the coaching process, insofar as it requires a special sensitivity and knowledge of the interaction rules and formulation patterns of the respective culture by the coaches. They have to take these factors into account in the coaching process and deal with them in a appreciative and utilising way.

The setting factors are listed in ◘ Fig. 10.2. This overview was created with a tool from the CAI® World. The different colored cards can be pulled onto the geometric object in the middle, depending on whether they play a role in a certain coaching format or not. They thus form the "outside world" of the spatial object, in whose interior the respective format can crystallize. In the following representation, a crystalline structure is therefore also chosen as a symbol for the format.

While the setting factors represent a framework for coaching, the form of implementation is determined by additional criteria. These are presented in the following chapter and also summarized in an overview. Examples are presented with different combinations of format criteria. This different composition differentiates the formats.

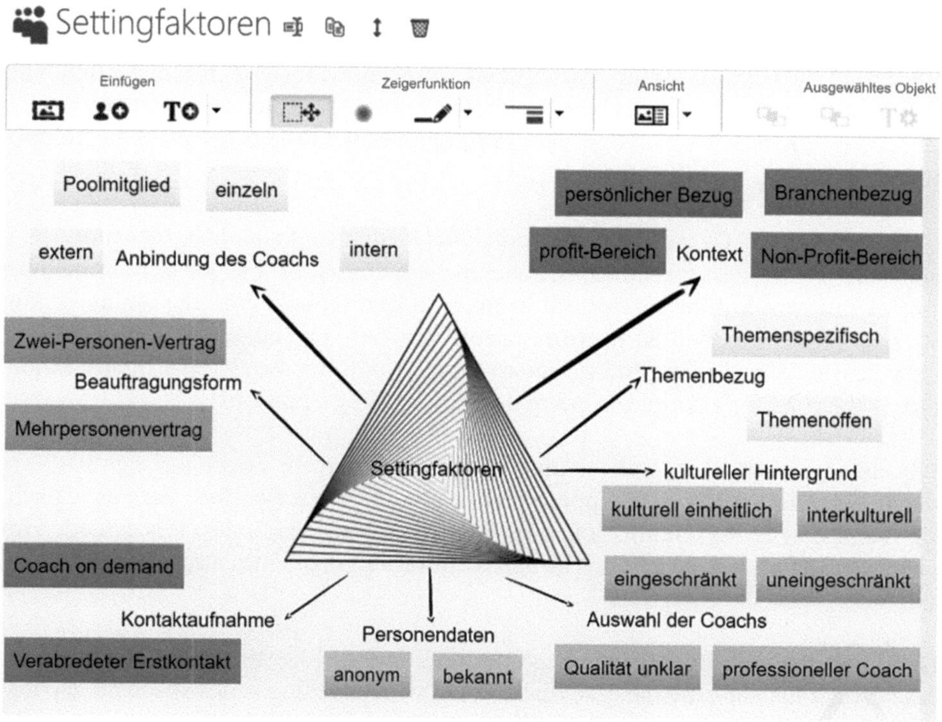

Fig. 10.2 Overview of setting factors created with the arrangement tool of the CAI® World. (© CAI GmbH)

10.3 Format Criteria

Differentiating between different coaching formats can only be schematically represented. The criteria for differentiation can be dichotomous, e.g. if it is a synchronous or asynchronous coaching. However, there can also be several variants within one category, e.g. if the number of persons involved determines the format. In addition, various hybrid forms are possible.

First, a list of possible criteria should be given, which represent different coaching formats in different combinations. Then some combination possibilities with concrete examples will be described.

▪ Embedding: Self-Contained—Program Component

Coaching as a self-contained measure Coaching can be used as a solitary measure. As a rule, a time frame (a certain number of sessions or duration of coaching) and the resulting fee are agreed. There may be goals for the coaching process or coach and client are free to set these goals independently (see two-person, triangular-quadruple contracts in ► Sect. 8.4.2). The same applies to group and team coaching processes if they are commissioned as self-contained measures.

Coaching as a program component The design of qualification programs, such as leadership development programs, trainee programs, culture development processes, change projects, etc. can contain a defined sequence of seminar-workshop- and coaching sequences. Coaching can be carried out in the form of individual coaching, group or team coaching. In contrast to the previously mentioned point, this coaching is thematically, temporally and in terms of sequence so defined that it serves the purpose of the overall program together with the other program components.

■ Duration of the Overall Measure: Individual Measure—Sequential Measure

Individual measure In special cases, coaching can consist of a single appointment or unit. A unit can also be carried out in time-delayed sequences in the online variant of coaching. An individual measure means that only one coaching unit is possible for a clearly defined topic. In the face-to-face variant, this would be a single session. This is the case, for example, in acute decision-making situations.

Sequential measure As a rule, a time frame is defined for coaching, e.g. 10–20 h, which is carried out in 5–10 appointments, etc. in the face-to-face variant. Coaching is ended after the commissioned time frame has expired, unless it is extended for a specific period of time again. The agreed duration of the measure is carried out in individual units or sequences.

Time-limited—unlimited (continuous) In addition to the time-limited sequential measures, it may also be the case that the end of a coaching is not specified. Coaching is used, for example, in top management, at the level of the management or the executive level, as a continuous quality assurance of the activity.

■ Duration of a Coaching Unit—Long vs. Short Units

In the face-to-face variant, coaching usually takes place in periods of 1.5 h, 2 or 3 h. In special cases, longer sequences can also occur, e.g. when coaching on the job. This accompaniment of the client in their work context (shadowing) requires a larger time contingent.

Greif and Benning-Rohnke (2015) speak of telephone shadowing (TS), which takes place in short telephone units between coach and client and is intended to support clients in difficult implementation situations. This corresponds to the virtual transfer coaching (VTC) by Geißler (2011).

The online variant is also particularly suitable for short units. The brevity of the individual interaction sequences can arise from the asynchronous, written-based approach or from the thematic limitations that result from a specific goal orientation of this approach. For example, it can be the transfer support in the implementation of goals or measures in the sense of VTC by Geißler or TS by Greif & Benning-Rohnke. But it can also be short units that take place as part of an asynchronous conflict coaching or, for example, a resource strengthening (► Sect. 10.4).

■ Frequency: High Frequency vs Low Frequency

Coaching is carried out more rarely (at intervals of several weeks) in longer units in a face-to-face approach. The possibilities of virtual units create further possibilities for variation. The short units mentioned above often allow for more frequent contact, which can excellent accompany clients in an implementation-oriented manner. The experiences that clients make when implementing previously agreed goals can be directly included in reflection processes and adjustments of goals and measures. More frequent online meetings in shorter units are currently changing the "face of coaching" quite drastically.

- **Participants (Role and Number)**

Coaching formats differ depending on the people involved in the coaching process and their defined roles.

Coaching by a Professional Coach A coaching conversation is a conversation on an equal footing, with the coaches responsible for the process design and the clients responsible for the content. The content refers to the introduction of an issue and thus the coaching topic, information about relevant people, circumstances and contexts, as well as their interaction, selection of goals and decision on solution measures. Coaches control a process that allows clients to clarify their topics in a results-oriented manner, find goals and solutions, and implement desired behavior. For example, business coaching strengthens self-reflection, problem-solving competence and action competence, and thus professional qualifications. Coaches are, according to this understanding, external sparring partners who do not have their own interests and goals in coaching.

The Leader as Coach A leader has their own goals and interests vis-à-vis their employees, represents the goals of the organization, and usually has responsibility for expertise and personnel. They make decisions, allocate resources, give feedback, solve problems, and assess performance. This does not correspond to the role of coaches in the sense described above. Nevertheless, increasingly, leadership skills are also expected to include coaching skills, particularly when it comes to developing, strengthening, and empowering employees, to inspiring and motivating them to proactive behavior. The current trend towards shorter, more frequent coaching sequences corresponds more to the everyday reality of leadership than the two- to three-hour coaching conversation. Nor is it necessarily a matter of following a complete coaching process, but rather of goal development or goal achievement coaching, of resource activation or results-oriented self-clarification.

In group and team settings, coaching skills can be used by leaders to promote the development of a constructive working atmosphere, to develop common goals and strategies, or to find creative solutions.

This can be done in both the face-to-face and online versions. In both approaches, tools can be used to facilitate process control. Coaching skills are particularly important for leaders in the area of "digital leadership" or "leadership at a distance". The big challenge here is the topics of digital transformation, target agreement in distributed teams, implementation of joint projects with spatial distance between participants, commitment and controlling, as well as communication styles and different leadership expectations in intercultural settings. Coaching skills and, in particular, skills in online coaching, are particularly helpful for leaders in this context.

Coaching Partnership or Coaching Tandem Persons of the same function, such as leaders, training participants or students acquire coaching competencies and carry out coaching units with each other in a coaching partnership. They take turns in the role of coach and client. They are equal, have the same prior knowledge and clarify the respective roles in each coaching unit anew. So it is a collegial coaching in pairs, where the participants should not be in a dependent relationship.

Collegial Group Coaching A group of persons in the same function meets regularly. The group has received an introductory training in the method of collegial group coaching, such as in the Collegial Coaching Conference® (Berg & Berninger-Schäfer, 2010; Berninger-Schäfer, 2012, 2014). In this training, the group learns about the process, the principle of role distribution and the communication skills for carrying out collegial group coaching. Several coaching sessions can take place during the individual group meetings, with approximately 90 min to be set for one coaching session. In such a coaching session, an individual receives coaching from the group. In the online variant, collegial group coaching can be carried out synchronously or asynchronously. A description can be found in the CAI®-World, if CAI®-Coaching Conference (▶ https://www.cai-world.com/cai-coaching-conference) is mentioned. A more detailed description is given in ▶ Sect. 10.4.1.

Self-Coaching J. Weiß (2001) described the optimization of personal competence in dealing with oneself and others as the supporting pillar of self-coaching. In self-coaching, methods for improving one's own self-management are used. For this purpose, background knowledge is acquired, for example by reading, i.e. tips for building competence in self-regulation and personal development are followed. Such tips relate, for example, to topics such as achieving solution trances (Mücke, 2004), effective work (Miedaner, 2001), self-regulation and mindfulness (Dietz & Dietz, 2008) or emotional management (von Elverfeldt, 2005). These are just excerpts from a large variety of topics that authors offer on self-management.

Self-coaching books therefore have the value of information provision and advice literature. In some cases, checklists are provided with which certain topics can be processed.

Online self-coaching applications offer further possibilities, especially if they can be used interactively. Examples of this are apps (see problem-solving app, resource tree, resource wheel, etc. for example under ▶ https://www.cai-world.com/apps#app-attentiveness-week) or self-coaching processes that are offered via platforms and allow for an interactive approach (see also the description of the Solution Finder in ▶ Sect. 10.4.6).

▪ Method Use in Coaching

The variety of tools described in coaching literature bears no relation to the actual tools used in coaching, as Deplazes, Schwyter and Möller (2016) describe. Coaches make use of the basic communication behavior, in which questions predominate. In addition to active listening and feedback, the basic communication behavior also includes (Berninger-Schäfer, 2018). With these basic conversation management skills, a coaching process can be designed and a constructive relationship management can be maintained. Nevertheless, coaching processes benefit when they are supported by tools. These enable creativity, condense information, activate resources and deepen experience and knowledge processes.

Tools include, for example, visualizations, systemic constellations, the resource tree, work with image materials, the inner team, etc. Since they are described in more detail elsewhere in the online version (▶ Chap. 9), only a brief mention is made here. Rather, the question arises to what extent the use of tools affects the format of coaching. This is most clearly seen in all those tools where coaches and coachees dissolve the classical arrangement of sitting on a chair or sofa because the tool requires it. With floor anchors, large cards or sheets are placed on the floor and the clients stand on or next to them. It takes a lot of space to even notice differences between the experiences on the individual cards. The coaches stand next to the clients, look in the same direction, speak a little quieter in order to not disturb the inner processes of the coachees, but to support them, possibly with the targeted induction of trance phenomena. If a time line is laid out on the floor with a crepe band, this also means that coaches and coachees move around in the room. This changes the form of coaching in that the conversation posture of sitting opposite each other is dissolved. You go or stand next to each other, which changes the direction of view and the type of interaction. This also has an effect on the design of physical proximity and distance or on the volume and modality of speech. Physical mirroring requires high flexibility and trust. This physical mirroring takes place, for example, in problem-solving gymnastics (Schmidt, 2014). The clients go pantomimically exaggerated into the body posture of the problem and later into that of the solution state and are mirrored by the coaches in doing so.

A change in the behavior of the coaches also arises with experience-activating tools. These include, for example, creative design by coachees, for example by painting, creating collages, working with clay or picture materials, focusing on inner images through trance induction or focusing, photo telling or scenic representation. When using such and similar methods, there are longer phases in which coaches remain silent in order to give the inner processes of the clients space. They second and explore the associative spaces of the clients. It is about emotional and associative work, less about cognitive-reflective. Some of the listed methods are accompanied by changes in the spatial setting. In ◘ Table 10.2 you will find some examples of different methods.

◘ Table 10.2 Example of method use in coaching

Basic behavior	**Experience-activating tools**	**Methods that come with spatial changes**
Active listening Questioning techniques Feedback Sitting setting	Inner images (trance phenomena) Outer images (image material, photos of the coachees, etc.) Design with paper, colors, sound Visualize on flip chart or with cards on pinboards Arrangement on a board or table Inner parts	Ground anchors Time Line Arrangement in space Flipchart, pinboard, Hot seat Problem solving gymnastics Movement

Table 10.3 Places where coaching takes place

Coachroom	On the job	Movement coaching	Online
Classic coaching	Accompaniment at the workplace	Walking, walking, running together	In different places

- **Location of Coaching**

The location where coaching takes place can influence the format. In the face-to-face variant, coaching usually takes place in the premises of the coaches or in the working environment of the clients. A meeting room is often used for this purpose. However, coaching sometimes also takes place in conference houses, hotels or any other meeting place where the participants can save travel time. According to the definition of setting presented above, these would initially be setting criteria if coaches are able to act professionally at such a location and can ensure confidentiality. The professionalism of the procedure concerns the control of coaching processes via communicative basic behaviour (see above) and also the use of tools that are transportable or on-site (cards, figures, pens, paper, etc.). Online tools can also be used in the face-to-face variant via a laptop or tablet. However, the location of coaching affects the format if, for example, it is a coaching on-the-job. In this case, the coach is visible in the context of the clients and thus becomes part of the system he observes. The personal accompaniment at the workplace leads to a different form of encounter, e.g. by clients showing or demonstrating something to their coach, introducing them to other people, possibly eating together and coaches participating in everyday work activities, e.g. meetings, in an observing capacity. The online variant of coaching on-the-job, i.e. the high-frequency, short reflection and feedback loop to current experiences at work, also represents a special format.

Another special feature arises when coaching takes place outdoors. Not only in health coaching or sports coaching do clients and coaches agree to go for a walk, to a place in nature, or they run/jog/walk together. Being together in movement changes the direction of view, has a direct physiological effect and can be used methodologically. This can be done, for example, using the metaphor of "being in motion", activating movement or the environment as a resource, or using "tools" that can be found on the way. These include, for example, plants, stones or sticks with which "drawings" can be made or with which systemic visualizations can be made.

In the online variant, clients and coaches can, for example, go to a certain place with their laptop, smartphone or tablet, which can be used for coaching, for example, to activate resources and change the pattern state (◘ Table 10.3; see also the example "Walk and Talk" in ► Sect. 10.4.5).

The location where coaches and clients are located, especially in the online variant, is to be considered independently of the location as a format criterion. It can be helpful for all parties involved to exchange information about where they are, what it looks like there and how it affects their well-being. This creates closeness and trust and makes it easier for coaches to empathize. Such information is omitted if clients value their anonymity.

■ Table 10.4 Use of media in coaching formats

Co-presence/face-to-face	Synchronous, mediated presence	Asynchronous, mediated presence
Flipchart Bulletin boards Pens and paper Figures Picture cards	Audio Video Written (email, chat, white-board) Interactive 2-D and 3-D spaces (additional coaching tools, possibly meeting of avatars)	Written Interactive 2-D and 3-D spaces (tool support)

■ Use of Media

The term media is used in a variety of ways in connection with coaching. If flipcharts, bulletin boards and cards are used in coaching, on the one hand media are spoken of, on the other hand the digital support of coaching is meant. Classical or traditional coaching is characterized by copresence (simultaneous presence in the same room) of two or more people. With a media-mediated simultaneous presence (synchronous communication of people who are in different places), it can be telephone coaching, coaching via video or text-based coaching, such as in a chat, or a meeting in virtual 2-D or 3-D spaces (■ Table 10.4).

In a mediated asynchronous presence, the communication partners act at different times and are in different places. This is done in a writing-based and possibly tool-supported manner, such as in mailings, forums or virtual coaching rooms (2-D or 3-D), which allow the use of coaching tools.

Geißler and Kanatouri (2015) speak of digital support for so-called basic media and mean by this the conduct of coaching via telephone, video, chat or avatars. They speak of problem-solving tools when online tools are used to design coaching processes.

Mixed forms of all these variants are possible in coaching processes.

■ Structuring of the Coaching Process

The process control in coaching is carried out as described in ► Chap. 8, a quality feature of professional coaching. The competence of the coaches lies in knowing the phases of a coaching process and being able to initiate and carry out the process in a methodological way and nevertheless remain free for the current needs of the coachees and the many feedback loops that take place in such an interaction. It is the task of the coaches to combine an individual process design with a clear process control. This represents a royal road between two extremes. One pole of the continuum is the complete process openness, which lets the conversation degenerate into the arbitrariness of a nice encounter at best. The other pole is a rigid structuring, as is the case, for example, with online applications when questions have to be answered and processed in a predetermined order. The extent of the process structuring therefore has a significant influence on the format in which a coaching can be carried out (■ Table 10.5).

The format criteria described so far are shown in ■ Fig. 10.3. There is a symbol in the middle that connects various points to each other in a circular shape and resembles a crystalline structure. There can be any number of points that are

Table 10.5 Extent of process control in coaching

Complete openness, No process control Arbitrariness	Process control and openness to the development path of the counterpart Client centered and process-determined approach	Rigid structure Predefined path Limited development

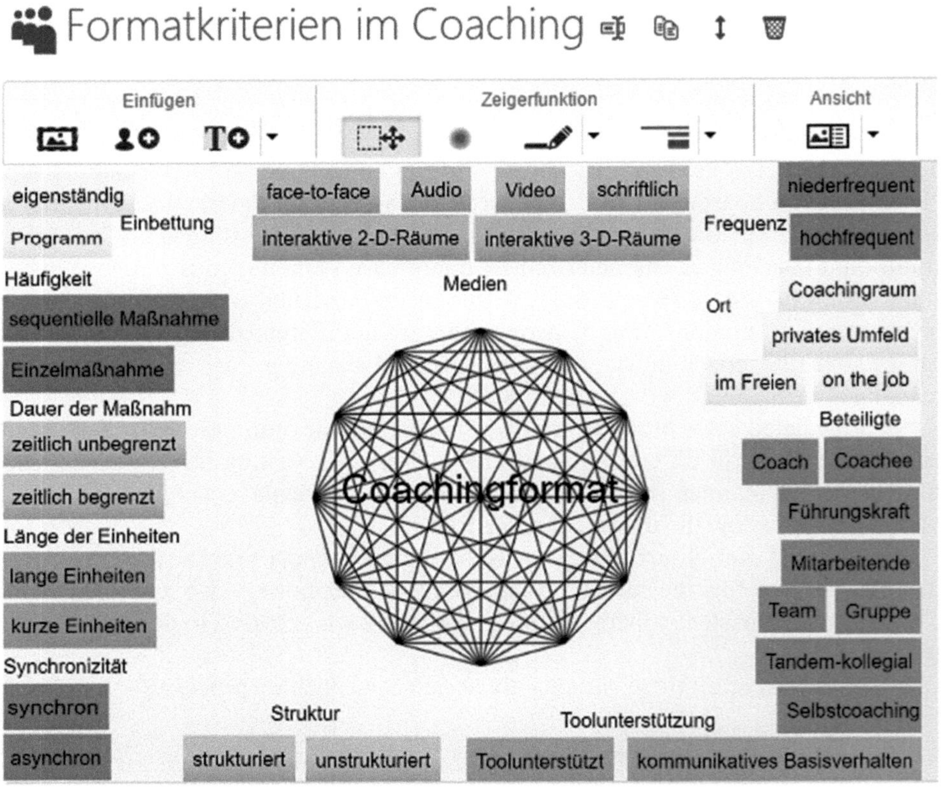

Fig. 10.3 Representation of the format criteria in coaching

connected to each other, so that depending on the format a different figure (shape) results.

This representation of the format criteria in coaching was carried out in the same way as the representation of the setting factors (Fig. 10.2) with an online tool from the CAI® World. As with a pinboard with meta cards, these "cards" can now be clustered in different combinations. This makes it possible to map different formats flexibly.

10.4 Format Examples

10.4.1 Group Coaching Online—Coaching Conference

Group coaching is usually carried out in groups whose members are equal and who, unlike team members, are not in a mutual dependency, e.g. of a hierarchical nature. The group members come together for different reasons, e.g. because of a similar function (e.g. department heads, managing directors, students, project managers, etc.) or a common topic (e.g. environmental protection, school development, change management, succession planning, etc.).

The task of group coaches is to empower the group and the individual members to work on topics independently, resourcefully, goal- and solution-oriented. For this purpose, a structured approach and the observance of rules are essential. In the online variant, topics such as commitment, appreciation and the definition and observance of rules are even more challenging than in the face-to-face approach. For example, one group member may be logged in but not participate. If no clarification takes place, the other group members have to form hypotheses about this behavior. Perhaps this person is not present at all, perhaps the topic is not interesting to him, perhaps he is so affected that he cannot react.

The moderator function of the group coach is therefore particularly important in the online variant. This also includes dealing with devaluation or disrespectful comments, which are easier to make because of the lower self-censorship. Dealing with "talkative people" and "silent people" is also a great challenge here. The groups need clear and communicated rules of the game that not only concern the coaching process, but also the form of interaction, the group ethic and the consequences of non-compliance. Helpful support are role icons, emoticons and other symbols (e.g. hand signals, pause request, desired tempo) with which the group members and the coaches can express themselves without directly interfering with the process. The symbols that can be used for this purpose are shown in ► Sect. 9.2.

Ploil (2009) describes phases that occur repeatedly within chats:

1. Welcome and getting to know each other phase
2. Impressing and nonsense/fun phase
3. Content-related phases/consultation phases
4. Farewell phases

While the impressing and nonsense/fun phase described by Ploil as 2nd phase occurs rather among younger participants, in the coaching context in the online variant often still an uncertainty phase can be observed. It happens that clients find themselves in an online group process for the first time and are confronted with both the technical challenges and the new social environment and its interactions. It is the task of the coaches or group moderators to establish the workability of a group and, if necessary, to enable new group members to join.

The technical competence of the individual group members can be very different, just as their technical connection. Different bandwidths, for example, lead to different performance when communication takes place via the Internet. Therefore, a technical check is required or the assurance that all group members are able to

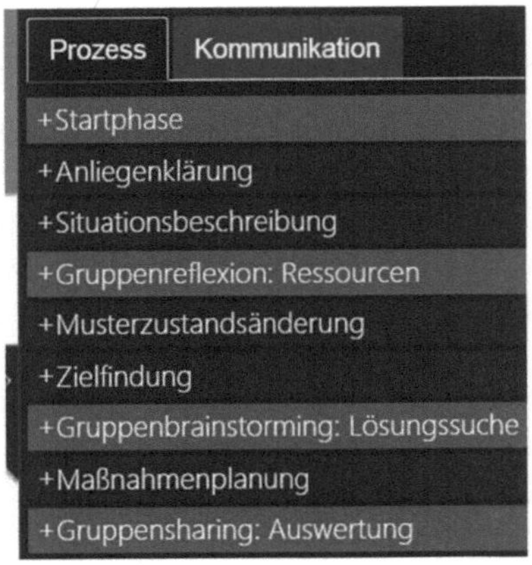

◘ **Fig. 10.4** Process of the CAI® coaching conference. (© CAI GmbH)

follow the group process online. For online coaching, the process described by Ploil (2009) can be adapted as follows:
1. Technical check and, if necessary, technical assistance
2. Welcome and getting to know you phase
3. Uncertainty phase
4. Working phase
5. Evaluation phase
6. Agreement and farewell phase

Within group coaching, different formats can in turn be distinguished. In the CAI® World, they are referred to as CAI® Coaching Conference and abbreviated as CCC. Two forms are presented below, CCC-with coach and CCC-collegial.

▪ CAI®Coaching Conference (CCC)—with Coach

Persons of equal rank meet online, with one person always receiving coaching in a structured manner. This coaching unit can be carried out synchronously or asynchronously, or in mixed form. The resources of the group are used by the coach for the concerns of the coachee defined in this round in certain phases of the coaching process. The coaching process is controlled in the CAI®-World, which is illustrated in ► Sect. 8.4. In ◘ Fig. 10.4a screenshot of the process depicted in the CCC is shown. The phases can be clicked on by the coach and the question sets assigned to the phases can be used if necessary. The other usable online tools are shown in ◘ Fig. 10.5.

Procedure In a first pass, the coach leads the clarification of concerns and description of the situation with the client and decides which tools to use for this purpose. If the process runs synchronously and the group members are present, a group round will take place immediately after these first two phases. This is a resource feedback from the group members or their associations with the topic. The group is asked to forego interpretations and their own explanations in their contributions. Open questions can be raised by the group, which are, for example, collected on

Fig. 10.5 Tools for the CAI® coaching conference. (© CAI GmbH)

a whiteboard. The group members can also choose a figure/symbol for themselves and contribute with cards in the placement tool.

In the asynchronous variant, a time is set by when the feedback described above (resource feedback, associations, open questions) is desired by the group members.

In the next step, the coach develops, together with the client, the goals that are appropriate for the client—synchronously or asynchronously—after the change in pattern state has been achieved. They are visualized (e.g. with cards on a whiteboard or within a placement) and form the basis for the solution brainstorming to which the group is asked in the next step. In the asynchronous variant, another time is set by when the tips of the group members should be taken into account for the achievement of the goals. Afterwards, the coach develops, together with the client, those implementation measures which are desirable and realistic for the client on the basis of the solution brainstorming. The coaching unit ends with the concrete planning of the first implementation steps. All participants in this unit are asked for a final sharing. This includes feedback on the experienced coaching process and information from the individual group members on their personal learning experience through participation in this process.

The phases of the process, tools that can be used and the interplay of the participants in the CAI® Coaching Conference are schematically illustrated in Table 10.6:

Figure 10.6 shows a solution brainstorming from different perspectives, the symbolism of which the group members have chosen themselves.

If the group members wish, they can write their name to the symbol that represents them, but they can also carry out the brainstorming "anonymously". The choice of symbols is not evaluated, it is simply a collection of ideas in the sense of a brainstorming. The coach uses this collection to work out implementation steps with the client in the following phase.

Overall, the coach's task is to moderate the process, work out the topics with the client, involve the group members and select the appropriate tools.

Table 10.6 Sequence of phases of the CCC, participants and tools

	Phase	Participants	Potential tools
1	Clarification of concerns	Coach/Client	Set of questions Chat window Whiteboard Picture gallery Lineup
2	Description of the situation		
3	Resource activation/reflection support	Coach/group members	Question set Whiteboard Chat window during setup or picture gallery
4	Change of state	Coach/client	Question set Image gallery Constellation Question set Whiteboard
5	Goal setting		
6	Solution brainstorming	Coach/group members	Whiteboard Symbolization of the advisors in the Aufstellungstool
7	Planning measures	Coach/client	Question set Whiteboard
8	Evaluation/Sharing	All participants	Chat window Whiteboard

The group decides when to meet again. As a rule, certain time slots are agreed for the individual coaching units in the group and it is clarified in each case who wants a coaching. The group members can also contact the coach ad hoc in the event of an acute need and ask him to convene the group for a coaching unit.

As a rule, this is the format of the CAI® Coaching Conference shown in Fig. 10.7 with a coach.

The format may look different if, for example, it is an unlimited measure or a measure within a program, or if asynchronous work is also carried out.

▪ CAI Coaching Conference—Collegial

In the collegial variant of the CCC, coaching of each group member by the group takes place. The CAI® Coaching Conference is also based on the Collegial Coaching Conference®, which has been described in detail many times (Berg & Berninger-Schäfer, 2010; Berninger-Schäfer, 2012; Berninger-Schäfer, 2014a). It runs according to the same scheme as the Coaching Conference with a coach. However, the role of professional coaches is divided among the group members in the collegial variant.

In each coaching session, these roles are newly assigned. The group member who receives coaching has the role of the client. A group member takes on the role of moderator, controls the process flow and moderates the two group phases "resource feedback/associations/open questions" and "solution brainstorming". One person has the role of an interviewer and, in a first round, carries out the

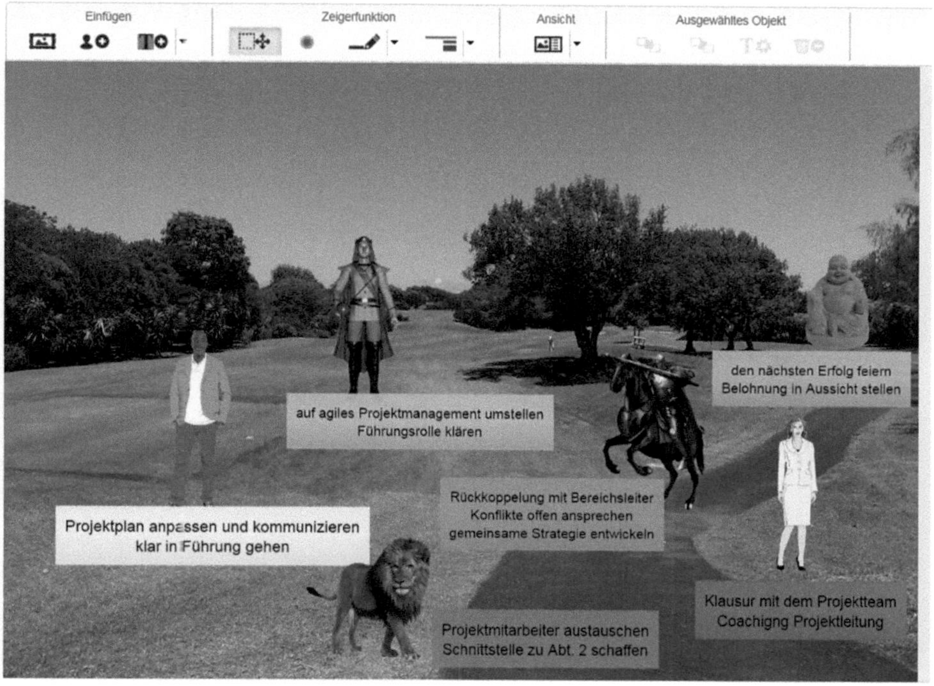

Fig. 10.6 Solution brainstorming by the group members in the CCC in the alignment tool. (© CAI GmbH)

clarification of concerns and description of the situation with the person receiving the coaching (client), in a second round the change of the pattern state and target finding and in the third round the planning of measures. The flow and the distribution of roles in the CCC-collegial are shown in Table 10.7.

In order to be able to take on the roles in the collegial CAI® Coaching Conference, the participants take part in an introductory training. They practice the operation of the CAI® World, learn about the background of the integrated coaching process and acquire the repertoire of methods necessary for the implementation of the coaching units.

The groups give themselves their own rules about the way they want to work together. These include, for example, the form of convening a coaching unit and the planned frequency of coaching units. It has been proven that fixed dates are spread over the year and that in addition, each group member can activate the group for a coaching unit ad hoc at the so-called group manager or the group manager. The group manager organizes the dates and the distribution of roles for the respective coaching units. He/she exercises the office for a period of one to two years, while the other roles (interviewer, moderator and client) change in each coaching unit.

Analogous to the face-to-face variant of the collegial coaching conference®, the groups can determine a scribe for the individual coaching units, who protocols verbal interview sequences.

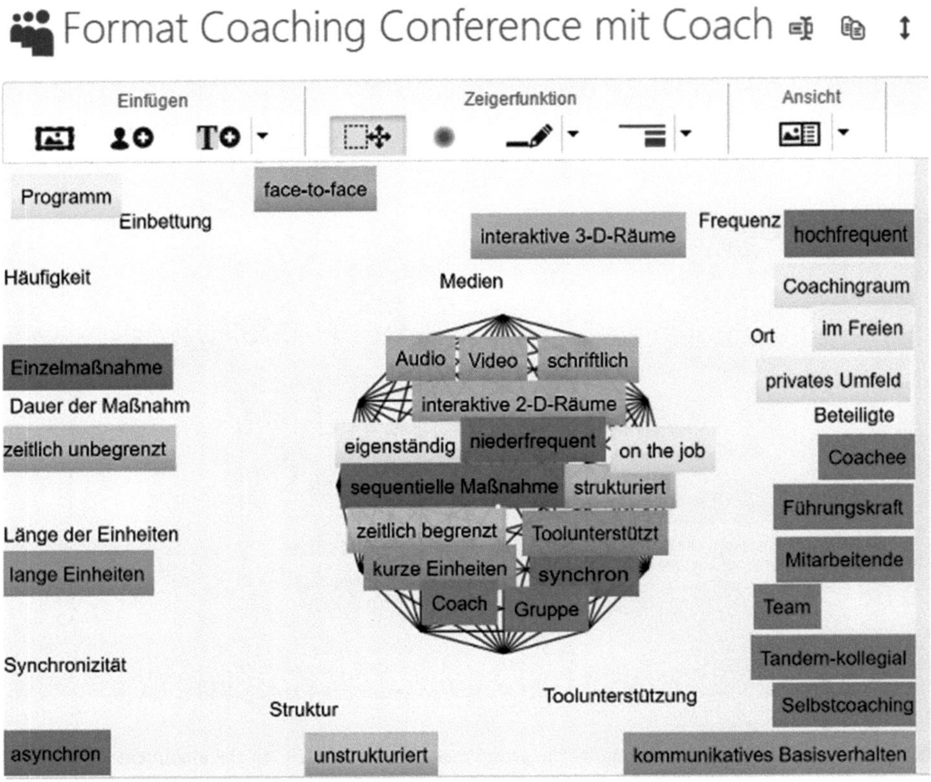

Fig. 10.7 Format of the CAI® coaching conference with a coach. (© CAI GmbH)

Table 10.7 Phase sequence of the CCC collegial and the active roles

Phase	Participants
Clarification of concerns Description of the situation	Interviewer/Client
Activation of resources/Reflection support	Group members and Host
Change of Pattern state Goal setting	Interviewer/client
Solution brainstorming	Group members and moderator
Measures planning	Interviewer/client
Evaluation/sharing	All participants

If the groups meet at previously agreed dates, it is clarified who has a coaching concern before the further roles are assigned.

Many groups give themselves additional rules for the desired form of cooperation.

If professional coaches or coaches within coaching further education are involved, a diverse use of the coaching tools is advisable, because in the protected area of their own collegial CCC, these tools can be practiced.

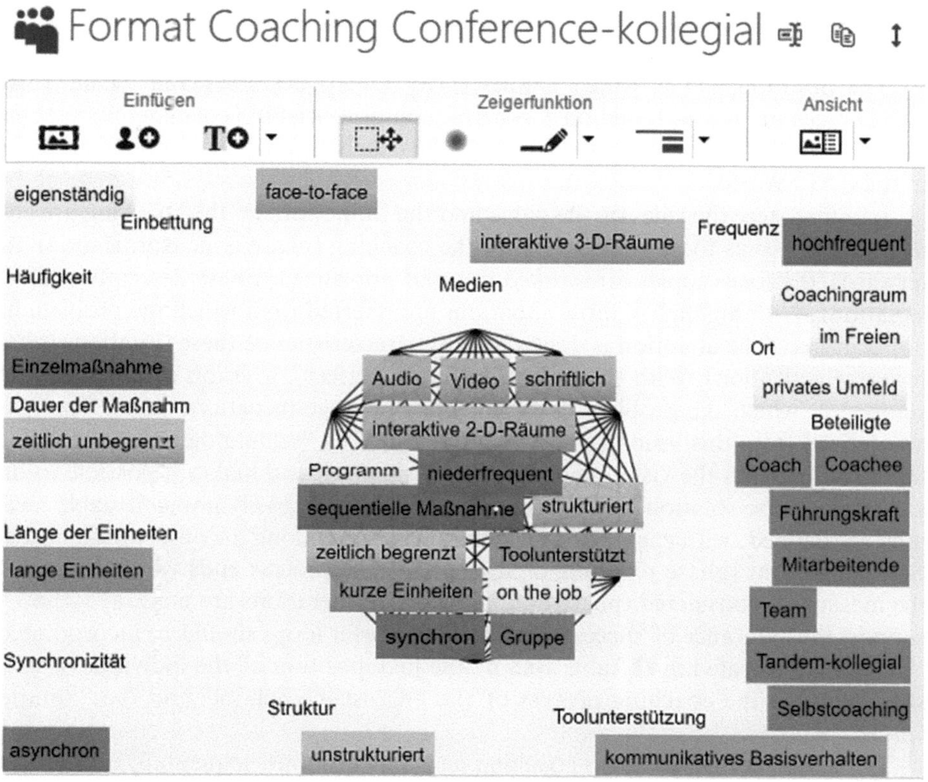

Fig. 10.8 Format of the CCC-collegial as part of a program. (© CAI GmbH)

Therefore, participation in the CCC is part of the qualification to become an online coach, because the participants regularly carry out this format in distributed roles, both in terms of process flow and methods in the online environment, without immediately assuming the entire and sole responsibility for the coaching unit, as is the case with professional coaches.

The format of the collegial CCC is therefore also related to a program in Fig. 10.8, although this does not necessarily have to be the case. There are now a number of groups that use this form of accompaniment, for example, to support their everyday leadership. As part of a program, it is a time-limited measure.

Participants in the collegial CCC who have learned this method as part of a program often voluntarily decide to continue to use the CCC autonomously. It can run asynchronously or synchronously with different media.

10.4.2 Team Coaching

In team coaching, professional coaches accompany a team with a common task, common goals and mutual dependencies.

In contrast to group coaching, in which a group member receives coaching from a coach involving the potential of the group, in team coaching the whole team is in the role of the coachee. In team coaching, it is about an issue of the team and that means that all team members have to be included.

The Solution Circle, which Daniel Meier (2004) describes and which Topan (2011) picks up, is also based on a systemic solution-oriented coaching understanding and can be very well carried out with the coaching process mapped and usable in the CAI® World.

In a first step, the rules of the game and the framework of the coaching are clarified, or the issues to be addressed with the coaching (phase issue clarification). Afterwards, the focus topics are worked out and prioritized (phase description of the situation). With highlights, those situations are referred to in which the problem has not occurred. The attention is drawn to the characteristics of these situations (phase resource activation). With the so-called "future perfect", a vision of a future is developed in which the problem is solved (phase change in pattern state). The goals are derived from this vision (phase goal finding). The "scaling dance" serves to differentiate between the vision and the current situation and makes it possible to find solutions (phase solution brainstorming). Subsequently, easily implementable measures are defined, with each team member also taking along an observation and action assignment (phase planning of measures). The process ends when the gain of the measure is considered (phase evaluation). Considerations are made as to how to support the assurance of success, i.e. whether transfer loops should be incorporated.

This is illustrated in ◻ Table 10.8 by the juxtaposition of the individual process steps between the coaching process of the "Karlsruhe School" and the "Solution Circle".

◻ Figure 10.9 shows team coaching as a synchronous, sequential, independent format.

Team coaching can also be carried out as a program component, in 3-D spaces and longer units, or asynchronously. Asynchrony is recommended, for example, in team conflicts, which are carried out under the heading "Conflict coaching online".

◻ Table 10.8 Process steps in team coaching

	Coachingphase	Solution Circle
1	Declaration of intent	Clarification of the framework and what is to be achieved with the coaching Define rules
2	Description of the situation	Hot spots: Clarification of the topics to be addressed and their prioritization
3	Resource activation	Sternstunden: in welchen Situationen ist das Problem nicht aufgetreten und was hat dies unterstützt?
4	Pattern state change	Future perfect: Vision der Zukunft, in der das Problem gelöst ist
5	Goal finding	Deriving goals from the vision
6	Solution brainstorming	Scaling Dance: Scaling for differentiation
7	Planning measures	Appointment of quickly implementable solutions with a personal observation and action mandate
8	Evaluation	View of the benefit of the measure, support for success assurance

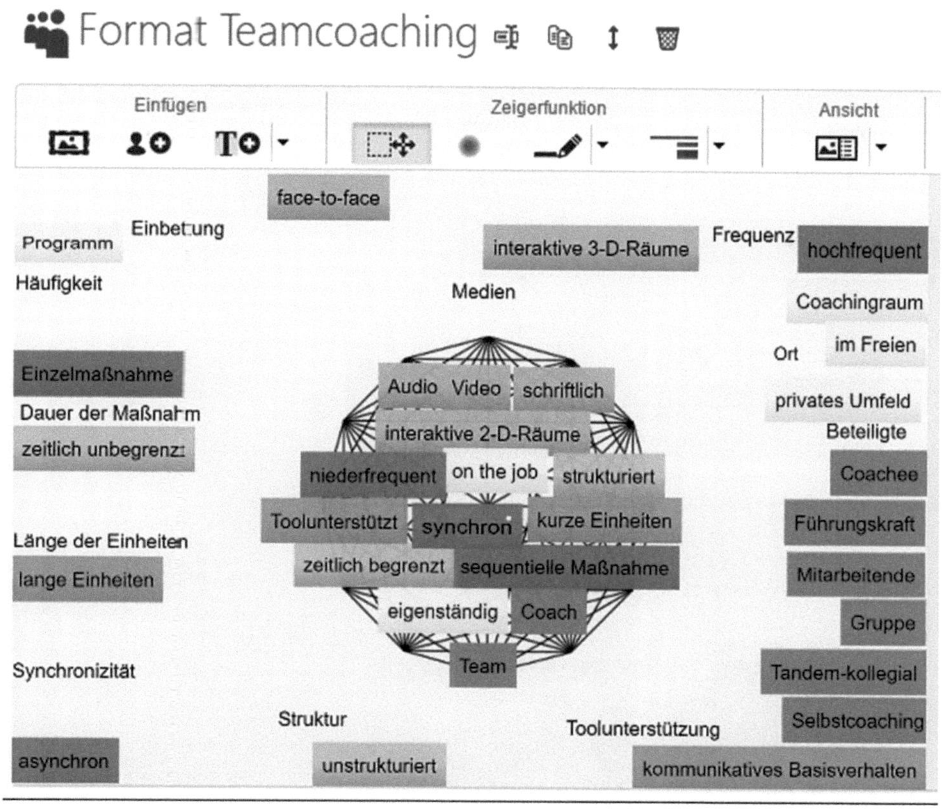

Fig. 10.9 Format teamcoaching. (© CAI GmbH)

In team coaching, it is also advisable to work with online tools. Purely writing-based processes take a very long time if a coach wants to be fair to each team member and bring together concerns, visions, goals and measures.

10.4.2.1 Example of the Use of Online Tools in Team Coaching

- **The Image Gallery in Team Coaching**

The selection of images from the image gallery can be done individually by each team member and symbolize the team climate, as it is perceived by this person. The individual images are introduced and the associations are recorded in the chat window. This is done in the phase of describing the situation.

The images are not questioned or evaluated. In the Figs. 10.10, 10.11 and 10.12 pictures of three different team members are shown on the same topic.

This approach represents an important mutual feedback and serves to clarify the situation.

Images can also be selected so that they reflect team resources. This selection can also be made by each team member individually or in a process of agreement on an image with which everyone can identify.

Fig. 10.10 Image association of a team member (1). (© CAI GmbH)

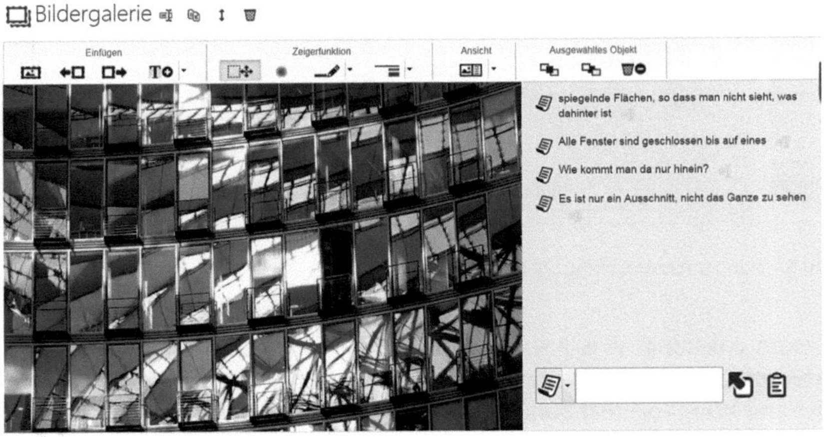

Fig. 10.11 Image association of a team member (2). (© CAI GmbH)

In the phase of change of the pattern state, a positive future scenario can be developed very quickly with image material. Even if this is initially done by each team member individually, it is important to find a common image for a successful team future. The step that each team member individually chooses a future-feeling image can also be omitted. What is decisive is that an agreement is reached on a common future vision, from which goals can then be derived in the phase of goal finding. The probability that these will then be goals that everyone can share is increased.

Working with the image gallery supports the following coaching phases:

- Situation description,
- Resource activation,
- Change of pattern state,
- Goal finding.

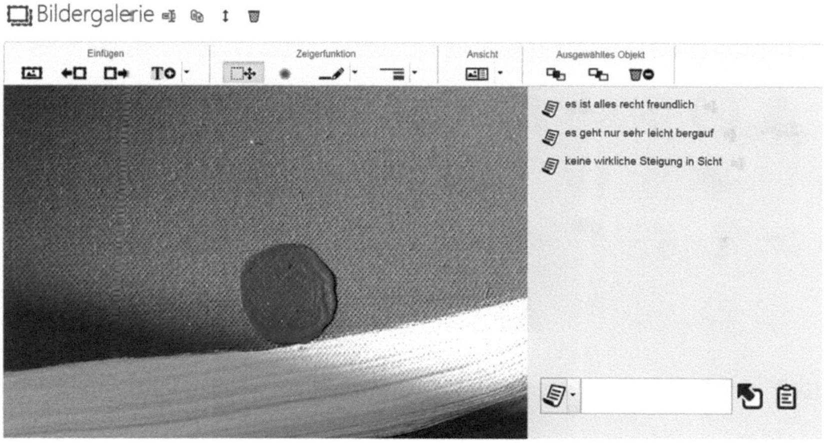

Fig. 10.12 Image association of a team member (3). (© CAI GmbH)

▪ Constellation in Team Coaching

The arrangement tool can be used in a similar way to the image gallery in the phases of situation description, resource activation and change of standard state. In addition, solution brainstorming can be designed with it.

There are also several variants here in principle. For example, each team member can make his own arrangement to describe the actual situation. For this purpose, he chooses a background image that expresses the subjectively perceived mood. The other team members are represented by figures or symbols, they can be identified by cards if desired. With the cards, other written messages can also be placed in the image. They can refer to topics, where topics can also be symbolized.

Even with this approach, it is a powerful feedback from the individual team members to each other.

In another variant, everyone agrees on a common image or only one person creates an image of the current team situation, while the others only observe the arrangement process. The other team members give feedback on how the arrangement affects them. The coach can decide whether more team members should arrange.

In an arrangement, resources can also be represented. For this purpose, various symbols can be selected in the CAI® World; examples are shown in ◻ Fig. 10.13 (▶ Sect. 9.3.6).

The change in the desired state leads to a change in the arrangement, since this should now represent a desired situation. For this purpose, it is recommended to copy the actual arrangement so that the actual state can be recorded. For the desired image, changes can now be made in the copied arrangement. A new arrangement can also be opened by clicking on the tool.

In team coaching, it is crucial that the phase of pattern state change ends with an arrangement with which everyone can identify and which is an desirable situation for everyone. This is the basis for finding goals that are usually written on a whiteboard.

For the solution brainstorming, an arrangement can be used again. The team members look for a figure/symbol for themselves and write their solution proposal

Fig. 10.13 Symbols in the arrangement tool of the CAI® World. (© CAI GmbH)

on a card that they draw to their figure. This can also be done anonymously, as the arrangement does not require personal identification (see also the remarks on group coaching).

The arrangement tool thus supports the following coaching phases:

- Situation description
- Resource activation
- Pattern state change
- Solution brainstorming

The Resource Tree in Team Coaching

The resource tree can be used in team coaching from the resource activation phase (Fig. 10.14). The clarification of concerns and description of the situation usually take place via chat or on the whiteboard.

If the resource tree is used in team coaching, those aspects that give the team orientation, are important for team retention and promote the team climate are written on cards on the root level. Positive events and developments are recorded on the trunk. The team vision is placed at the top of the crown in the next step. The resulting goals are represented as "goal branches". The measures that lead to this represent the link between trunk and crown.

Case Example

Team P (Product Introduction and Consulting) consists of 7 people and has formed itself anew due to an internal restructuring. Four people have worked together before, while three have been added new. Various measures for personnel development are offered to the teams as part of the restructuring process. Team P has decided on coaching. The team wishes for the development of a positive working atmosphere and a high acceptance of their services within the organization and among the customers. Up to 12 h of coaching can be used in total. A special challenge for the team is that a lot of work has to be done outside and this is associated with travel. Everyone has been granted permission to work from home and two team members work part-time.

Due to this special situation, team coaching was carried out online. For this purpose, the coach opened a common virtual space for the entire team and himself.

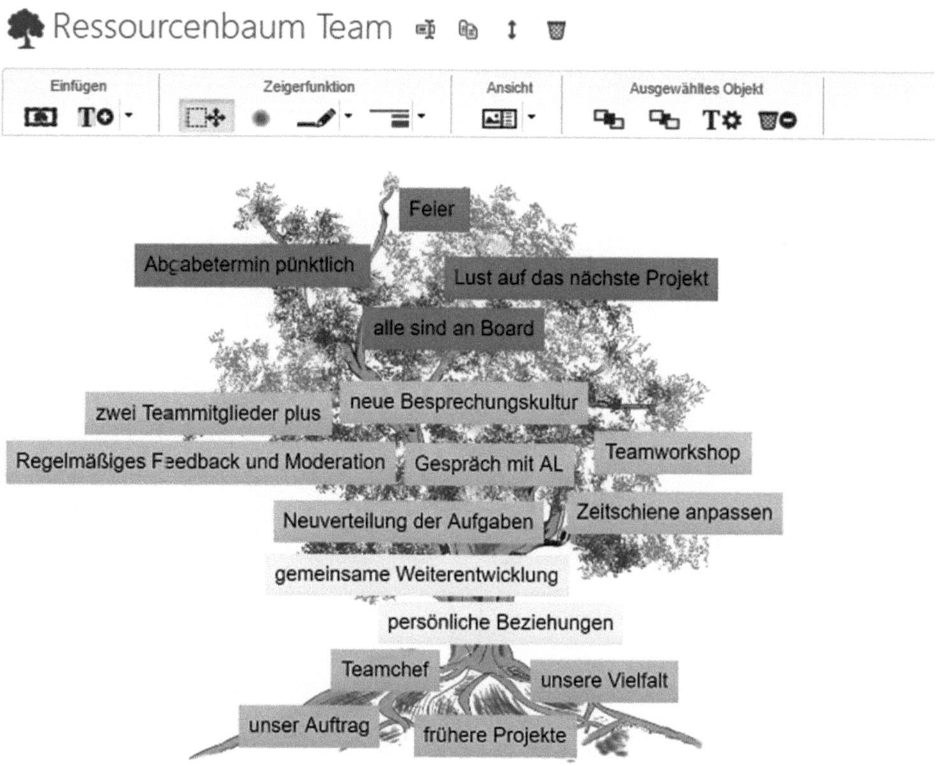

Fig. 10.14 Resource tree team. (© CAI GmbH)

While the concerns were quickly and consensually clarified, different topics arose during the description of the situation, which were prioritized with points. Each team member could award four points. All marked the topic "positive team climate", so that it was started in coaching first. In order to capture the current team climate, each team member created a sociogram. It turned out that there was already a long-standing conflict between M and F. The sociogram of M is shown as an example (Fig. 10.15). M's relationship to the other team members was surprisingly similar in all sociograms. The sociograms were created asynchronously. For this purpose, the coach defined a time frame.

- **Text in the Subordinate Chat**

» There is an open conflict between M and F. M suffers from the fact that F has a close relationship with L. L has a good working relationship with N, while it is unclear how the relationship with M is. S, B and E come new to the team. M has a good relationship with B from previous work contexts. Since B has a very good and close relationship with S, and S in turn has a good relationship with F, M fears that B will turn away from M and could go into coalition with S and F. E is still not assessable for M, in particular M can not say anything about the relationship between E and N.

In the conflict analysis it became clear that it was a conflict limited to F and M. In order not to generalize it, it was agreed that a conflict management between F and

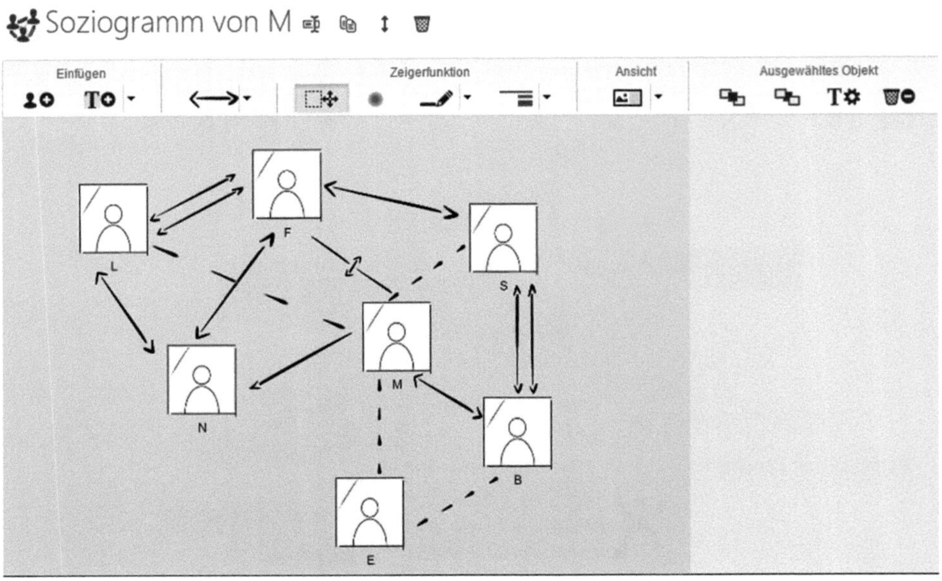

Fig. 10.15 Soziogram of a team member. (© CAI GmbH)

M should be carried out without the presence of the team. For this purpose, the coach opened a common virtual space for F, M and himself. At the same time, there was also a room for the coach and F, as well as for the coach and M. In these separate rooms, the coach helped the two parties to reformulate their accusations into needs. Afterwards, work was continued in the common room. For both, this approach was very helpful, especially that the conflict was not carried out in the team. This was welcomed by all team members. F and M received positive feedback for their conflict solution.

In the next step, a resource activation was carried out throughout the team. For this purpose, associative work was carried out. Each team member chose an image and shared their own associations with the team resources in a chat window associated with the image. For example, Fig. 10.16 shows the image with the associated associations of a team member.

Text in the Subsidiary Chat

> A stream flows in its bed. There are no larger obstacles. The whole landscape looks balanced and beautiful. Here you would like to stay. There are trees, bushes, benches, bridges and a path. Everything is very inviting. The sky is blue. For our team this means that we can make progress in calm waters. We are in a fertile, well-kept environment. It also means that there is a clear path.

In the arrangement tool, the team members worked out a positive future vision (Fig. 10.17). For this purpose, they agreed on a background image and positioned themselves in this image. The characteristics of the positive future image were also described in the subsidiary chat window.

Fig. 10.16 Image association with team resources. (© CAI GmbH)

Fig. 10.17 Future vision of the team worked out together. (© CAI GmbH)

- **Text in the Subordinate Chat**

» We are on the right track. The river has now flowed into the sea. We have arrived and are going in the same direction. Even if we are different, we belong together. Everyone has their place and their right. We need each other and can rely on each other.

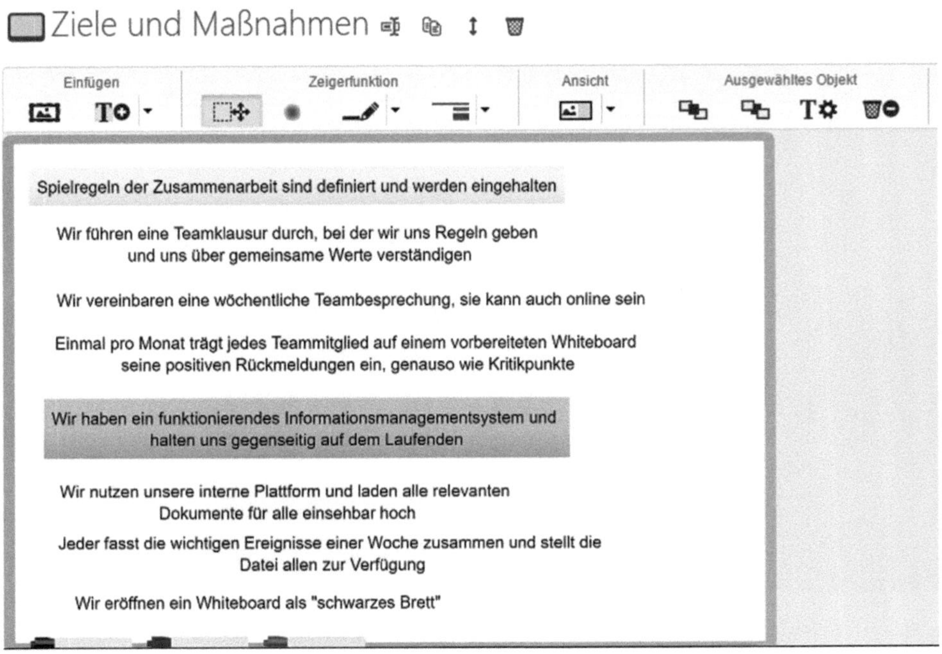

Fig. 10.18 Whiteboard with goals and measures. (© CAI GmbH)

In the next step, goals and measures were derived from this image. These filled several whiteboards. One is listed here by way of example (Fig. 10.18).

The case study of a team coaching shown in excerpts, which was carried out online, corresponds to the format shown in Fig. 10.19.

10.4.3 Conflict Coaching Online

Conflict situations are accompanied by high emotionality and a specific communication behavior. Conflicts that cannot or cannot be processed in time can lead to great personal suffering, to performance losses, to a bad working atmosphere or even to illness. Conflicts bind energy and resources.

Conflict coaching presents coaches with the challenge of maintaining their impartiality, regulating emotions and interrupting conflict patterns. Online procedures are particularly helpful for this.

An example of this are Zezula and Beer (2012), who describe the online portal "Theratalk®", which has been developed and evaluated as a scientific project at the University of Göttingen for couples and partnerships since 1996. It is based on the short-term couple therapy of Halford et al. 1996 (cited according to Zezula & Beer, 2012, p. 233) and is carried out by means of a chat.

If the contact between the parties to the conflict takes place exclusively in writing at least at the beginning, the resulting slowdown results in a decoupling of entrenched conflict patterns. In face-to-face events, escalation occurs very quickly because the conflict behavior between the parties to the conflict is automated. These automated processes are interrupted by the online procedure. Conflict coaches can

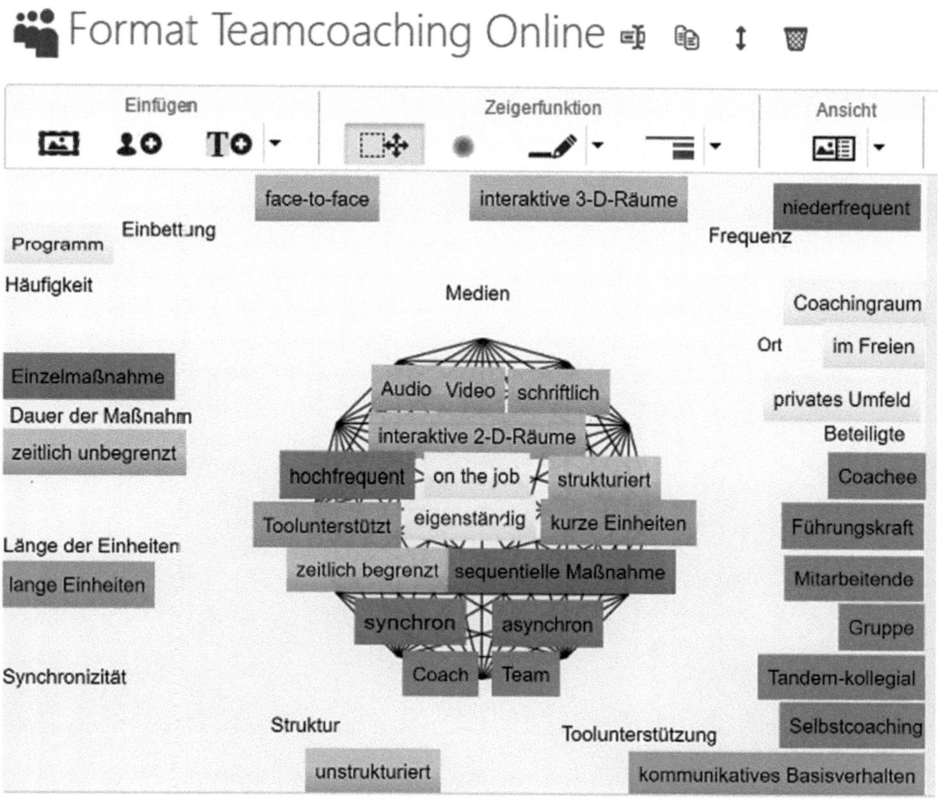

Fig. 10.19 Format Teamcoaching online/Fallbeispiel. (© CAI GmbH)

work with the people individually and work out the needs behind the accusations. The parties can reflect and work on their formulations so that accusations are reformulated into wishes. Online tools such as the sociogram, constellations and associative work with symbols and images facilitate and shorten the process flow. A close transfer accompaniment can take place during the implementation of the objectives and measures agreed between the parties concerned, which positively supports the realization of a changed communication behavior.

Case Example: Conflict Coaching in a Team Leadership Standem

After the order clarification and the consent of the two parties to the conflict (team leader A and team leader B) to carry out the conflict coaching online, the coach prepared the virtual "workplaces".

Several virtual rooms were created.

- Room 1 for A, B and Coach,
- Space 2 for A and Coach (Fig. 10.20),
- Space 3 for B and Coach (Fig. 10.21).

In the respective direct communication spaces for the coach and conflict partner A or the separate space for the coach and conflict partner B, individual coachings took place. Here, the conflict experiences were processed individually. Own

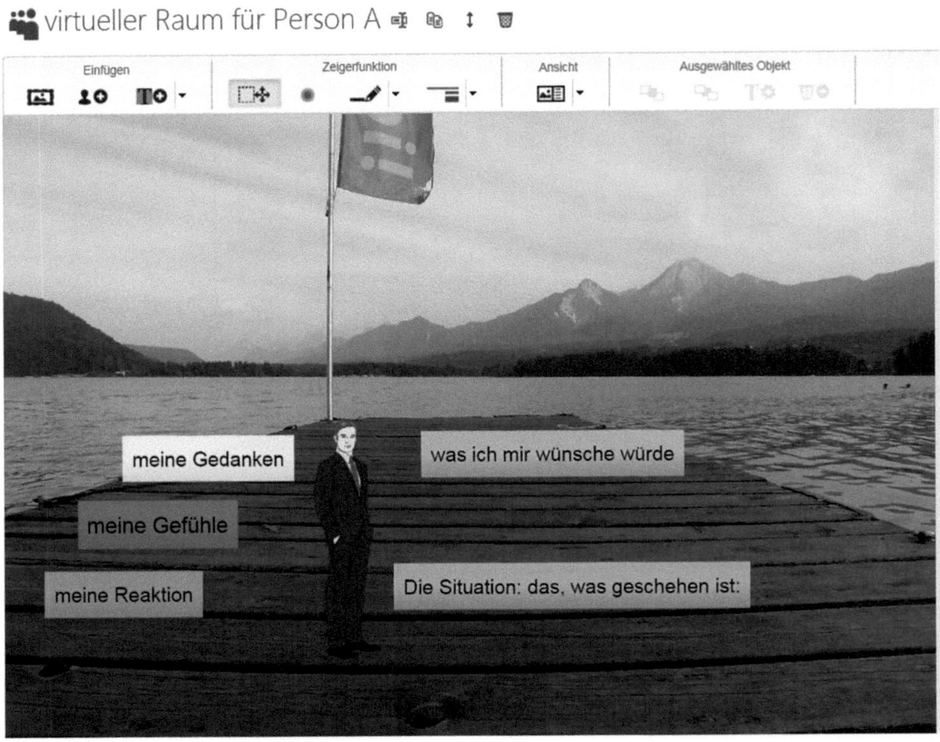

Fig. 10.20 Reflection space for person A in conflict coaching. (© CAI GmbH)

thoughts, feelings and reactions were reflected and considered in their systemic interactions. Needs could be identified and formulated.

After that, the conflict resolution process took place in a common, virtual space, created for the coach, person A and person B.

The coach created a whiteboard based on the information provided by the parties in conflict, on which the people involved in the conflict, the type of conflict, its effects and the situation were briefly outlined and with which the two parties in conflict could identify (Fig. 10.22). This first alignment of perceptions and interpretations was a valuable, mutual feedback of the parties in conflict and the basis for further work.

Another step in the joint conflict resolution process was an associative feedback that condensed information and identified key sentences. Person A represented person B symbolically and found a striking sentence that describes the disturbance from the perspective of A. The same applied to person B. The symbolic representation of the conflict situation between A and B is shown in Fig. 10.23.

In the separate coaching rooms, the coach worked with the participants on their respective symbolic and verbal feedback.

In the sense of resource activation, "moments of glory" were sought, i.e. positive, shared experiences. It was worked out what the respective persons did in these situations or which of their properties and competencies they brought in so that positive experiences with each other were possible.

Fig. 10.21 Reflection space for person B in conflict coaching. (© CAI GmbH)

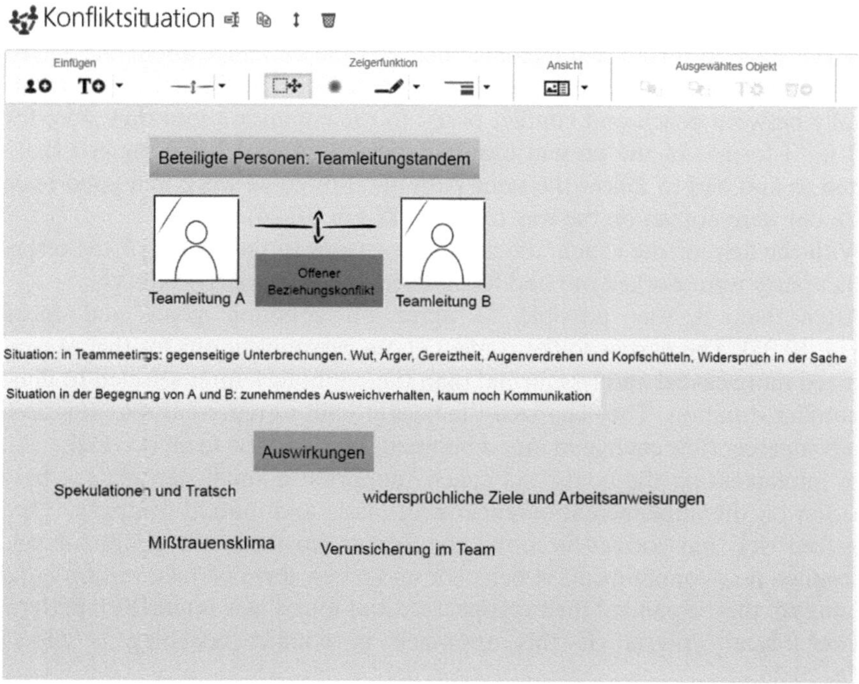

Fig. 10.22 Description of the conflict on the whiteboard. (© CAI GmbH)

Fig. 10.23 Symbolic representation of the conflict situation between A and B. (© CAI GmbH)

A key stage in further conflict coaching was the exchange about the needs that lay behind the mutual accusations. These were reflected in the individual rooms bilaterally between coach and conflict party. In the common room they were formulated in "I-form". In the present example, persons A and B had agreed that they wanted to and had to follow the same path (goal-oriented work in a good team climate), but were not yet on the way together (Fig. 10.24).

With the help of the coach, the mutual reactions to the wishes of the respective conflict party were worked out and formulated as constructive feedback.

After that, it was possible to agree on common goals and measures (Fig. 10.25). The parties to the conflict chose personifications for themselves that appeared more casual and less formal than the symbolic figures selected to illustrate the conflict situation. They changed the background to represent the intention and already a perceptible change in mood between them and the team occured.

In implementing the goals, the coach supported a small-step change between reflection on the implementation experience made and mutual feedback. Through these feedback and correction loops, the former parties to the conflict developed and trained new communication behavior and a new form of relationship building. In doing so, they expanded their competence and found new interaction patterns.

The format criteria of this approach in conflict coaching is shown in Fig. 10.26.

Conflict coaching online can also be carried out synchronously. In this way, audio and video can also be used between coach and client in synchronous stages in

Fig. 10.24 Exchange about needs in conflict coaching. (© CAI GmbH)

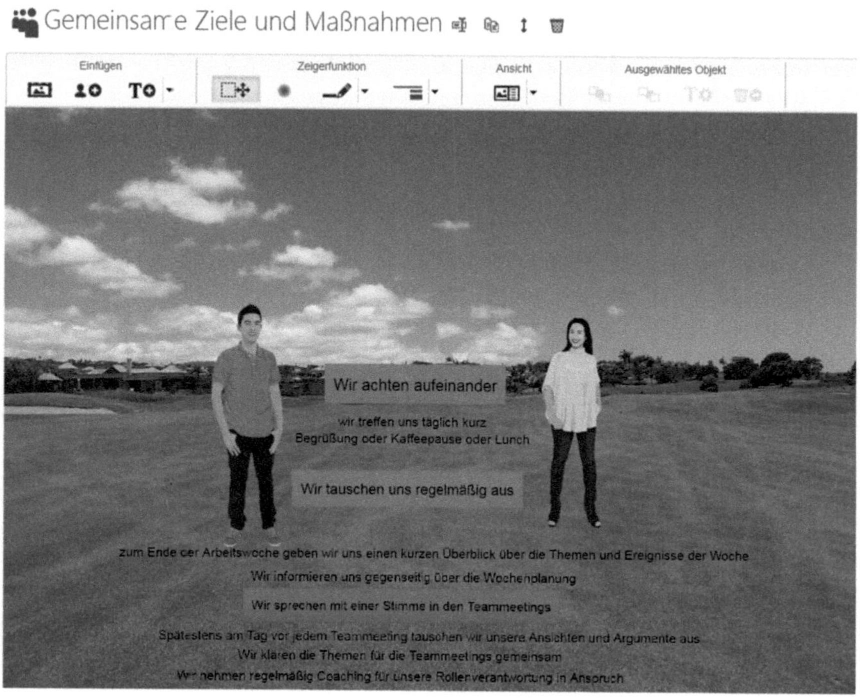

Fig. 10.25 Common goals and measures in conflict coaching. (© CAI GmbH)

10

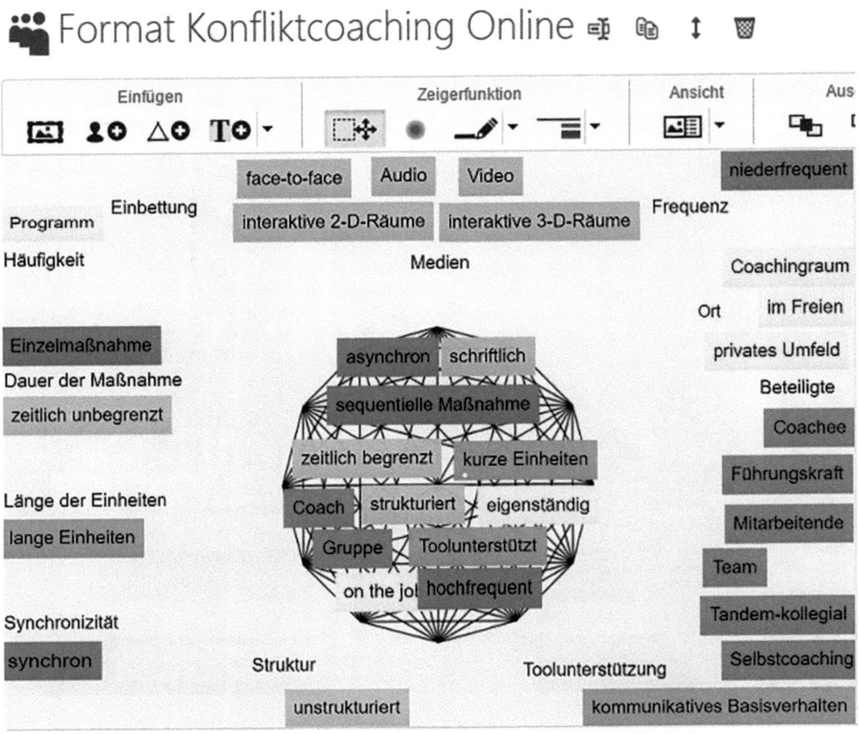

Fig. 10.26 Format conflict coaching online with arrangement. (© CAI GmbH)

the individual coaching rooms. The same applies to the shared group room. Nevertheless, it is recommended to carry out some sequences between the conflict parties at different times, as the special charm and advantage of online applications in conflict coaching lies in the emotional distance and the time available for reflection and reformulation of accusations into needs.

10.4.4 Transfer Coaching

As already described (► Sect. 8.4.4) transfer coaching is used to support the implementation of measures to achieve goals. For this purpose, a short format is suitable, which is carried out online. Transfer coaching is therefore often part of qualification programs. Transfer coaching increases the effectiveness of training by two to three times (Geißler, 2011).

Transfer coaching can be used for various personnel development measures and also as part of a sequential coaching process as an intermediate stage (Fig. 10.27). Goals that are shared with other people increase the chance that the goals will be successfully implemented. This also includes a regular update on the degree of goal achievement. This update takes place when the current status of goal achievement is assessed and communicated in transfer coaching.

Geißler (2011) also uses virtual possibilities in transfer coaching. This is an Internet tool with preformulated questions, which coaches accompany the clients by

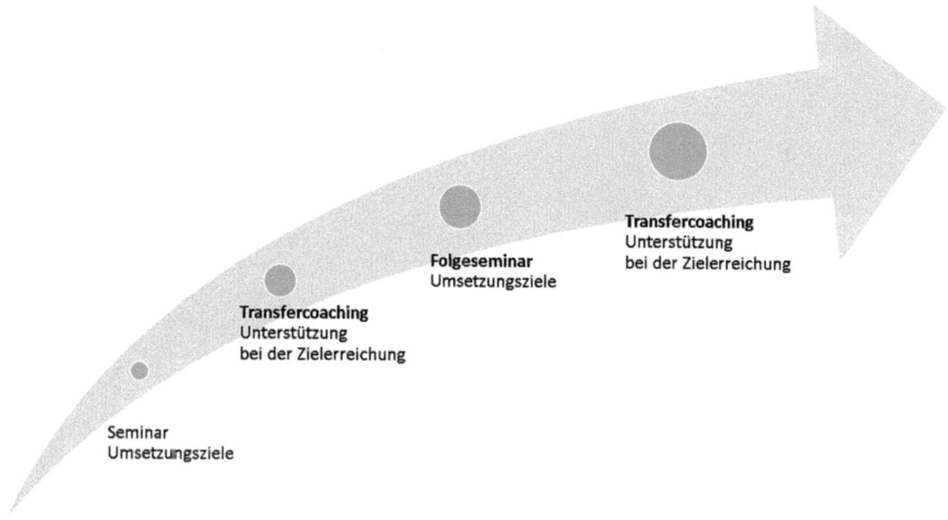

Fig. 10.27 Transfer coaching. (© Berninger-Schäfer)

telephone when answering them. Geißler was able to prove that approximately half-hour virtual transfer coachings significantly improve the achievement of participants.

In the CAI® World, transfer coaching is offered as a separate coaching format. This makes it flexible to use when it comes to supporting the implementation of action intentions. These can relate to goals that have been developed in a coaching, as part of a further education module or, for example, in a performance agreement.

For this purpose, the coaches select the format transfer coaching. After that, a process menu opens, the individual steps of which are backed by questions. These are not static, but can be selected as needed. Custom questions can also be formulated precisely. Tools such as chat, whiteboard, presentation and desktop sharing support the process.

Transfer coaching is implemented as a separate format in the CAI® World in accordance with Geißler (2012) and Offermanns (2004) in 4 phases (Table 10.9).

These phases can be clicked individually. Depending on the selected communication medium, communication takes place in writing and/or by video/audio (Fig. 10.28). A set of questions is stored for each phase, so that individual questions can be clicked or spoken (Fig. 10.29). Coaches have the freedom to ask their own questions or to make the process client-centered. In this respect, the given questions are of a suggestive character. In this coaching format, a selection of tools is offered, since this is a short format in which the whole coaching process should not be redesigned. Rather, a previously defined goal should be worked on very focused.

The format criteria of transfer coaching are shown in Fig. 10.30.

This format is also particularly suitable for managers when they support their employees in achieving goals. The role of coach is then replaced by the role of manager.

Table 10.9 Phases of transfer coaching

1	Assessment of target achievement	Description of the target Target achievement Hindering conditions Helpful conditions
2	Lessons learned	–
3	New target	Implementation planning Measures planning Hindering conditions Helpful conditions Resources
4	Target review	–

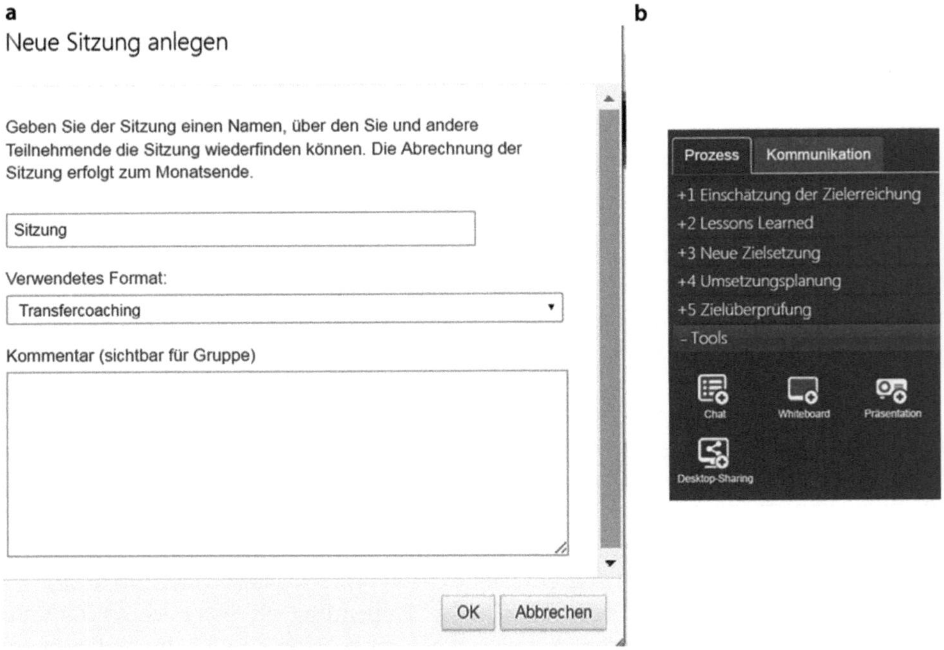

Fig. 10.28 **a**, **b** Creating the session format Transfercoaching and process menu in the CAI® World. (© CAI GmbH)

10.4.5 Walk and Talk

Both in the context of health coaching and in business coaching, coaching appointments are made between clients and coaches in the outdoors. It may be that they walk or run together. The movement itself is a metaphor that has to do with development and change, namely "getting in motion". Coaches use routes that are familiar to them. There are usually rest breaks, e.g. at a bank, in a clearing in the forest, in a hut and the like. There sticks, leaves, stones and the like can be used for visuali-

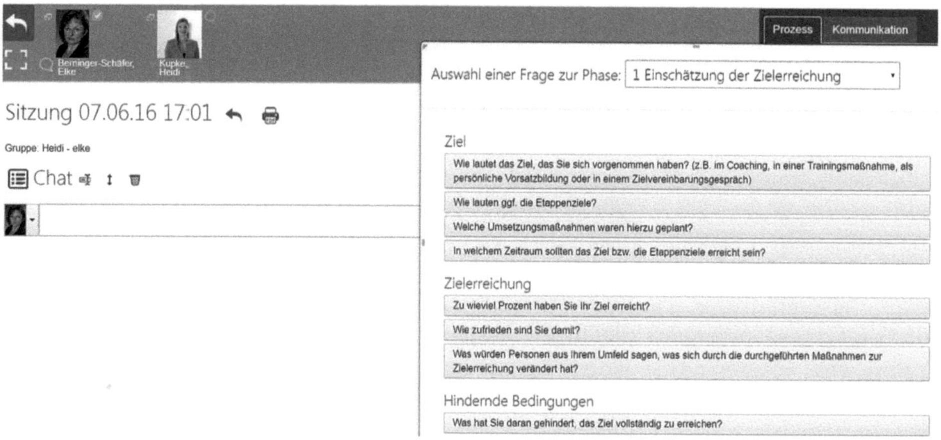

Fig. 10.29 Communication space and exemplary question set for transfer coaching. (© CAI GmbH)

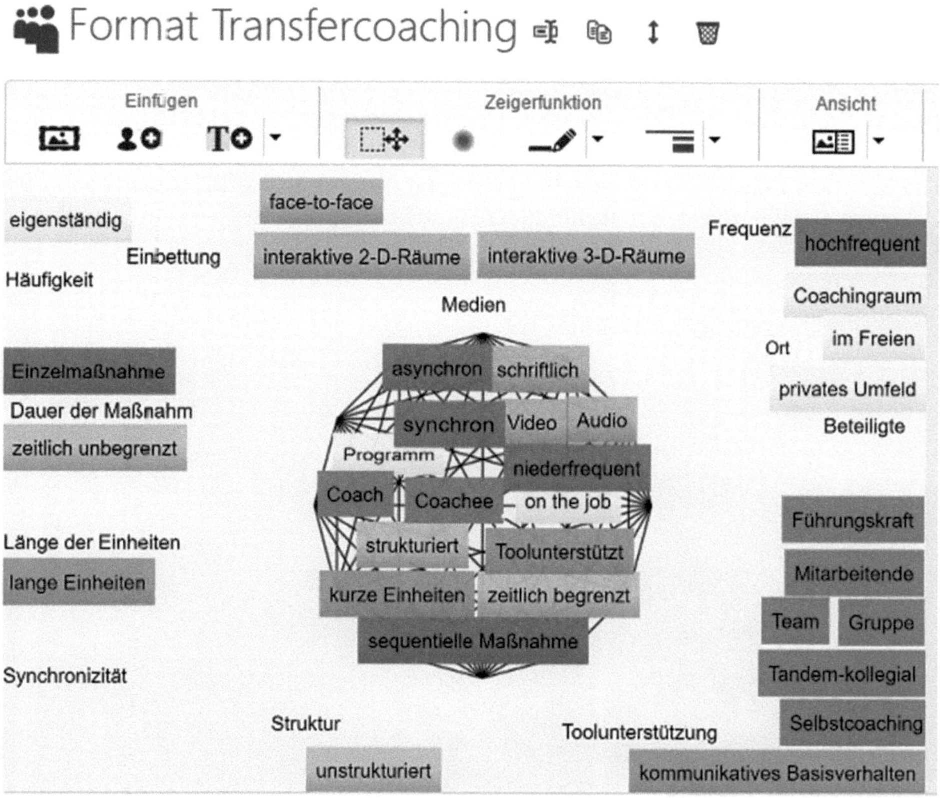

Fig. 10.30 Format Transfercoaching. (© CAI GmbH)

zations. A tablet or a laptop can be taken along as a "toolbox" and used. Photos of the route can be created and worked on with online tools. Popular in this context is, for example, the tool "resource tree".

■ **Example**

Mr. O is responsible for a department with over 300 employees in a corporation. He hardly manages to integrate sport into his busy everyday life and to plan time for coaching. But both are very important to him. He is extremely enthusiastic about the idea of combining both. For him, this creates a new quality of his further development. As part of such a walking sequence, coach and client stop at a certain point in the forest that has been chosen by the coach beforehand. They sit on a tree trunk. The coach asks the client to look around and choose a tree that particularly appeals to him. The coach carries a small laptop in a backpack. There he opens the online tool "resource tree". While the client has a real tree in front of him, the coach documents the client's statements on the virtual tree. He guides him to find what locates him, just as the tree finds support and food with its roots. In the next step, the strengths, skills and experiences are gathered. The coach notes these statements on the trunk of the virtual tree. The upper part of the crown stands for a fulfilled life. Some branches already reach that far, some have to grow still. The branches are symbolically for already achieved or still to be achieved goals (◘ Fig. 10.31; see also ► Sect. 9.3.7).

◘ Figure 10.32 shows the format implemented in this example.

10.4.6 Solution Finder—Self-Coaching Plus Peer Coaching

The Solution Finder is a self-coaching tool that is combined with excerpts from the Coaching Conference-peer coaching format at a certain point.

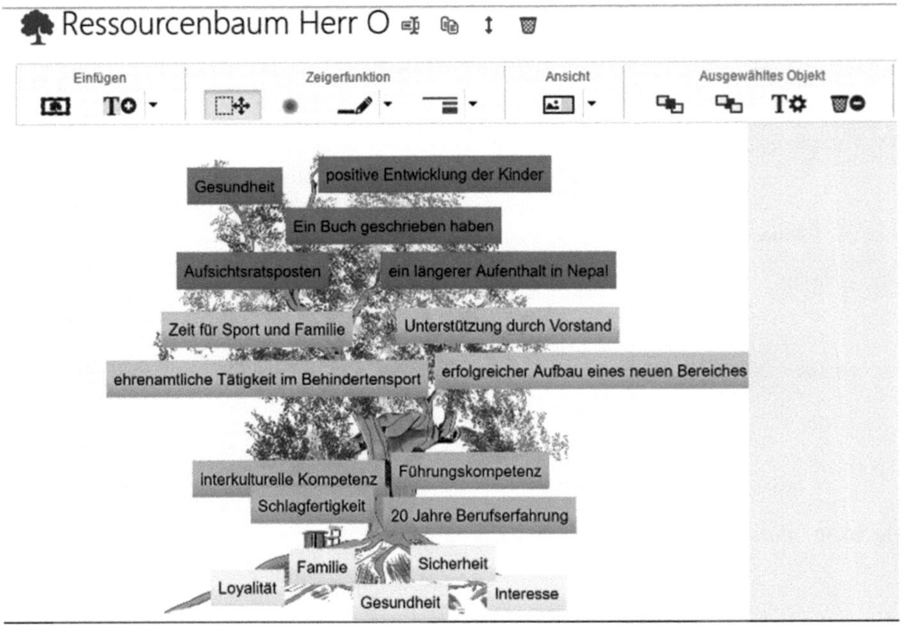

◘ **Fig. 10.31** Resource tree in case study. (© CAI GmbH)

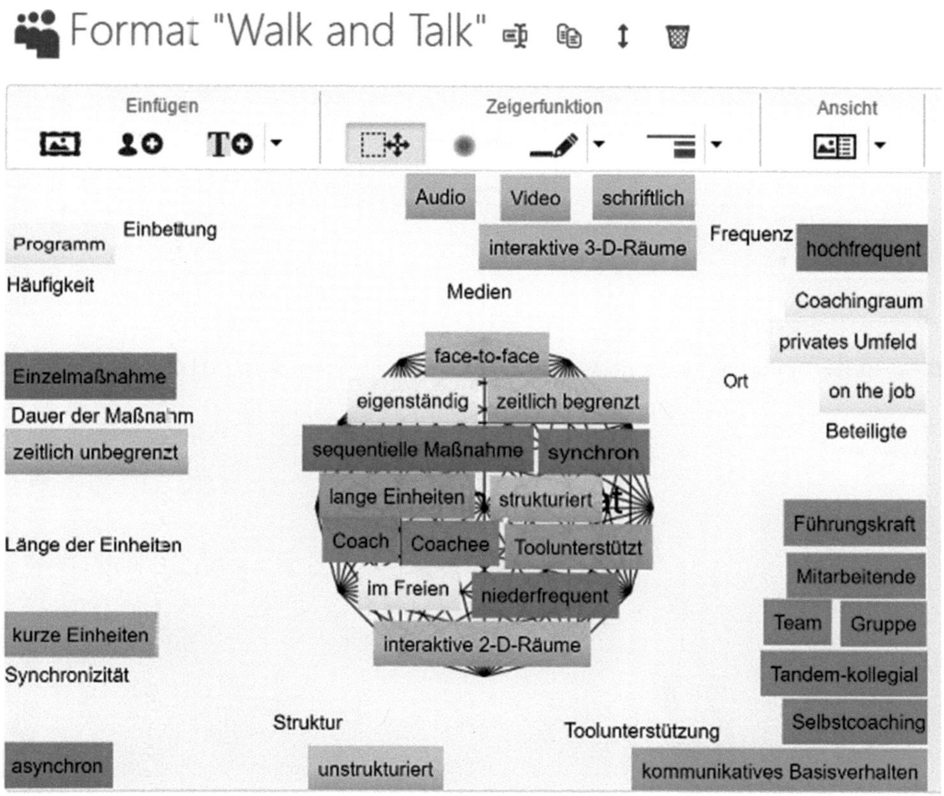

Fig. 10.32 Format "Walk and Talk". (© CAI GmbH)

People who want to use the Solution Finder find a user-friendly guide and are led through the coaching process already shown in Fig. 10.33; see also ► Sect. 8.4.4). Various tools are available for this purpose. Each step is explained to the user by means of a short guide. First, they are guided to describe their situation and work out their question.

The placement tool (Fig. 10.34) can visually represent the problem. There is a guide and a preset.

In contrast to the alignment tool, which is used in coaching with the coach or in coaching conferences, only a few single-color backgrounds are available in the Solution Finder. For visualization, a selection of figures (symbols) is available (Fig. 10.35).

In the next step, the users are guided to create a solution image using the placement tool as well (Fig. 10.36).

Goals should be derived from the solution image. For this purpose, a whiteboard is used and the goals are entered with cards (Fig. 10.37). Next to the whiteboard is a manual.

Up to four people can be invited as consultants at this point. They are asked to give tips on what the person concerned should do to achieve their goals (solution brainstorming; Fig. 10.38). These selected consultants receive a preconfigured

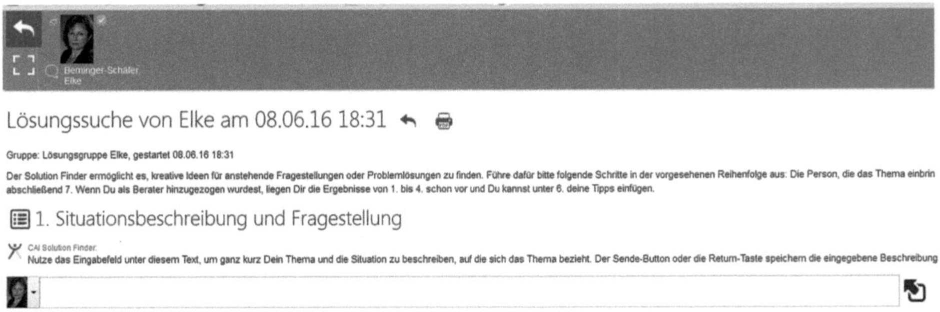

Fig. 10.33 Instruction for describing the situation in the solution finder. (© CAI GmbH)

Fig. 10.34 Placement tool in solution finder. (© CAI GmbH)

Fig. 10.35 Symbols in the solution finder. (© CAI GmbH)

e-mail in which they are introduced to their role. This mail can be edited by the sending persons and thus adapted individually.

In a final step, the person who uses the Solution Finder selects the solutions that are right for them and thanks their consultants.

They are asked to submit feedback on the Solution Finder, which is to serve the continuous improvement of this self-coaching format.

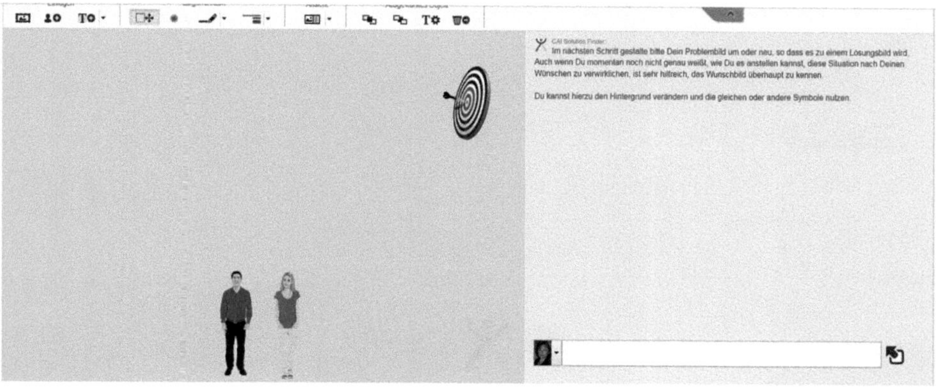

Fig. 10.36 Instructions for creating a solution image in the solution finder. (© CAI GmbH)

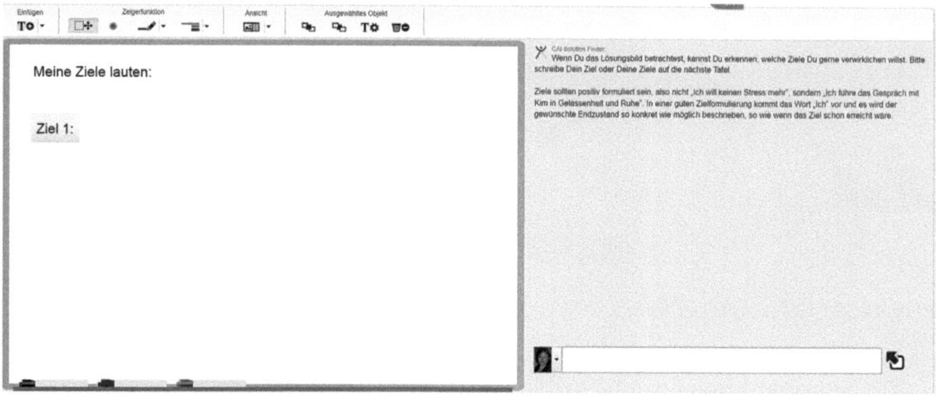

Fig. 10.37 Goal formulation in the solution finder. (© CAI GmbH)

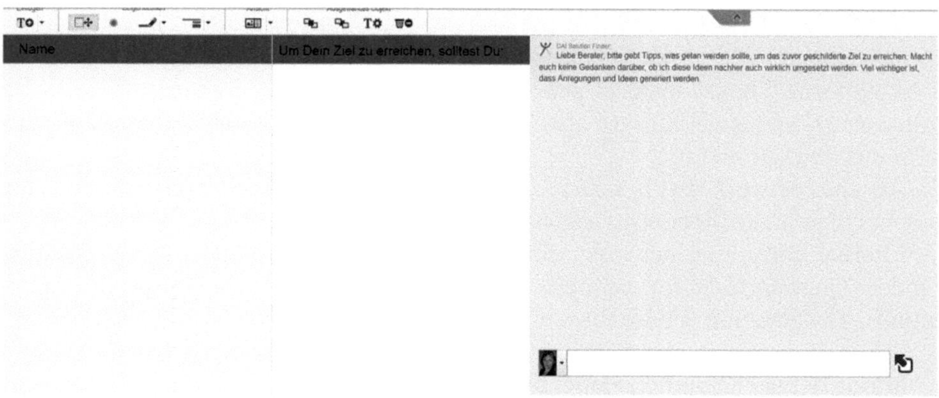

Fig. 10.38 Solution brainstorming in the solution finder. (© CAI GmbH)

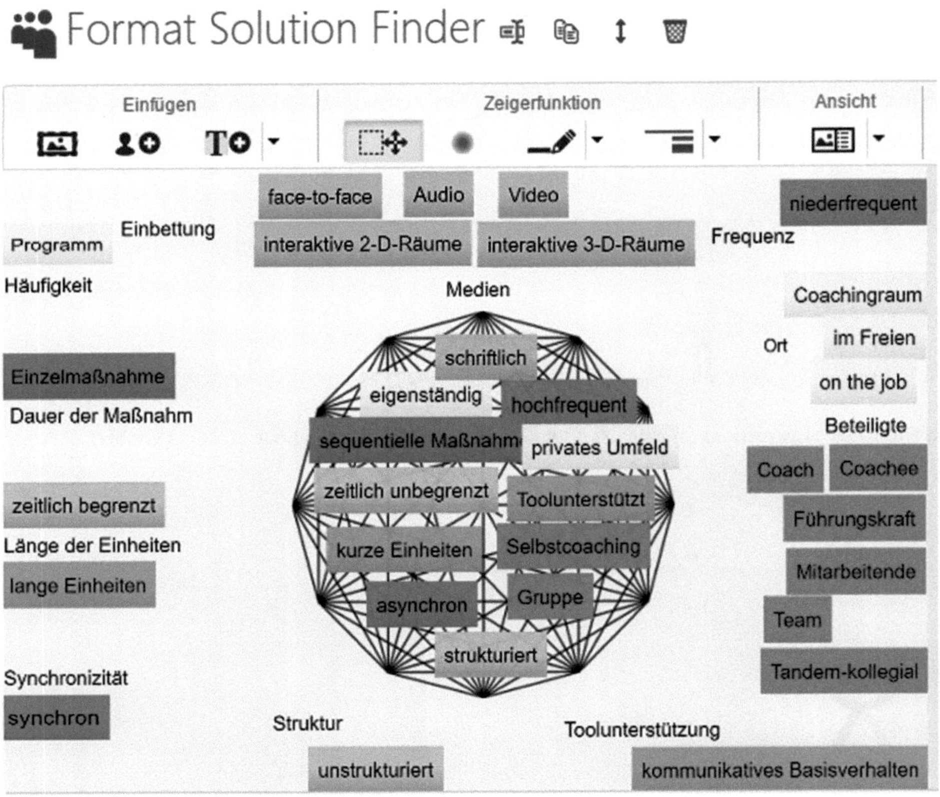

Fig. 10.39 Solution finder format. (© CAI GmbH)

The Solution Finder can be used as often as desired. The processing of the Solution Finder can be interrupted at any point. Since everything is stored, the users can design their self-coaching process at their own pace.

Advisor Network

In addition to the possibility that the users of the Solution Finder can invite freely chosen people to brainstorm solutions, an advisor network is being set up on the CAI platform. These consist of people who have already been invited to brainstorm solutions by someone and are also available to others. Advisors are asked if they wish this on their first use.

Another network that is asked for a contribution in brainstorming solutions are coaches who make themselves available for this.

Internal consulting networks also arise in organizations that use the Solution Finder. These include, for example, universities, companies and non-profit organizations. The Solution Finder format is shown in Fig. 10.39.

Bridge between Solution Finder and Coach Database

The coaching with the Solution Finder reaches its limits when the self-reflections of the users do not lead to the usual patterns or the consultants do not provide helpful solution ideas.

Then it can be very useful to involve a professional coach. If a user wishes this, the processing steps of the Solution Finder can be made visible to the coach in the shared virtual space.

10.4.7 CAI®-Business Coaching as a Format

In ► Sect. 4.3 Business Coaching was presented in the tree metaphor as an application area for coaching. Business coaching is an umbrella term for very different fields, such as leadership of employees, inter- and intraindividual conflict management, potential development, strategic planning, change management, etc. Business coaching refers to coaching in a professional context. This can be implemented with very different formats for different target groups.

In the CAI® World, business coaching is implemented with a defined process flow and certain online tools available, thus structured and conveyed in a medial way. As a result, it already has a certain format, which is further concretized in actual application (◘ Fig. 10.40). An example case is presented in ► Sect. 9.3.10.

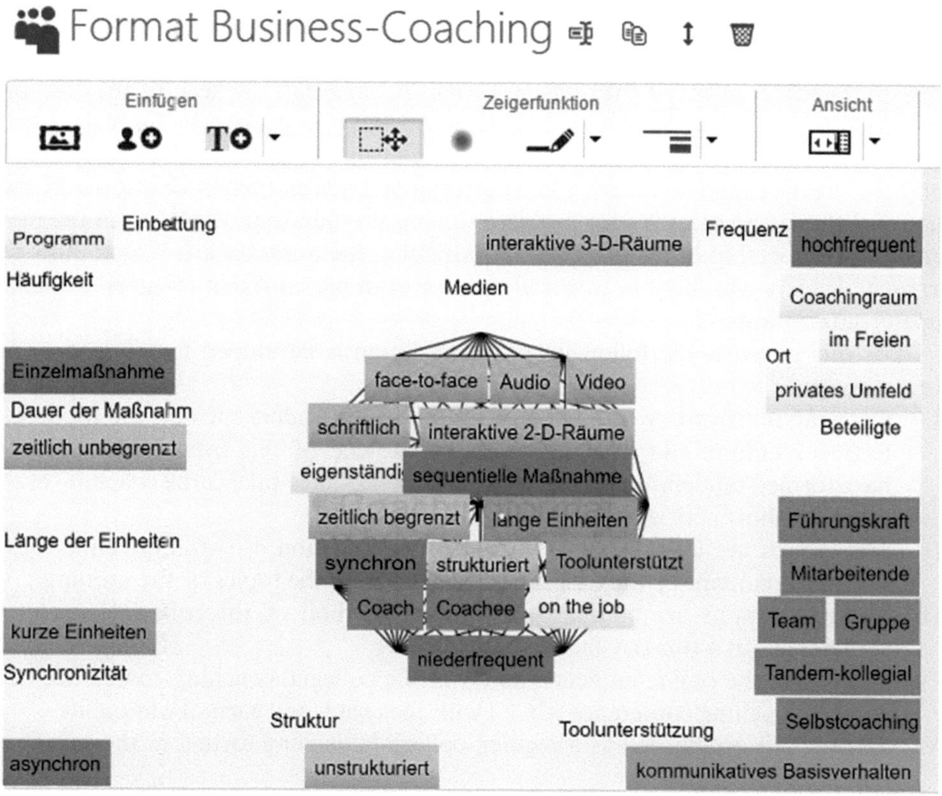

◘ **Fig. 10.40** Format business coaching. (© CAI GmbH)

- **CAI®Business Coaching as a Tool**

CAI® Business coaching becomes a tool when coaches open the Business Coaching session format on their computer in the face-to-face variant. Instead of writing on a flipchart, they can write on the whiteboard and use all the tools together with the clients. This makes it easy for coaches to orient themselves in the process and structure the coaching session transparently for the clients.

The entire coaching session is documented and there is no need to write a subsequent protocol. Coaches can send a link directly from the session to the clients, so that they can also enter this virtual meeting room. This can support the self-reflection of the clients and significantly increase the likelihood of implementation. Clients usually work on their sessions and document their experiences and progress, so that valuable material for the next steps in the coaching process is created as a whole.

10.4.8 Coaching Program for Developing Culture in a Corporation

The head of a division has the task of leading departments that are located on different continents. He is very familiar with the intercultural challenges that come with it. His department heads are located in Asia, South and North America, Germany and the Czech Republic. He wishes for the development of a culture of trust and feedback, so that despite intercultural differences, an exchange is possible at the level of department heads, which supports cross-departmental projects and contributes to the achievement of the division's goals. At an event, the head of the division gets to know the collegial coaching conference® and is impressed by the structured, goal- and solution-oriented process, the appreciative and resource-oriented attitude and the creative methods used. The respectful attitude in communication and the use of different perspectives for problem solving should expand and enrich the repertoire of leadership in his division. In particular, the question arises as to how to animate leaders who have been socialized, for example, in Asian cultures, to make open contributions.

For this purpose, the following program design is developed for 60 leaders in several steps:

I. Carrying out two-day training courses for 10–15 leaders each on the topics of feedback culture and coaching skills. At the end of this training, the leaders have formed tandems and in the following weeks they take turns coaching each other for short periods of about 30 min with a guide.
II. The groups are introduced to virtual communication in two-hour online sessions. The content of the training is transferred to the topics of the training.
III. The participants are familiarized with the method of the collegial coaching conference® in a two-day face-to-face training.
IV. They learn the online implementation of the collegial coaching conference® as a CAI® coaching conference (CCC) with the coach and carry it out online.
V. The CCC is established as a regular, collegial coaching format at the management level.

Even if the participants in a coaching conference are known to each other and have "committed" to this approach, feedback can be given and suggestions made in individual phases of the coaching process using symbolic figures or simply by attaching

Fig. 10.41 Brainstorming with figures and symbols. (© CAI GmbH)

cards to a virtual bulletin board (Fig. 10.41). The person "behind the cards" or "behind the figure" does not have to reveal themselves.

By using feedback, coaching skills and the CCC, managers practice appreciative, goal-oriented communication, find solutions to pending problems and learn to see their differences not as an obstacle, but as a valuable resource. The possibility of conducting the coaching conference online reduces the fear of revealing oneself, which is also indirectly and to a certain extent anonymous.

This program there is a connection between coaching competencies in everyday leadership, online coaching and distance leadership, a topic that is becoming increasingly important. In many organizations, online communication is a matter of course in everyday work and leadership, but the competencies required for this are often not trained, so that managers sometimes try to transfer face-to-face behavior directly into online action, which leads to frustration.

Thus, Katrin Schöpf, Senior Leadership Consultant IBM, stated in her address as part of the event "Leading in Distributed Teams" on October 22, 2015 in Karlsruhe:

> » We experience the 'digital pain' when trying to transfer face-to-face behavior directly into online action (Katrin Schöpf, 2015, oral statement).

The importance of online coaching competencies for the topic of distance leadership represents another valuable research field.

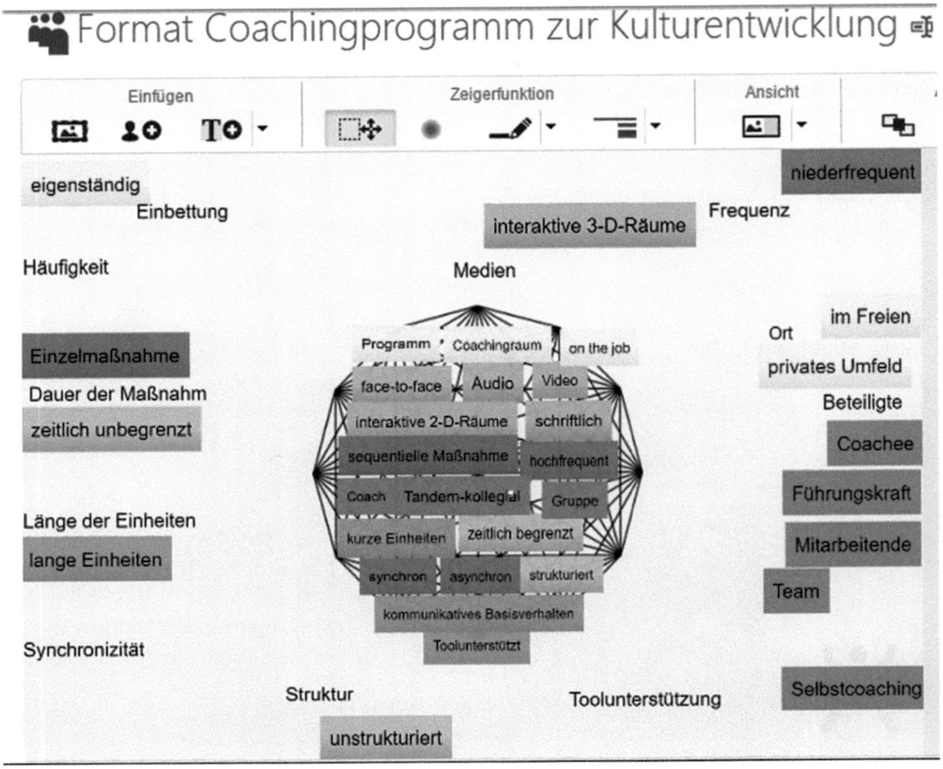

Fig. 10.42 Format of a coaching program. (© CAI GmbH)

The format of the presented coaching program for culture development combines different format criteria (Fig. 10.42).

This example shows to a particular extent that, with the increasing variety of format criteria and the associated combination possibilities, design competence of the coaches must be added to the format competence.

- **Design Competence**

The differentiation and segmentation of the coaching field makes new coaching offers possible and arouses a wide range of expectations of potential clients and commissioning organizations. The "coaching jungle" is not becoming more transparent as a result, but rather larger. It is therefore all the more important for the future viability of coaches to have a sound knowledge of different coaching formats, their possibilities and their limits. This knowledge should lead to a continuous review and, if necessary, expansion of one's own qualifications. Likewise, professional coaches should be able to provide information about which coaching formats are suitable for which concerns. On the basis of knowledge about setting factors and format criteria, coaching products can be developed that fit the wishes and needs of the contracting parties exactly. The design competence thus realizes the format competence. It enables a careful clarification of the concerns and the development of the appropriate coaching format. It thus forms the basis for the successful service coaching. Likewise, professional coaches should realistically assess their own competence, experience and preferences for certain formats and offer them both seriously and transparently (see ethical guidelines).

A proven format and design competence in coaching are necessary components of a successful presentation of one's own coach profile on the Internet (on databases and on homepages); this will become increasingly relevant in the future if the function of coach-on-demand is requested to a greater extent.

Quality in Online Coaching

Contents

E. Berninger-Schäfer, *Online Coaching*,
https://doi.org/10.1007/978-3-658-39133-1_11

Quality standards in online coaching are based on the quality requirements in coaching in general. These can be formulated from different perspectives. These include the perspectives of practicing coaches, coach pool providers, coaching training providers, contracting persons or organizations, and the perspective of coaching research (Berninger-Schäfer & Wolf, 2011).

In online coaching, additional requirements are added.

The starting point is first the definition of quality as it can be found at the DGQ (German Society for Quality):

"Quality is the totality of characteristics (and characteristic values) of a unit with regard to its suitability to meet specified and required requirements" or according to the revision of the standard in 2000: "Quality is the degree to which a set of inherent characteristics meets requirements" (Steinke, 2012, p. 114).

This means that quality can then be assessed if certain requirements are defined. These are listed in the tables on requirements for structural, process and result quality in relation to online coaching and are based on characteristics that Kühne (2012) has found for psychosocial online counseling.

Reindl (2015) and Engelhardt (2013) also describe the need for universally applicable quality standards or a quality seal for online counseling and name various associations as predecessors, e.g.:

- BDP: Association of German Psychologists (2001)
- FKOB: Federation of Swiss Psychologists (2003)
- VWS: Association of Viennese Social Projects (2006)
- German Caritas Association e. V. (2007)
- DAKJEF: German Working Group for Youth, Marriage and Family Counseling (2010)
- DGOB: German Society for Online Counseling (2015)
- Advisory Board and Certification Committee for Online Counseling Training (2015).

In his master's thesis on "Quality Management in Psychosocial Online Counseling", Kühne (2012) carries out a systematization and evaluation of existing concepts of further education in online counseling.

He relies on the definition of the German Counseling Association (DGfB):

> Counseling is a person- and structure-related social service. It therefore requires a joint effort and performance by all parties involved (counselor/client and possibly payer) and clear target agreements (DGfB, 2010, p. 3, quoted from Kühne, 2012).

Online counseling takes place over the Internet and, like face-to-face counseling, has the goal of supporting clients in their self-reflection, self-regulation, and ability to act.

Quality management in online counseling means that measures to ensure the quality of structure, process and results are also taken into account in mediated communication.

11.1 Structural, Process and Result Quality

Kühne (2012) evaluates offers of psychosocial online counseling, specifically counseling centers for education, using an analysis grid. Therefore, not all criteria and their assessment fit online coaching and, following Kühne, its own presentation is made. A challenge here is the diverse use of the term online coaching. This can mean the specific offer of an online coach, but also a platform or an online coaching tool. The collection listed in ◘ Table 11.1, 11.2 and 11.3 for online coaching refers to coaching platforms, specifically the CAI® World, and is intended as an encouragement—without claiming to be complete.

Because of the potentially very positive quality of online approaches, Reindl (2015) pleads for the definition of uniform quality standards that allow users to assess Internet offers. These include:

- Target group orientation
- Accessibility
- User-friendliness
- Selection of suitable communication media (mail, forums, chat, video)
- Presentation of the counseling concept
- Qualification of the counselors
- Performance spectrum and limits
- Data protection and IT security
- Anonymity
- Documentation
- Costs and payment modalities
- Information on quality assurance
- Responsibilities and rights/roles system
- Processes
- Technical equipment and requirements
- Networks
- Feedback and complaint management
- Support
- Barrier-free
- Ethical standards

This list shows that a platform for online coaching can contribute significantly to quality assurance in coaching, if it actually implements the above requirements. Online coaching can then be superior to face-to-face coaching in terms of redeeming quality promises, as some of the requirements are already implemented through the construction of the platform itself (see also ▶ Chap. 12). The foundation for a successful coaching is the relationship between coach and client. For this you need—in addition to the possibilities that such a platform offers—the competence of the coaches to create a media-mediated, appreciative, empathetic and respectful relationship with clients. Special skills are needed for this, which require qualification (▶ Sect. 11.2). The necessary conditions are specified in the ethical guidelines for online applications in coaching, supervision and therapy (▶ Sect. 11.3).

Online competence and ethical behavior correspond to the requirements of the DGOB (German Society for Online Consulting), which defines the continuous

Table 11.1 Structural quality

Criterion	Online coaching	Face-to-face coaching
Low-threshold access	Yes	Usually not
Ad hoc or short-term intervention	Yes	Usually not
Availability	Potentially always, defined by the coach	Scheduling Office hours
Multimedia	For multimedia platforms, when a combination of different communication channels is given (video, audio, mailing, chat, forums)	No
Security and data protection	Security standards are assessable, e.g. SSL encryption Anonymity possible	Up to the coaches Anonymity not possible
Barrier-free	Legally required and assessable	Unclear
Coaching concept	Indicated and verifiable	Oral or written information from the coaches
Transparency of procedure	Visible, inspectable and controllable	Oral or written information of the coaches
Transparency of time and cost	Available with automated client management and payment systems, minute-by-minute measurement	Agreement between coach and client
Equipment	Computer, notebook, tablet, smartphone; Internet connection, multimedia Online coaching tools client management system integrated process flow Knowledge management Forums Feedback instruments Document templates	Rooms Flipchart Notice boards, moderation materials Tools, such as image material, pens, figurines, etc.
Human resources	Coach Technical support	Coach Back office
Expertise	Additional competence in online coaching Ongoing development	Coaching competence Ongoing development
Contact frequency	Frequencies determine the clientele (low to high frequency)	Low frequency
Transfer support	Frequent, direct feedback "on the job" possible	Limited, Shadowing expensive
Evaluation instruments	Integrated online instruments, Anonymous possible for research purposes	Obliges the respective coaches or contracting parties

(continued)

Table 11.1 (continued)

Criterion	Online coaching	Face-to-face coaching
Formats	Small units Frequent units Asynchronous and synchronous work Anytime Anywhere Combination of apps, media-mediated coaching units and face-to-face sessions Format diversity	Longer sessions Low frequency At the same time Location-based Multiple formats
Tool diversity	Visible present	Possible

commitment of online consultants to quality assurance in its quality guidelines through the following three points (▶ http://dg-onlineberatung.de/wpcontent/uploads/2015/02/Richtlinien_Anerkennung_von_24_11_09.pdf, accessed on 21.08.2016):

1. Supervision for regular reflection of activity in individual, group or collegial supervision (intervision)
2. regular professional development
3. Orientation to ethical standards

These points are elaborated in the following sections.

11.2 Professional Development

Schermuly and Graßmann (2015) explain that for successful coaching from the clients' perspective, motivation, willingness to change and commitment to coaching, and from the organization's perspective, financial and temporal resources, as well as support from the management, are necessary. From the coach's perspective, in addition to experience and field competence, professionalization in an adequate further education is essential. However, there are great differences here. In the study conducted by Schermuly and Graßmann (2015), 20% of coaches had experienced a coaching education that included no more than 10 training hours. The authors refer to the German Federal Association of Coaching (▶ www.DBVC.de), which demands at least 150 h of training without self-study over a minimum duration of 12 months for a qualified coaching education. In addition to formal criteria, the DBVC's quality requirements for coaching further education include information on the recognizable theoretical concept, the development of a coach identity, evaluation, ethical guidelines and quality assurance.

In their survey on online supervision, Reindl et al. (2016) found that only 17.2% of supervisors had received further training in online procedures, while 90% of respondents had received training in supervision. Interviews were also conducted with British supervisors, 60% of whom had received online training. In Germany, there seem to be few such offers. The resulting lack of knowledge is also reflected in

Table 11.2 Process quality

Criterion	Online coaching	Face-to-face coaching
Outstanding process control	Integrated coaching process with outstanding and activatable phases	Up to the coaches
Process clarity and openness for individual process design	Integrated coaching process creates maximum transparency Process steps and tools can be varied to fit	Obliges the coaches
Templates for contract design/order processing	Forms are available online	Obliges the coaches
Order clarification and target definition	Independent, designated phases with supporting tools	Obliges the coaches
Evaluation instruments	Visibly present	Obliges the coaches
Client management system	Automatic documentation of sessions, times and invoices Forms and documents are possible and can be assigned to clients	Up to the coaches
Documentation	Automatic documentation of the coaching process	Protocol, photos, video and audio recordings possible
Reflection support	In the coaching session itself, controlled by the coaches Documentation, this allows for high reflection support Clients can work alone Written form facilitates structuring and distancing	In the coaching session itself, controlled by the coaches Activation by homework possible
Self-determination of the clients	Clients decide when and how much they work, even without a coach, can carry out individual process steps in agreement with the coaches also alone	Dominance of the interaction between coach and client
Method Use	The visible availability of many tools makes orientation and selection easier	Up to the coaches
Supervision	The supervisor can see the whole coaching process anonymously or can be actively included in a session	Case discussion, format open
Collegial exchange	Group setting available Format and tools for collegial coaching available Networking in forums	Obliges the coaches
Professional development	Knowledge management available Forum exchange Offer of further education modules Certifications	Obliges the coaches

Table 11.3 Result quality

Criterion	Online coaching	Face-to-face coaching
Statistical processing of work	Automated in client management system	Obliges the coaches
Evaluation	Scientifically standardized evaluation instruments are integrated	Up to the coaches or the contracting parties
Feedback	Feedback tools are integrated into the individual coaching phases	Up to the coaches
Scientifically researchable data material	Documentation of coaching processes can be made available to research and evaluated anonymously by agreement	Up to the coaches

the fact that many supervisors use unsecured email connections when talking about online applications (Reindl et al., 2016).

Qualification as an online coach can be a additional qualification for already professionally trained and active coaches, or the acquisition of online competence can already take place during coaching further education.

A further education as an online coach should train the following competences:

- Knowledge and skills to be able to carry out coaching as a professional measure virtually and multimedia, synchronously and asynchronously
- Building the ability to carry out coaching with professionally developed online coaching tools
- Ability to control online coaching processes that activate resources, are goal- and solution-oriented, and realize the associated ethical requirements
- Design of empathic, appreciative relationships in online encounters
- Holistic online guidance using cognitive, emotional and physiological information and their interactions
- Realization of structure, process and result quality in online coaching
- Acquisition of the necessary technical know-how to be able to control and accompany clients in their application in a sovereign, responsible and up-to-date manner
- Further development of one's own media and media communication competence
- Expansion of format and design competence in coaching
- Marketability in the provision of online coaching as an extension of one's own portfolio and the competitive positioning

An example of the additional qualification for the CAI® certified online coach is presented in excerpts. It is carried out in 3-h online modules with a lecturer/a lecturer. In addition, peer coaching takes place with and without a coach as well as individual teaching coaching, in which one's own online coaching case is supervisory. The participants practice in collegial coaching units, partly accompanied by teaching coaches. The contents of the online modules are shown in the following overview:

Contents of the Online Modules

Module 1: Technical instruction and competence development

- Possibilities of using a virtual platform for online collaboration
- Operation of different communication channels in online media
- Knowledge of necessary technical equipment for online coaching, consulting, training and leadership
- Management of participants, groups and sessions
- Operation of online tools in accompanying processes

Module 2: The coaching process in CAI® World

- Implementation of the systemic solution-oriented coaching concept in CAI® World (definition, process, effectiveness variables, quality)
- Overview of phases and virtual implementation
- Dealing with increased self-revelation of clients
- Particularities of written communication in online encounters

Module 3: CAI® Coaching Conference

- Working with groups in online coaching
- The concept of the collegial CAI® Coaching Conference
- Procedure and roles
- Implementation synchronous/asynchronous

Module 4: The online encounter

- Ethics guidelines and competence fields in online events
- Constructive relationship management
- Targeted use of communication media
- Specialties of the auditory channel

Module 5: Media Selection, Technical Quality and Quality Assurance

- Technical Refresh
- Management of Personal Data and Documents
- Use of Individualized Content
- Use of Automated Statistics
- Use of Secured Media and Devices
- Knowledge Management and Community

Module 6: Online Coaching Methods

- Use of specific methods in online coaching
- Working with a whiteboard and sociogram
- Systemic constellation
- Use of pictorial materials
- Resource tree
- Working with different perspectives in problem solving
- Working with inner parts
- Drawing tools

Module 7: Coaching formats
- Overview of consultation formats
- Overview of coaching formats
- Transfer coaching
- Order clarification

Module 8: Group dynamics online (optional)
- Online coaching with groups
- Coaching circle
- Team accompaniment
- Process control synchronous/asynchronous
- Reflection and exchange of experiences

Module 9: Marketing (optional)
- Marketing of Online Coaching
- Market analysis
- Benefit argumentation
- The customer perspective
- Your own coaching profile

More modules are offered, e.g. specifically for self-employed people: Business and legal aspects of the activity as an online coach.

The contents of the modules are adapted according to the feedback of the course participants and can thus change. For this purpose, the regular evaluations for the process control of further education are of decisive importance.

In the meantime, there is also the possibility to acquire these competences in a basic coaching further education to the "business coach" or to the "health coach". These further education courses are offered as recognized further education courses of the DBVC in cooperation with the Mannheim Business School (HdWM) as contact study and as part of master's programs.

The acquisition and use of the described competences is a prerequisite for fulfilling the ethical guidelines listed in the following chapter.

11.3 Ethics Guidelines

The ethics guidelines formulated here represent minimum requirements for self-commitment by professionally working coaches, therapists and supervisors who offer and provide their services online. They are incorporated into further education and certification. They are based on the following ethical guidelines formulated elsewhere:

- Guidelines for the Recognition of Online Advisors of the German Society for Online Consulting (DGOB)
- Ethical Standards of the International Coach Federation (ICF)
- Guidelines of the German Federal Association of Coaching (DBVC)

- Media Guidelines of the European Federation of Psychologists' Associations (EFPA)
- Professional Ethics of the Professional Association for Coaching, Supervision and Organizational Consulting (bso)
- Ethics Guidelines of the German Society for Systemic Therapy, Counseling and Family Therapy (DGSF)
- Ethics Guidelines of the Karlsruhe Institute

Basic Attitude and View of Man

Professional service providers in coaching, therapy and supervision meet their clients with respect, empathy, care and respect, regardless of origin, gender, sexual orientation, skin color, world view, ethnic origin, nationality, age, religion, language, culture, lifestyle and status.

They consider people as independent, autonomous personalities who are able to learn and develop, as well as make autonomous decisions and act responsibly. They respect and observe the inviolable dignity of their clients.

Professional service providers in coaching, therapy and supervision create a trusting, protected and supportive relationship that recognizes and strengthens resources and potentials, increases self-control and responsibility of clients in a way that is appropriate for the clients, and leads to a solution-oriented transfer to the personal context.

They strive to use their knowledge and skills to improve the living conditions of individuals and society. They respect and protect the rights of all parties involved, in particular the right to self-determination. They distance themselves from fundamentalist and/or sectarian positions.

Professional service providers in coaching, therapy and supervision practice their professional behavior in such a way that it serves the reputation of the entire profession.

Expertise

The range of services is based on scientifically sound concepts (e.g. psychology, counseling and economics, educational sciences, media research, neuroscience, medicine, communication sciences, etc.), depending on the focus of the services. They determine the type of process support, the understanding of roles, the approach and the methods used. This requires content-related, personal, communicative, social, emotional, technical and economic competence.

This knowledge and ability has been acquired in verifiable qualifications, both in face-to-face and in virtual, media-mediated settings.

The limits of one's own competence are recognized and not exceeded.

The individual support processes are evaluated.

Scientific research is supported.

One's own knowledge and ability is regularly further developed, e.g. through training courses, supervision and quality dialogues.

Technical Competence

The basic knowledge about different virtual, media usage possibilities is regularly updated.

For work with modern media, in-depth knowledge about media communication forms and their impact on interpersonal communication and relationship formation—as well as their targeted application to control helpful accompaniment processes—is available.

In order to be able to carry out virtual offers sensibly and professionally, sufficient technical equipment is available—as well as the ability to advise clients on the necessary equipment.

Clients are professionally supported in the application of the media necessary for the professional encounter and, if necessary, instructed.

At the beginning of a virtual session, a relapse scenario is set, e.g. by clarifying the desired and possible communication channels that can be used in the event of technical problems.

The knowledge of the legal and ethical requirements for data protection and data security is available, both of a technical and organizational nature and is always up to date. The necessary technical requirements for the use of secure media, devices and communication channels are created.

- **Confidentiality**

The technical requirements for protected data management and data transmission (encryption, firewalls, passwords, virus protection) are known and taken into account.

The data protection regulations regarding confidentiality and data backup are observed. Information is only passed on to third parties with the express approval of clients and in the form desired by clients.

It is ensured that personal data, material worked out content-wise and passwords are stored inaccessible and destroyed after a certain period of time. This applies to both digital and analogue storage.

Data material can be used anonymously for research purposes, for further and continuing education and publications with the prior written consent of clients and coaches.

- **Transparency and Integrity**

Clients are informed about the procedure for providing the service, the procedures and media used, their effects—as well as the data backup carried out. They expressly agree to the corresponding data protection declarations.

Information about own qualifications, certifications, experiences, skills and membership is correctly represented.

The order clarification, the type of communication, the definition of financial framework conditions, the choice of media, the contract design and other agreements are carried out honestly and appropriately.

Professional competence is used to the benefit of the clientele, avoiding dependence and manipulation (e.g. by satisfying sexual, economic, social and spiritual needs).

The cooperation is regulated by a service contract, which, for example, contains the objectives, the working method, the time frame, the fee arrangements and statements on the preservation of professional secrecy and data protection.

In order to be able to realize these ethical claims in the online approach, coaches are dependent on the quality of the technical environment, for example, in order to be able to fulfill their promises of data security, confidentiality and the implementation of professional competence. Therefore, the next chapter is dedicated to the media concept for online coaching.

Media Concept for Online Coaching

Contents

E. Berninger-Schäfer, *Online Coaching*,
https://doi.org/10.1007/978-3-658-39133-1_12

Discussions on media conception can be found in particular in connection with teaching and learning with multimedia and the internet (Köhler et al., 2008). This knowledge can be used as a basis when designing media-assisted coaching. This transfer seems legitimate because coaching is often also described as learning accompaniment (Wolf, 2014). This is based on an understanding of coaching as the activation of resources and helpful patterns (see resource activation and pattern state change in ► Sect. 8.4.3), which enable and support new behaviour through techniques of perspective change. The intention is less the transfer of information and knowledge than the empowerment to be able to act in possibly blocked or new situations. In online applications, knowledge can also be made available, for example in the form of documents, videos, audio files, checklists, etc., which can be processed by the clients during the coaching process. Another aspect of coaching as learning accompaniment takes place explicitly when coaching is used explicitly for this purpose. This has to do with the increasing individualisation of learning paths. With the possibilities of e-learning, individual learning paths can be created, for example by assembling e-learning elements according to a competence assessment and determination of the development needs, the acquisition and application of which is accompanied by personal coaches using coaching methods. Training elements can also be integrated with trainers or instructors. Platforms can offer this connection between e-learning, virtual classrooms and virtual coaching rooms and thus enable holistic, socially supported, individually tailored learning (◘ Fig. 12.1).

◘ **Fig. 12.1** Virtual academy and coachroom on the CAI platform. (© CAI GmbH)

When designing the media used for this purpose, certain aspects of media design must be taken into account, as well as their effect on the development of new behavior, that is, the development of progress or learning progress. Whether this is possible depends on the type of information processing. This in turn is influenced by the way it is designed or processed media.

12.1 Information Processing

A influential construct from psychology is the schema concept (Seel & Ifenthaler, 2009; see also ► Sect. 7.2). It is assumed that people organize their entire knowledge on all abstraction levels via schemas. Existing schemas influence how new information is processed and for which information preferences exist.

Stimuli that do not fit into an existing schema (inconsistent items) receive more attention, are perceived more consciously and are better remembered.

Learning occurs when stimuli are assimilated. In this process, new knowledge is integrated into existing structures, e.g. by expansion, refinement and reorganization. Furthermore, learning takes place through accommodation when knowledge is restructured or a new mental model is constructed. First of all, existing knowledge is used, whereby a search is initiated in the semantic memory. If the facts can be explained on this background, the model formation is completed, even if it is a subjectively plausible but false model. A new formation arises when there are strong contradictions, when the requirements of a new situation require this and when alternative models can be tried out. For this purpose, certain environmental conditions are important, which enable alternatives and experimentation. This must be taken into account when designing the virtual coaching environment. In coaching, it is often about problem solving. This means that there is a situation in which clients cannot get any further with their previous behavior. So it's about developing and trying out an alternative behavior. In the evaluation of coaching sequences, clients often say that they feel confirmed by the solution path, that they had already thought of it (assimilation) or that there are "aha" experiences, new ideas and surprising twists and turns (accommodation).

In order to enable effective communication, it is important to match the task and the medium (Boos & Jonas, 2008). The goal is to convey the necessary information and at the same time to ensure a contribution to the reduction of ambiguity and complexity. In addition, the media function as external memory storage, which relieves the working memory (Schwan & Bruder, 2007).

When it comes to transmitting and compressing information, Boos and Jonas (2008) refer to the Media Synchronicity Theory by Dennis and Valacich from 1999, according to which media can be described by five characteristics:

1. Immediacy of feedback, support for bidirectional communication through the medium
2. Symbol variety, communication through multiple channels
3. Parallelism, simultaneous processing of a topic by multiple people
4. Revisability, editing function for messages before they are sent
5. Reusability of a message, possibility to view and possibly edit again (Boos & Jonas, 2008, p. 208)

Boos and Jonas (2008) conclude that media with low synchronization are more suitable for pure information transfer, while high synchronization is desirable for information compression when several people have to agree on communicatively transmitted meanings at the same time.

All five criteria apply to online coaching, so the media used for this purpose must be designed accordingly to meet them. Schwan and Buder (2007) also conclude that human understanding of various communication channels increases cognitive performance if certain media design principles are taken into account.

12.2 Media Design Principles

Köhler et al. (2008) describe effective media design principles, for example. Many other authors also refer to the following categories.

▪ Multimedia Principle

Multimedia is used when information or stimuli are presented both visually and auditorily through media (Seel & Ifenthaler, 2009).

> Multimedia allows for a diverse verbal and pictorial communication and provides access to a wealth of information and resources via the Internet (Seel & Ifenthaler, 2009, p. 68).

Multiple types of signs (e.g. text and image) lead to richer mental representations of a situation than just one.

Multimedia applications combine multimedia (various communication channels) with multicodality (different sign forms related to each other, e.g. language and image). This places special demands on working memory, so that the question arises as to what leads to meaningful use and what represents an overload or what generates optimal benefits for learning processes. Schwan and Buder (2007) refer to the theory of multimedia learning and its empirical validation to show that linguistic and pictorial information use two separate processing paths in the cognitive system.

In this context, Seel and Ifenthaler (2009) also describe the importance of audio-video redundancy in their discussion of online learning and multimedia psychology. They state that multi-channel communication is superior to single-channel communication for learning processes when important information is summarized and the material is presented both visually and auditorily.

This is not the case when the information relates to the same meaning, i.e. is redundant.

A deterioration or inferiority of multi-channel communication occurs when irrelevant stimuli or stimuli that have nothing to do with each other are combined and interference occurs. Attention must then be divided.

The authors refer to studies which show that "an active, effortful information processing leads to better learning results than passive reception" (Seel & Ifenthaler, 2009, p. 38). Another important aspect is the social interactivity between learners, which is possible via computer-mediated communication.

In their presentation of the cognitive prerequisites of online learning, Seel and Ifenthaler (2009) refer to Allport's concept of cognitive styles. They describe cognitive styles as the "habitualized and typical way in which an individual perceives, remembers, thinks and solves problems" (Seel & Ifenthaler, 2009, p. 47).

According to this, learning materials are particularly helpful when they correspond to the cognitive styles or the preferred sensory modalities (visual, auditory, kinesthetic) of the learners.

While using a multimedia approach, there should not be any preselection of the platform, to allow for individual preferences. This applies first of all to both the coaches and the clients. It is the task of the coaches to determine the preferences of the clients and to adapt to them. For this, coaches must acquire competencies that relate to seeing, hearing, speaking and writing (▶ Sect. 9.2) and have the technical possibilities to be able to switch between different media. The media used in online coaching should therefore serve different communication channels (multimedia) and connect language with image (multicodality), in order to summarize important information without being redundant. This happens in online coaching, for example, when working associatively with image material, symbols and layouts and reflexively-cognitively through linguistic expression. It is exactly this connection that coaches have to design in order to be able to accompany clients meaningfully.

▪ Contiguity Principle

The contiguity principle is the principle of spatial and temporal proximity. Learning is facilitated when words and images that belong together are presented in spatial and temporal proximity. This requires fewer cognitive resources.

These three principles are implemented in the CAI® World, for example, by presenting the interactive chat next to the image chosen by the client. The image associations can be written down immediately. The client's gaze can alternate between the written word and the corresponding image, which stimulates further reflection processes. In ◘ Fig. 12.2 an example from the CAI® World is shown. The desired situation was associated with a bird's-eye view by a client and a corresponding image was chosen. The questions and associations were recorded by the coach in a chat that is built up next to the image.

▪ Coherence Principle

Omitting irrelevant information facilitates the learning of multimedia content.

In the coaching process, which is designed and documented using images, layouts, chats, etc., the clients themselves generate the content. It is the coaches' task to steer a goal-oriented process here, i.e. to orient themselves clearly on the clients' concerns and thus on the order for the respective coaching unit and to avoid side paths as far as possible that do not relate to this or are not conducive to the progress of the process. With the asynchronous approach, it is, as already explained in ▶ Sect. 9.2.1. it is particularly important to make the message to be sent clear in advance and then to reduce, focus and formulate it positively.

▪ Modality Principle

The use of different sense organs supports learning. Content that is presented in a combination of spoken language and image (auditory and visual channel) can be learned more easily than in the combination of written text and image (only visual channel).

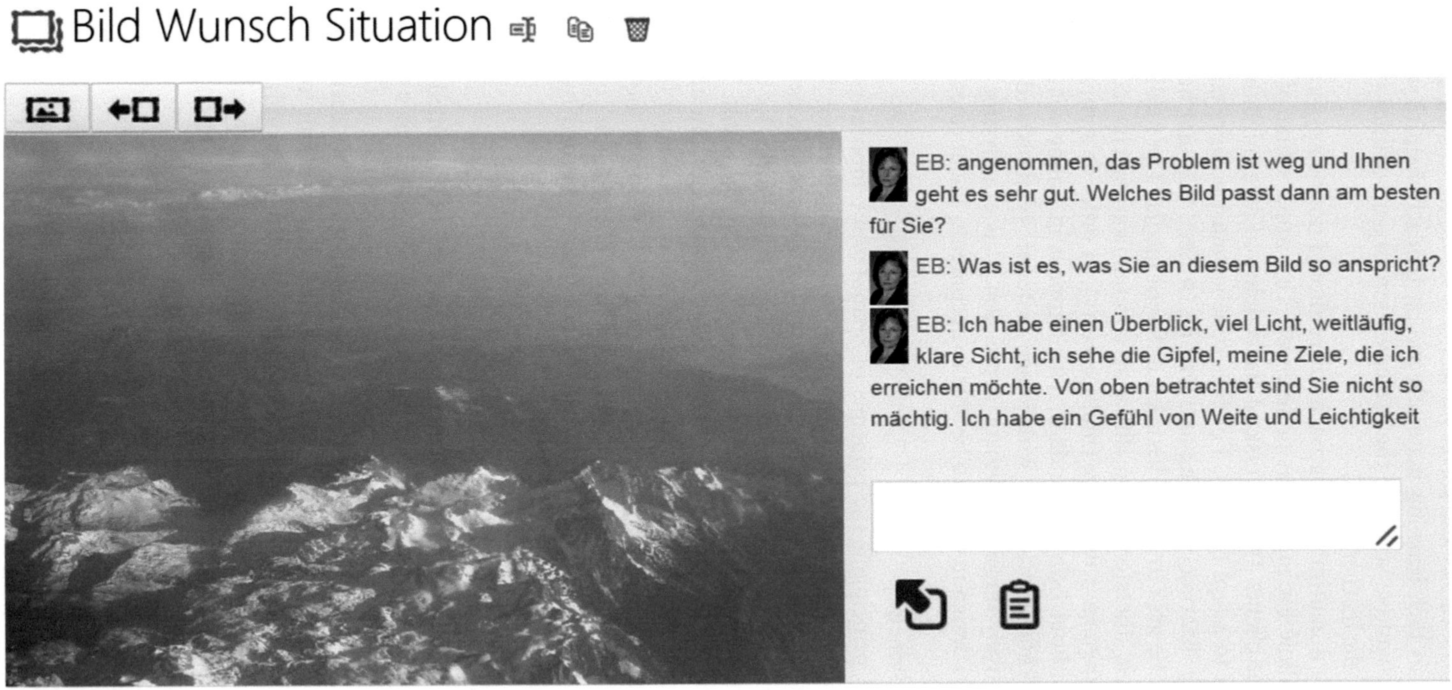

Fig. 12.2 Arrangement of image and chat. (© CAI GmbH)

In order to realize this principle, coaches should work with flexible, multimedia platforms on which they can use visualization tools and at the same time communicate verbally with the clients.

- **Segmentation Principle- Self-Regulation Principle**

Learning is supported when learners can control their learning process themselves.

In computer-mediated learning, it is all about the balance between pre-structuring and interactive events. This is also emphasized by Geißler, who works with predefined questions in his "Virtual Coaching" tools (Geißler, 2015). The questions increase the efficiency of coaching and can be easily used for self-coaching purposes. It is advantageous if the given structure is so flexible that it allows individual adaptation.

It is recommended to alternate between a structured approach (e.g. phases and predetermined or suggested questions) and the freedom of the coaches to react immediately to the expressions and the perceived experience of the clients.

"Creativity and cooperation in communication can arise when both actors coordinate their communicative action with each other and also develop a minimum of coherence, i.e. take into account the other's utterances. In order to realize this reference, they must deviate at least partially from their own communication plans" (Boos & Jonas, 2008, p. 194).

In the CAI® World, coaching phases and corresponding questions are offered as options. Coaches have the freedom to use them, reformulate them, or replace them, depending on what the situation requires. By allowing coaches to give each tool and each phase section a heading that is visible to clients, the respective sections are clearly visualized for everyone. The structure of the process can be seen in Fig. 12.3. On the side is the process menu, where phases can be clicked. The headings can be adopted or changed.

In contrast to face-to-face coaching, segmentation in online coaching is given in a special form when clients can also work in the virtual coaching rooms without the coaches, when they can choose between synchronous and asynchronous units, and when they can transparently recognize the process steps. They thus have the opportunity to decide on the tempo, the tool use and the form of the contact (with). Thus, the segmentation principle becomes a self-steering principle.

This is also in line with the results of a study by Kiili (2005), in which variables were also sought which influence digital learning environments in such a way that effective learning experiences result. These included the activity of the learners and participation in the creation of learning content, which was associated with a Flowerleben. In coaching, the content of the clients is anyway worked out.

- **Personalization Principle**

The activation of communication-related, social schemata supports learning. This includes, for example, a dialog-oriented writing style, a personal address, for example with one's own name or by a human voice (see also ► Chap. 9).

- **Exercise Principle**

What practicing acquired knowledge in learning tasks is in the learning process, is in coaching the execution of the planned problem-solving measures in the real situation. Especially online coaching offers good opportunities for transfer support,

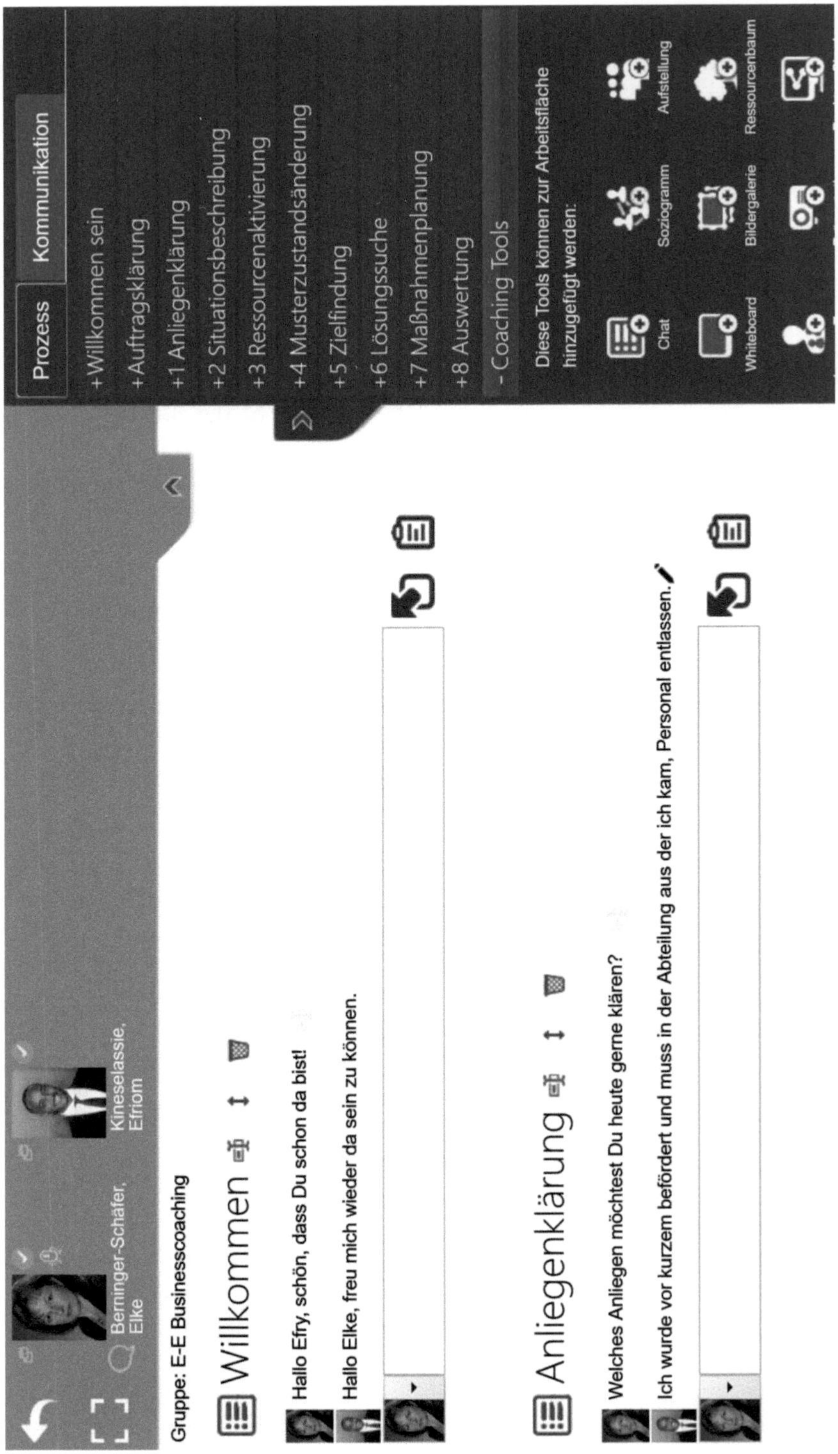

Fig. 12.3 Segmentation of the approach. (© CAI GmbH)

as already mentioned several times (see also ▶ Sect. 10.4.4). The exercise principle is also implemented in online coaching when clients can work independently on the topics and with existing tools in virtual rooms between contacts with the coaches. Platforms that offer this possibility do justice to this principle in a special way.

The criteria mentioned so far can be integrated into the grid which Six et al. (2007, p. 24) represent for the categorization of new media. The authors list the following criteria:

Criteria for Categorizing New Media

- Degree of interactivity
- Type and spectrum of addressed senses and degree of multimedia
- Number of participants and degree of publicity (dissemination and clear division)
- Degree of synchronization (simultaneous and delayed communication)
- Degree to which reality and "experience of presence" or "awareness of mediality" are induced
- Requirements for cognitive activities and media competence

From this one can conclude that it is important for an effective to find not only ready-made pages, but rather tools that enable clients to design themselves that communication can take place over several channels in protected rooms synchronously and asynchronously and that for clients subjectively appropriate processes of experience, thinking and doing are possible.

3-D Worlds

Brunner (2009) provides an orientation framework for theoretical foundations that professional offers in 3-D worlds can build on. For this purpose, he describes four central topic areas:

1. Communication/Interaction
2. Relationship/Feelings
3. Context/Space
4. Person/Identity.

In coaching with avatars, various interactions are possible that depend on the equipment of the 3-D world. When communicating, which is transmitted synchronously via audio function, the same variables have to be observed as in ▶ Sect. 9.2.2. (e.g. modulation, voice, volume, positive emotional deepening language, descriptions and rewrites). Communication can also take place exclusively or additionally based on text. Here, a special competence of the coaches in dealing with the written word is important (connotations, emotional charge, cultural peculiarities, etc., see also ▶ Sect. 9.2.1).

The 3-D space can be designed contextually very differently. It can be set up like a real coaching room, there can be indoor and outdoor spaces, landscapes or moods that can be accentuated by colors or seasons.

Since 3-D worlds can be designed specifically and diversely in principle, this offers a rich potential for intervention that exceeds the possibilities of the real world.

When designing three-dimensional rooms and landscapes, the principles of action described in ▶ Sect. 7.4 are important.

Via the possibility to choose or design avatars oneself, a play of identities can take place. This opens up new perspectives that can be used in coaching.

In summary, Seel and Ifenthaler (2009) can be referred to again when they describe the opportunities that arise for learning processes through today's computer technology:

- Enabling productive and creative learning through multimedia learning environments that allow knowledge to be constructed independently
- Solving problems with the computer tool and not simply acquiring factual knowledge. This is made possible in particular by alternative reality games that use collaborative tools and allow entertaining approaches.
- Simulation of situations and behavior
- Direct learning feedback
- Control by the users
- Enabling individual approaches
- Spatial and temporal independence
- High flexibility as a superordinate characteristic

All of these aspects must also be implemented in online coaching. This also corresponds to the quality requirements described in ▶ Chap. 11.

Döring and Ingerl (2008) also describe various steps and features that are necessary in a media concept in order for the goals to be achieved with the medium. They represent this design competence (purposeful design of media offerings) with various characteristics. These include:

- Screen design (information architecture that refers to how the information contained in the medium is structured and displayed on the screen)
- Usability (ease of orientation and navigation)
- Experience design (fun that is had while using it)
- Corporate design (possibility of adaptation to the individual situation/presentation in color design, icons, image material, etc. of the users)

In addition, gender-appropriate formulation, the possibility of international use of the medium and accessibility must be considered.

12.3 Accessibility

Since there are legal regulations on the subject of barrier-free accessibility, this subject is given its own section here.

The Federal Equal Opportunities Act (BGG) requires that information technology be designed so that it can be used without restriction by disabled people, because the Internet represents an enormous advance for people with impairments. Internet accessibility means that people with disabilities can navigate the Internet, understand everything, and interact.

In addition to disabled or temporarily restricted people who use the Internet, accessibility also means the independence of special technical requirements for all users. This includes, for example, software independence, the presentation of content in an easily understandable language, and the use of the Internet on different devices.

Barrier-free Internet requires the separation of the structure of a document from its presentation. Furthermore, for example, the following aspects (without claiming to be complete):

- Understandability of texts
- Scalability of the font
- Structured, clear layout, orientation and navigation aids
- meaningful links
- interactive buttons
- Text alternatives for non-text content
- Alternatives for audio and silent video
- Videos with subtitles
- Audio description for videos
- Facilitating the distinction between foreground and background
- Adjustable time limits
- Predictability of structure and use
- Support for error avoidance and correction

Web accessibility guidelines are defined by the European Union and at the national level. The Web Accessibility Initiative (WAI) publishes the internationally recognized standard "Web Content Accessibility Guidelines" (WCAG) (Caldwell et al., 2008).

12.4 Data Security

One requirement that is agreed upon by all in online coaching is the security of data and the confidentiality of the process. This is an ethical requirement and a basic prerequisite for professional coaching. At the same time, it is a legal requirement under the Federal Data Protection Act and the data protection guidelines of the respective countries. Data protection refers to the protection of personal data from abuse and is regulated in the Federal Data Protection Act (BDSG, § 1) (▶ https://www.gesetze-im-internet.de/bdsg_1990/, accessed 21.08.2016). Data security is the technical guarantee of this protection.

The principle of data security applies to spoken, video-transmitted, and written information.

As current discussions show, different countries have different ideas and regulations on data protection. Since German law is very demanding here, the data of the CAI® World are stored exclusively in a German data center.

Even if data security is an apparent self-evident, it can only be surprising how carelessly and perhaps also unknowingly coaches deal with this topic and conduct coaching via free chat and video conferencing providers or via classical email programs. With free services, either the user pays with their own data or advertising is displayed, unless the provider explicitly waives this (see their terms of use).

With classical email programs, data is usually sent unencrypted and passes through several stations on the Internet where copies can be made or where data

Fig. 12.4 Security key on the internet. (© CAI GmbH)

can be easily intercepted by third-party access. This can be compared to sending a postcard.

Security vulnerabilities can arise if the transmitted data can be intercepted, the browser addresses the wrong server, or the data can be manipulated in transit.

This is why SSL technology is used. SSL stands for Secure Sockets Layer and is the predecessor to Transport Layer Security (TLS). The German term is Transportschichtsicherheit.

The protection of data transmission by an SSL encryption is also used in online banking and creates an encrypted data channel between senders and receivers.

If an encryption protocol is secured with SSL, a green lock and the protocol https:// are displayed in the browser. HTTPS stands for Hypertext Transfer Protocol Secure (Fig. 12.4).

In order to prevent language and video messages from being intercepted by intermediate servers, CAI® World uses a so-called end-to-end encryption.

In the data center, an automatic data backup is performed so that the coaching processes are backed up (obligation to preserve). The metadata of the session data is automatically stored, but not the creation history. This ensures that deleted data in an online session is really deleted.

This information should be present in the terms of use of websites. It should be clear how the data is transferred, which data is stored for how long and where it is located.

Furthermore, it is necessary for data security that an account is protected by a password. This account relates to data that is stored on a central computer and to which only authorized persons have access with their password.

Technical security standards also include the possibility of anonymization and pseudonymization (Rinsau, 2009).

A coaching session can also be exported to PDF in the CAI® World. Then everything that has happened verbally and in writing is visible. It should be noted that when downloading content to your own PC, the security standard of the platform is abandoned. Here the users themselves are responsible for data security.

Advantages and Disadvantages of Online Coaching

Contents

E. Berninger-Schäfer, *Online Coaching*,
https://doi.org/10.1007/978-3-658-39133-1_13

13.1 Advantages of Online Coaching

The advantages of online applications in coaching, consulting and supervision are investigated and described by many authors (Borlinghaus, 2010; Engelhardt, 2013, 2014; Geißler, 2008, 2012; Kühne & Hinterberger, 2009; Ploil, 2009; Ribbers & Waringa, 2015, etc.).

Due to the time and location independence, various effects occur. First, this leads to a reduction in costs, as travel and downtime as well as travel costs are saved.

By eliminating the need for arrival and departure, the sessions are more timely, ad hoc possible, so that coaching can take place exactly when needed and not according to the free schedule.

Coaching can be carried out and continued synchronously (simultaneous presence of coach and client) and asynchronously, which facilitates integration into everyday work life. The client can work asynchronously, which increases the effectiveness of coaching.

Mobility and flexibility are given a positive meaning by online coaching. Coaching can take place at any location in the world at any time in the desired format. The experts and not the locally available or the cheapest coaches can be used. Cultural and linguistic requirements are met by the right coaches. Coaches can also accompany their clients when they change location (e.g. during long business trips or transfers), so that no coach change and the associated new onboarding is necessary.

Ribbers and Waringa (2015) refer to studies that show that the frequency of contacts between clients and coaches has a significant impact on the success of coaching. This is not possible in the form that online sessions allow with traditional coaching, which is usually carried out in several-hour sessions with a multi-week interval. These can be switched so that they allow the greatest possible transfer support in everyday life and lead to a acceleration of the coaching process. Through the faster and more frequent contact, the factors that occur in the clients' everyday and working life can be taken into account more in coaching. On-the-job accompaniment is possible in a simple way. This allows immediate feedback, which in turn can be used as a feedback loop and lead to faster correction of goals and measures, resource activation and increased success probability. The intensive accompaniment in shorter and smaller units counteracts possible overstrain and strengthens motivation, as faster successes become visible. For this purpose, there is targeted, positive feedback from the coaches, which in turn strengthens solution-oriented behaviour in a timely manner.

Clients can decide for themselves when and how often they want to carry out a coaching sequence, as it is no longer the two- to three-hour coaching session that has to be agreed and organised. Coaching can thus be used even more client-centred.

Clients experience stronger control over the process in that they can decide for themselves when to send a message, how much time they want to spend on formulations (and thus reflection) or self-work. They also decide much more strongly when to take a break. This is unusual in face-to-face coaching. This strengthens the autonomy, activity and self-efficacy of clients.

By using certain communication technologies (e.g. writing-based coaching), by changing time formats (short units, self-work by clients) and by the possibility of accompanying clients step by step "on the job" in the sense of transfer support, new coaching formats arise. The automatic documentation of the coaching process increases the value of coaching for the clients, as self-reflection is supported and all aspects of coaching, possibly also for later questions, are always accessible. The documentation obligation of the coaches is thus fulfilled and their work is made easier.

Writing in coaching has a strong structuring and immediately effective effect on increased self-reflection of the clients. They can distance themselves, take different perspectives and assess topics in different contexts. This is both a cognitive performance and a strong emotional approach, which can be supported by the corresponding behavior of the coaches. Reindl et al. (2016) also describe these advantages for online supervision.

If an online coaching has a process structure, this provides for high transparency and efficiency.

If appointments are cancelled at short notice in face-to-face coaching, this is associated with corresponding cancellation costs. These are reduced by the shorter agreed session times. In addition, there is often the possibility to communicate for 10–15 min or to prepare the missed appointment so that content is already provided in the virtual rooms. Coaches can thus use at least part of the agreed time window for online coaching.

Organizations have the opportunity to see the status of the retrieved coaching hours up to date. In face-to-face coaching, organizations often only find out with the invoice whether coaching has taken place.

Other advantages of online coaching lie in the efficiency and effectiveness. The warming phase, which takes place in particular in the first contact with clients, serves to clarify the relationship so that clients can trustfully enter the coaching. With online coaching, clients are usually in a familiar place (workplace, at home) and therefore feel safe. Socially desirable behavior and role-conform behavior are less in the foreground, especially when the visual channel is not used. There are fewer distractions, which helps clients focus on the coaching process. They accelerate their development path and get to the point much faster. This is due, among other things, to the extremely high focus and the holistic, interactive address of the clients during the coaching session.

If several sessions take place, as is the rule, online coaching allows a faster re-entry and connection to the last session, since, in contrast to face-to-face coaching, the online space is found again as it was left last. If work has been done individually in the room, this builds on and is immediately visible.

People who work from home can take coaching for themselves at home. Employees who travel for work (e.g. field employees, traveling or flying employees) can be coached in their temporary locations. People in crisis or epidemic areas can be intensively accompanied from a distance without the coaches having to go to these areas.

Group or team coaching is easier to organize because participants do not all have to be available at the same geographical location at the same time and work can also be done at different times. This is particularly important for groups and teams that are spread across time zones (Asia, Europe and America).

By means of online coaching, coaching can be done anonymously, so that further target groups, which could not or could not be optimally served in face-to-face coaching so far, can be reached. First experiences show that, for example, people with physical disabilities react very positively to online coaching, because in the virtual space the coaching performance is in the foreground and not their disability. The possibility of anonymous coaching also leads to the fact that self-revelation is much higher and faster achieved by the clients. The openness of the clients is generally greater in the online process. It is easier to write about burdensome and possibly embarrassing things than to express and open up to another person verbally when this person is sitting opposite and maintaining eye contact. Social anonymity also reduces socially desired behavior in coaching, as concerns about appearance and possible interpretations by the coaches are eliminated. The greater openness is particularly advantageous with shame-related issues. This makes it possible for people to have access to coaching services that they would otherwise not use. Anonymity allows not only the hiding of one's own identity, but also the testing of other identities, e.g. of another gender, other roles, other professions, etc. Anonymity is given in all forms of virtual encounter, limited in the use of audio and video functions.

Anonymity and the low level of effort support the low threshold in the use of online coaching.

The generation of digital natives, that is, people who were already confronted with IT in their youth and who master the virtual, multimedia worlds, expect their employers and/or consultants to offer and use modern and IT-supported methods. In the fight of employers for skilled and managerial staff or of coaches for clients, the use of a professional platform for coaching can be an advantage.

In order to realize these potential advantages of online coaching, certain framework conditions must be observed, which have been described in the previous chapters. It is also important to ensure that possible disadvantages are minimized.

13.2 Disadvantages of Online Coaching

Online coaching requires a stable internet connection and it can also lead to unintended, unexpected failures during a coaching process. A fallback solution should always be provided for this, e.g. the email address or telephone number to have at hand. It is important to discuss with the clients at the beginning of a coaching what should happen in the event of an interruption of the connection.

It cannot be assumed that there will be a professional working environment without disruptions. The participants can be tempted to engage in secondary activities in a synchronous process without video transmission (e.g. reading mails if the other person's writing process takes too long, leaving the room, distractions by what is on the desk, etc.). The competence of the coaches is required here to maintain the relationship and contact with the clients as well as to make written statements very short and concise (see ► Sect. 9.2.1).

If, on the other hand, a video image is available, the illusion of eye contact is created, which is not possible virtually (Ribbers & Waringa, 2015). The video image can also be a distraction, as can the image of oneself.

When coaching online, it is still important to keep in mind that there is a greater potential for misunderstanding. This is a significant difference from copresence, where the perceived environment of the participants overlaps with each other, creating a shared frame of reference that allows for the interpretation of gaze and pointing gestures (Schwan & Buder, 2007). This is even more possible in virtual, three-dimensional spaces, where avatars can interact with each other, for example by relating to each other's movements. Otherwise, when working purely based on writing, it is important to be precise in the formulation of communication content and messages. In general, many feedback loops are necessary in professional online interactions. The editing function of the chat supports the avoidance of misunderstandings.

The potentially constant availability of coaches can lead to the expectation that they would need to respond seven days a week at any time. Here, coaches need to know their own offers, limits and possibilities, and communicate them clearly.

The possibility of also doing short sessions, for example five to ten minutes of feedback, creates the risk that these times will not be invoiced and the coaches will give them away. In face-to-face coaching, these usually only occur rarely, so they are not invoiced for reasons of courtesy or evidence. Here, new business models are needed on the part of the coaches.

As Marzschesky (2015) found in her survey on the acceptability of online coaching, clients (in contrast to coaches) expect that the coach's fee will be lower in online coaching than in face-to-face coaching. This expectation could be interpreted as online coaching still being seen as a "lesser" coaching that should at best be an addition to face-to-face coaching. However, with increasing experience, this perception changes significantly.

In order to make up for the possible disadvantages of online communication, certain competencies of the coaches (▶ Chap. 9) and good information about the possibilities of online coaching are required. This includes the identification of quality standards in the content and technical approach and the compliance with ethical guidelines. Furthermore, in the professional implementation, the potential advantages of online coaching should outweigh any possible disadvantages.

13.3 Final Recommendations

The following recommendations supplement or focus on the many aspects that have already been extensively presented.

- Dock, embed, and take online coaching into your existing repertoire and profile.
- Calculate the time investment that is needed in the initial phase to be able to work professionally online.
- Choose the tool or platform that you want and can work with.
- Acquire working technology (computer equipment, headset, internet connection).
- Take advantage of further education and ongoing supervision.
- Specify your own offer, also in terms of good time management, in theory one could work 7 days, 24 h a day.
- Be open to changing your own coaching behavior.

The online coaching practice and experience influence the face-to-face behavior of the coaches. For example, Ribbers and Waringa (2015) report on a survey of online coaches that through the practice of online coaching, they also become more aware of their use of language and ask different or fewer questions in the face-to-face setting. They also give more positive feedback.

- **New Business Models**

The business models of face-to-face coaching cannot be transferred 1:1, as the requirements for the duration and availability of coaching have changed and coaches have to reckon with worldwide competition. Contracting parties and coaches are here required to agree on appropriate agreements and performance evidence, as well as to ensure ad hoc availability.

- **Technology Check Before**

It is very annoying when technical problems have to be fixed in an agreed online session or when there is still effort to clarify the technical procedure. This affects the relationship design and the concentration on the content. Therefore, it should be clarified before the start of the coaching unit whether all technical possibilities, in particular video and audio, work or whether a telephone is used in addition to communication via a platform.

- **Clarification of the External Framework**

It is important that the coach and client have clarified that they are undisturbed for the agreed time. Likewise, there should be an agreement for a fallback solution if, for example, the Internet fails or other technical obstacles arise. This could be the switch to the telephone or a defined postponement.

- **Confidentiality and Documentation**

If the clients have not already informed themselves about this prerequisite for professional online coaching in advance (e.g. by examining the specified security standards of platforms, see also ▶ Sect. 12.4), it should be clarified during the first contact that the creation of the coaching room defines who has access to the contents of this coaching process. These are usually the coaches and the clients who belong to a joint coaching process (e.g. in group, team or conflict coaching). If, for example, another person is given access to a coaching room for supervision purposes, this is only with the express consent of the clients. Everything that happens during the coaching session is automatically documented and can be viewed, closed, copied or further processed at any time. Only the previously defined persons still have access. If this centrally stored documentation is not desired, the contents are deleted at the end of the session, possibly after creating a PDF.

- **Inquire About Environment**

A appreciative exploration already begins when a coach shows interest in the environment in which the clients are currently located, for example at home, in a professional context, on vacation, at the airport, in the park, in a conference hotel, etc. It can be just as important to get an idea of the time of day, time zone and season that prevails with the clients, or in which cultural environment and physical space they are located and what this means for their well-being.

■ Transparency of the Process Steps

This should be illustrated once again using the example of online coaching in the CAI® World. Online coaching in the CAI® World is characterized by a high transparency of the process steps, inasmuch as the process is always visible to the coaches and they can tell the clients exactly which phases and tools are appropriate from their point of view. They can also design the individual, visible phases with process headings that are visible to the clients (see also case study in ► Sect. 9.3.10). Clients can also operate all the tools themselves, both synchronously and asynchronously. This gives clients a greater sense of control, as has already been pointed out.

■ Competent Use of Online Tools

The design of a systemic, solution-oriented coaching process is implemented using online tools. Knowing and being able to use them competently is part of the qualification of online coaches. Competent use also includes the flexibility of coaches to adhere to a process control while still using appropriate tools online in response to the immediate encounter with clients and their development steps. The goal is to transparently and safely control a defined process while virtuously using a wide range of existing coaching tools online that are tailored to the needs of clients. This should take into account the ten principles of process consulting, as Schein (2003) explains.

The 10 Principles of Process Consulting According to Schein (2003)

1. Always try to help
2. Never lose sight of current reality
3. Use your lack of knowledge
4. Everything you do is an intervention
5. The problem and its solution belong to the client
6. Go with the flow
7. Timing is everything
8. Be constructively opportunistic and work with confrontational interventions
9. Everything provides data; there will always be errors, they are the most important source of new insights
10. In doubt, share the problem with others

At point 8, Schein explains that it is about being open to the moment when clients indicate their willingness to open up to new perspectives. The most important thing is to focus on the strengths and positive motivation of the clients.

This is especially true for online coaching. Because especially with online coaching the use of provocative techniques or paradoxical interventions is to be avoided, since the risk of misunderstandings in online applications is greater and less controllable. In this context, in particular, Ribbers and Waringa (2015) emphasize the importance of the exclusive use of positive feedback in online coaching. This is in line with a solution-oriented approach (see also Schmidt, 2014; Szabo, 2015).

Final Remarks

E. Berninger-Schäfer, *Online Coaching*,
https://doi.org/10.1007/978-3-658-39133-1_14

The future of online coaching has begun. Coaching and online coaching are services that are part of standard procedures in the context of personnel development measures and for which further dissemination is predicted (▶ Chap. 2). The professionalization has progressed further and there is now a lot of research material available on which to build. If one looks at the beginnings of online coaching with first question tools and arrangement figures (▶ Chap. 6) up to the development of an integrated platform, one can say that online coaching is outgrowing its infancy and entering a next stage of development with great potential for development. In this context, the clarification of structure, process and result quality in online coaching is of great importance, as is the further development of concepts and procedures and their scientific research.

There are many exciting research topics that can be investigated in the various, already mentioned disciplines and may lead to an independent science of coaching.

The exemplary research questions of the following overview only represent small mosaic stones in the big picture of the science of coaching:

Example Research Questions

- Does online coaching require different theoretical concepts than face-to-face coaching?
- How can the effects of online tools be differentiated and empirically verified?
- To what extent are competencies in face-to-face coaching necessary or hindering for online coaching?
- What are the similarities and differences between face-to-face and online visualizations?
- To what extent are arrangements of representatives in a face-to-face group comparable to arrangements of avatars in 3-D worlds?
- Which groups of people make use of the opportunity to express themselves "anonymously" and does this change over time?
- Which competencies are trained by the use of 2D and 3-D worlds in coaching with clients?
- What should quality dialogues of coaches or providers of further education look like on the topic of online coaching?

The range of possible questions seems to be endless at the moment.

A reversal does not seem to be possible anymore, i.e. online coaching belongs to the present and future of coaching. If the development continues in the form corresponding to the social upheaval caused by the Internet with all its possibilities, then online coaching will become the standard and face-to-face coaching the special exception.

Who still knows the opening hours of banks or is dependent on them? Who is still dependent on standing in line at the ticket office? Who has never shopped online? Who has never used the knowledge available on the Internet, oriented themselves regionally, watched videos and TV shows, listened to music or read articles? Who has never communicated via the Internet and in social networks?

All this already belongs to everyday life.

In the work context, the use of an intranet, communication platforms, participation in telephone and video conferences are already self-evident.

The digital change of life and work worlds corresponds in its extent to a historical development jump, as it was triggered, for example, by the industrial revolution and led to powerful social changes with all their positive and negative effects.

The service coaching is just as affected as all other areas of human life. Coaching cannot remain on the island of apparent, unchangeable bliss. In this respect, the sentence may be true:

With online coaching, the future of coaching has begun!

Supplementary Information

E. Berninger-Schäfer, *Online Coaching*,
https://doi.org/10.1007/978-3-658-39133-1

References

Ahn, S. J., Bailenson, J. N., & Park, D. (2014). Short-and long-term effects of embodied experiences in immersive virtual environments on environmental locus of control and behavior. *Computers in Human Behavior, 39,* 235–245.

Aksu, Y., & Graf, E.-M. (2011). Beratung, Coaching, Supervision multidisziplinär-Eine Hinführung. In E. M. Graf, Y. Aksu, I. Pick, & S. Rettinger (Hrsg.), *Beratung, Coaching, Supervision. Multidisziplinäre Perspektiven vernetzt.* VS Verlag.

Ameln, F. von, & Kramer, J. (2007). *Organisationen in Bewegung bringen.* Springer.

Andersson, G., & Cuijpers, P. (2009). Internet-Based and Other Computerized Psychological Treatments für Adult Depression: A Meta-Analysis. *Cognitive Behaviour Therapy, 38*(4), 196–205.

Armutat, S., et al. (2015). *Virtuelles Coaching-Bilanz und Orientierungshilfe.* DGFP-Praxis Papiere.

Arnold, R. (2011). Lehrer Coaching-Herzstück einer transformativen Weiterbildung von Lehrkräften. In B. Birgmeier (Hrsg.), *Coachingwissen* (2. Aufl.). VS Verlag.

Bachmann, T. (2012). Coaching-Prozesse. In *Leitlinien und Empfehlungen für die Entwicklung von Coaching als Profession. Kompendium mit den Professionsstandards des DBVC* (4. Aufl.). DBVC Geschäftsstelle.

Bandura, A. (1977). Self-efficacy: toward a unifying theory of behavioural change. *Psychological Review, 84*(2), 191.

Berendt, J. E. (2008). *Das dritte Ohr. Vom Hören der Welt.* Traumzeit-Verlag.

Berg, T., & Berninger-Schäfer, E. (2010). *Die Kollegiale Coaching Konferenz®.* Boorberg.

Berninger-Schäfer, E. (2008). Erfolgsgeheimnis Coaching – Führungsqualität durch neue Führungskultur. In T. E. Berg & H. Wicker (Hrsg.), *Führen mit Leidenschaft.* Boorberg.

Berninger-Schäfer, E. (2011a). Coaching im Kontext Kirche – Möglichkeiten und Qualitätskriterien professionellen Coachings im kirchlichen Umfeld. *Pastoral Theologie, 3.*

Berninger-Schäfer, E. (2011b). *Orientierung im Coaching.* Boorberg.

Berninger-Schäfer, E. (2012). Die virtuelle Kollegiale Coaching Konferenz. In H. Geißler & M. Metz (Hrsg.), *E-Coaching und Online-Beratung. Formate, Koneztpe, Diskussionen.* VS Verlag.

Berninger-Schäfer, E. (2013). *Gesundheitskompetenzen für Führungskräfte.* Boorgberg.

Berninger-Schäfer, E. (2014a). Die Kollegiale Coaching Konferenz. In B. Schmid & O. König (Hrsg.), *Train the Coach: Methoden.* managerSeminare Verlags GmbH.

Berninger-Schäfer, E. (2014b). Lösungssuche mit Stellvertreter. Avatarbasiertes Coaching. *ManagerSeminare, 195,* 26–30.

Berninger-Schäfer, E., & Webers, T. (2010). *Hochschulreife von Coaching – Lehrgängen. Coaching Magazin, 2,* 34–39.

Berninger-Schäfer, E., & Wolf, C. (2011). Qualitätssicherung im Coaching. Was sich die Praxis von der Forschung wünscht. In E. M. Graf, Y. Aksu, I. Pick, & S. Rettinger (Hrsg.), *Beratung, Coaching, Supervision. Multidisziplinäre Perspektiven vernetzt.* VS Verlag.

Berninger-Schäfer, E. (2016). *CAI® Coaching Concept.* Unveröffentlichtes Manuskript als Teil der CAI®–Lizenz.

Berninger-Schäfer, E. (Hrsg.). (2018). *Interventionsmethoden im Coaching.* Boorberg.

Beushausen, J. (2010). *Ressourcenorientierte stabilisierende Interventionen. Kontext, 41*(4), 287–307.

Biocca, R., & Harms, C. (2002). Defining and measuring social presence: Contribution to the Networked Minds Theory and Measure. Paper of Media Interface and Network Design (M.I.N.D.) Labs, Dept. of Telecommunication, Michigan State University. ► http://citeseerx.ist.psu.edu/viewdoc/download?. Zugegriffen: 20. Juli 2016.

Blackman, C. (2010). Can avatars change the way we think and act? Hg. v. Stanford Report. ► http://news.stanford.edu/news/2010/february22/avatarbehavior-study-022510.html. Zugegriffen: 20. Juli 2016.

Böning, U. (2014). Business-Coaching mit Führungskräften. In R. Wegener, M. Loebbert, & A. Fritze (Hrsg.), *Coaching-Praxisfelder. Forschung und Praxis im Dialog.* Springer Fachmedien.

Böning, U., & Fritschle, B. (2005). *Coaching fürs Business.* managerSeminare.

Böning, U., & Kegel, C. (2015). *Ergebnisse der Coaching-Forschung.* Aktuelle Studien ausgewertet für die Coaching-Praxis.

Boos, M., & Jonas, K. J. (2008). Medienvermittelte Kommunikation. In *Medienpsychologie* (S. 195–217). Springer.

Borlinghaus, R. (2010). *Coaching 2.0. Handbuch TeleCoaching.* BORA TEXT.
Bozer, G., & Sarros, J. C. (2012). Examining the Effectiveness of Executive Coaching on Coachees' Performance in the Israeli Context. *International Journal of Evidence Based Coaching and Mentoring, 10*(1), 14–32.
Bredl, K., Bräutigam, B., & Herz, D. (2012). Avatarbasierte Beratung und Coaching in 3D. In H. Geißler, M. Metz, & H. Geissler (Hrsg.), *E-Coaching und Online-Beratung. Formate, Konzepte, Diskussionen.* Springer VS.
Brunner, A. (2009). Theoretische Grundlagen der Online-Beratung. In B. Caldwell, M. Cooper, L. G. Reid, & G. Vanderheiden (2008). ► http://www.w3.org/TR/2008/REC-WCAG20200812111/. Zugegriffen: 14. Aug. 2015.
Custers, R., & Aarts, H. (2005). Positive Affect as Implicit Motivator: On the Nonconscious Operation of Behavioral Goals. *Journal of Personality and Social Psychology, 89*(2), 129–142.
Damasio, A. (1997). *Descartes' Irrtum. Fühlen, Denken und das menschliche Gehirn.* List.
De Haan, E., Grant, A. M., Burger, A., & Erikssonn, P.-O. (2016). A Large-Scale Study of Executive and Workplace Coaching: The Realitve Contributions of Relationsship, Personality Match, and Self-Efficacy. *Consulting Psychology Journal: Practice and Research, 68*(3), 189–207.
Dehner, U. (2009). Beratung mit Ratschlag-Tabubruch im Coaching. *Manager Seminare, 131*(2), 46–49.
Deplazes, S., Schwyter, S., & Möller, H. (2016). Ein Blick auf Coachingprozesses-Die Interventionen des Coachs, dargestellt und analysiert mittels des KaSyCo-C. In E. Berninger-Schäfer, E.M. Graf, & H. Künzli (Hrsg.), *Coaching|Theorie und Praxis.*
Dietz, I., & Dietz, T. (2008). *Selbst in Führung. Wege zur Selbstführung in Coaching und Selbst Coaching.* Junfermann.
Dietz, T., & Müller, G. (2012). Coaching-Leistungen. In *Leitlinien und Empfehlungen für die Entwicklung von Coaching als Profession. Kompendium mit den Professionsstandards des DBVC* (4. Aufl.). DBVC Geschäftsstelle.
Döring, N. (2007). Vergleich zwischen direkter und medialer Individualkommunikation. In U. Six, U. Gleich, & R. Gimmler (Hrsg.), *Kommunikationspsychologie-Medienpsychologie.* Beltz Verlag.
Döring, N., & Ingerl, A. (2008). Medienkonzeption. In *Medienpsychologie* (pp. 403–424). Springer.
Drath, K. (2012). *Coaching und seine Wurzeln.* Haufe.
Eichenberg, C., & Kühne, S. (2014). *Einführung Onlineberatung & -therapie. Grundlagen, Interventionen und Effekte digitaler Medien* (S. 4131). UTB.
Eichenberg, C., & Ott, R. (2011). *Klinisch-psychologische Intervention im Internet. Psychotherapeut.* Springer-Verlag.
Eichenberg, C. (2008). Bedeutung der Medien für klinisch-psychologische Interventionen. In B. Batinic & M. Appel (Hrsg.), *Medienpsychologie* (S. 504–530). Springer Medizin
Elverfeldt, F. von (2005). *Selbstcoaching für Manager.* Orell Füssli.
Engelhardt, E. (2013). Qualitätsmerkmale guter Onlineberatung–Aktuelle Anforderungen an Forschung und Praxis. *Zeitschrift für systemische Therapie und Beratung, 31*(3), 111–115.
Engelhardt, E. M. (2014). Online-Supervision-neue Perspektiven für die Praxis. *Kontext, 45*(2), 172–185.
Filk, C. (2014). Plädoyer für eine Social-Media-Ethik in der Medienwirtschaft. ► http://www.medienpolitik.net/2014/02/medienethik-wir-sind-mit-ethischmoralischen-problemen-und-dilemmata-konfrontiert/. Zugegriffen: 14. Aug. 2015.
Förderland. Wissen für Gründer und Unternehmer. ► http://www.foerderland.de/gruendung/gruendungsvarianten/geschaeftsideen/ideepc-internet/online-coaching/2016. Zugegriffen: 20. Juli 2016.
Fritze, A., Loebbert, M., & Wegener, R. (2014). Coaching-Praxisfelder. Annäherung an einen Arbeitsbegriff. In R. Wegener, M. Loebbert, & A. Fritze (Hrsg.), *Coaching-Praxisfelder. Forschung und Praxis im Dialog.* Springer VS.
Geißler, H. (2008). *E-Coaching. Baltmannsweiler.* Schneider Verlag.
Geißler, H. (2011). Coaching meets Training – zur Lösung des Transferproblems durch „virtuelles Transfercoaching (VTC)". In M. Loebbert & R. Wegener (Hrsg.), *Coaching entwickeln. Forschung und Praxis im Dialog.* Vandenhoeck & Ruprecht.
Geißler, H. (2012). Virtuelles Coaching-programmgeleitetes Coaching mit Internet-Support. In H. Geißler & M. Metz (Hrsg.), *E-Coaching und Online-Beratung.* Springer.
Geißler, H. (2015). Wer sollte denn eigentlich bei der Bewertung von Coachingprozessen das erste und wer das letzte Wort haben?-Eine gegenstandskonstitutive Analyse. In H. Geißler & R. Wegener. *Bewertung von Coachingprozessen.* Springer.
Geißler, H., Hasenbein, M., & Wegener, R. (2013). Virtuelles Coaching: Prozess- und Ergebnisevaluation eines internetbasierten Coaching-Formats. *OSC, 2,* 125–142.
Geißler, H., & Kanatouri, S. (2015). Coaching mit modernen Medien. In *Die Professionalisierung von Coaching* (pp. 399–419).
Geißler, H., & Metz, M. (Hrsg.). (2012). *E-Coaching und Online-Beratung.* Springer.
Geißler, H., & Wegener, R. (2015). *Bewertung von Coachingprozessen.* Springer.

Gieselmann, A., & Pietrowsky, R. (2016). Treating procrastination chat-based versus face-to-face: An RCT evaluating the role of self-disclosure and perceived counselor's characteristics. *Computers in Human Behavior, 54,* 444–452.
Gigerenzer, G. (2007). *Bauchentscheidungen.* Bertelsmann.
Gollwitzer, P. M., Kuhl, J., & Heckhausen, H. (1996). Das Rubikonmodell der Handlungsphasen. In J. Kuhl & H. Heckhausen (Hrsg.), *Enzypkopädie der Psychologie (Bd. 4). Motivation, Volition und Handlung.* Hogrefe.
Graf, E. M. (2015). Die Spezifika des Coaching-Gesprächs – der linguistische Beitrag zur Coaching-Prozessforschung. *Coaching|Theorie und Praxis, 1*(1), 5–14.
Grant, A. M. (2014). Autonomy support, relationship satisfaction and goal focus in the coach–coachee relationship: which best predicts coaching success? *Coaching: An International Journal of Theory, Research and Practice, 7*(1), 18–38.
Grant, A. M. (2013). The efficacy of coaching. In J. Passmore, D. B. Peterson, & T. Freire (Hrsg.), *The Wiley-Blackwell handbook of coaching & mentoring psychology.* Wiley Blackwell.
Grant, A. M. (2012). Making Positive Change: a randomized study comparing solution focused vs. problem-focused coaching questions. *Journal of Systemic Therapies, 31*(2), 21–35.
Grant, A. M., & Zackson, R. (2004). Executive, Workplace and Life Coaching: Findings from a Large-Scale Survey of International Coach Federation Members. *International Journal of Evidence Based Coaching and Mentoring, 2*(2), 1–15.
Grant, A. M. (2003). The impact of life coaching on goalattainment, metacognition and mental health. *Social Behavior and Personality 31,* 253–264.
Grawe, K. (2000). *Psychologische Therapie.* Hogrefe Verlag.
Grawe, K., Donati, R., & Bernauer, F. (1994). *Psychotherapie im Wandel. Von der Konfession zur Profession* (3. Aufl.). Hogrefe.
Greif, S. (2008). *Coaching und ergebnisorientierte Selbstreflexion.* Hogrefe Verlag.
Greif, S. (2015). Allgemeine Wirkfaktoren im Coachingprozess. Verhaltensbeobachtungen mit einem Ratingverfahren. In H. Geißler & R. Wegener (Hrsg.), *Bewertung von Coachingprozessen.* Springer.
Greif, S., & Benning-Rohnke, E. (2015). Konsequente Umsetzung von Zielen durch Coaching Praktisch nützliche Erkenntnisse aus der Grundlagenforschung und ihre Anwendung. In E. Berninger-Schäfer, E. M. Graf, & H. Künzli (Hrsg.), *Coaching|Theorie und Praxis.* Journal e-ISSN: 2364–5148.
Greif, S., Schmidt, F., & Thamm, A. (2012). Warum und wodurch Coaching wirkt. Ein Überblickzum Stand der Theorieentwicklung und Forschung über Wirkfaktoren. *Organisationsberatung, Supervision, Coaching, 19*(2), 275–390.
Gross, P. P., & Stephan, M. (2015). Der Coaching-Markt. In E. Berninger-Schäfer, E. M. Graf, & H. Künzli (Hrsg.), *Coaching|Theorie und Praxis, 1*(1), 15–24.
Grünbuch Arbeiten 4.0. Arbeiten weiter denken. (2015). ► http://www.bmas.de/DE/Service/Publikationen/A872-gruenbuch-arbeiten-viernull.html. Zugegriffen: 20. Aug. 2015.
Hauser, E., & Schlömer, S. (2014). Führung von Mitarbeitern. In A. Ryba, D. Pauw, D. Ginati, & St. Rietmann (Hrsg.), *Professionell coachen. Das Methodenbuch: Erfahrungswissen und Interventionstechniken von 50 Coachingexperten* (S. 132–146). Beltz.
Heckhausen, H., & Heckhausen, J. (Hrsg.). (2010). *Motivation und Handeln* (4. Aufl.). Springer.
Hinkelmann, R., & Enzweiler, T. (2016). Digitale Entwicklung: Chancen und Risiken virtuellen Coachings. *Coaching-Newsletter von C. Rauen, 7*(8).
Hinterberger, G., & Kühne, S. (2009). Veränderte mediale Lebenswelten und Implikationen für die Beratung. In G. Hinterberger & S. Kühne (Hrsg.), *Handbuch Online-Beratung. Psychosoziale Beratung im Internet* (S. 16). Vandenhoeck & Ruprecht.
Hüther, G. (2010). Wie Embodiment neurobiologisch erklärt werden kann. In M. Storch, B. Cantieni, G. Hüther, & W. Tschacher (Hrsg.). (2011), *Embodiment.* Huber.
ICF – Studie. (2011).Professional- Partners/Professional-Partner-Content/2013/06/2012-ICF-Global Coaching-Study- Top-Findings. ► http://www.astd.org/Professional-Resources/ASTD. Zugegriffen: 20. Aug. 2015.
ICF Globar Coaching Studie. (2012). ► http://coachfederation.org/about/landing.cfm?ItemNumber=828. Zugegriffen: 20. Juli 2016.
James, T., & Woodsmall, W. (1998). *Time line.* Junfermann.
Kaster, C. (2014). Systemische Einheiten zur Gestaltung eines lösungsorientierten Bilderbuchs im Kontext der stationären Jugendhilfe. Abschlussarbeit „Systemische Beratung" an der Heidelberger Akademie für Gesundheitsbildung (HAG) HD VI 2012–2014. ► http://www.claro-vita.net/pdf/texte/3-Systemische-BeratungHeilpaedagogische-Kinder-und-Jugendhilfe.pdf. Zugegriffen: 20. Juli 2016.
Kiili, K. (2005). Participatory multmedia learning: Engaging learners. *Australasian Journal of Educational Technology, 21*(3), 303–322.

Kindl-Beilfuß, C. (2008). *Fragen können wie Küsse schmecken. Systemische Fragetechniken für Anfänger und ortgeschrittene.* Carl-Auer.
Knatz, B. (2009). Medien der Online-Beratung. In S. Kühne & G. Hintenberger (Hrsg.), *Handbuch Onlineberatung* (S. 59–91). Vandenhoeck & Ruprecht.
Köbler, G. (1995). *Deutsches Etymologisches Wörterbuch.* Utb.
Köhler, T., Kahnwald, N., & Reitmaier, M. (2008). Lehren und Lernen mit Multimedia und Internet. In B. Batinic & M. Appel (Hrsg.), *Medienpsychologie* (S. 478–501). Springer Medizin.
König, E., & Vollmer, G. (2014). Der Blick auf das soziale System. In A. Ryba, D. Pauw, D. Ginati, & St. Rietmann (Hrsg.), *Professionell coachen. Das Methodenbuch: Erfahrungswissen und Interventionstechniken von 50 Coachingexperten* (S. 321–333). Beltz.
Kumbier, D. (2016). *Aufstellungsarbeit mit dem Inneren Team: Methoden-und Praxisbuch für Gruppen.* Klett-Cotta.
Kühne, S. (2012). Qualitätsmanagement in der psychosozialen Onlineberatung. Eberatungsjournal. *net Fachzeitschrift für Onlineberatung und computervermittelte Kommunikation, 2*(3).
Kühne, S., & Hintenberger, G. (Hrsg.). (2009). *Handbuch Online-Beratung. Psychosoziale Beratung im Internet.* Vandenhoek & Ruprecht.
Künzli, H., & Lohmann, A. C. (in prep.). unveröffentlichte, vorläufige Studie „Online Coaching mit der CAI-World – Ein Projekt am Departement Angewandte Psychologie der Zürcher Hochschule für Angewandte Wissenschaften ZHAW".
Künzli, H. (2009). Wirksamkeitsforschung im Führungskräftecoaching. *Organisationsberatung, Supervision, Coaching, 16*(1), 4–16. VS-Verlag.
Künzli, H., & Seiger, C. (2011). *Evidence-based Coaching und Wirksamkeit. Studientext zum Masterstudiengang Business Coaching und Change Management.* Euro-FH.
Küster, H. (2014). Entwicklungsorientiertes Coaching: Werte, Motive und Bedürfnisse klären. In A. Ryba, D. Pauw, D. Ginati, & St. Rietmann (Hrsg.), *Professionell coachen. Das Methodenbuch: Erfahrungswissen und Interventionstechniken von 50 Coachingexperten* (S. 252–266). Beltz.
Lehenbauer, M., & Stetina, B. U. (2009). Interaktive Programme und virtuelle Simulationen. In S. Kühne & G. Hintenberger (Hrsg.), *Handbuch Online-Beratung. Psychosoziale Beratung im Internet.* Vandenhoek & Ruprecht.
Loebbert, M. (2015). Wie gut gelingt die Steuerung eines Coachingprozesses. In H. Geißler & R. Wegener (Hrsg.), *Bewertung von Coachingprozessen.* Springer.
Marzschesky, J. (2015). Akzeptanz von Online-Coaching. Unveröffentlichte Abschlussarbeit im Kontaktstudium „Businesscoach" des Coaching Zentrums Karlsruhe und der SRH Hochschule Heidelberg.
Maturana, H. R., & Varela, F. J. (2009). *Der Baum der Erkenntnis.* Fischer Taschenbuch Verlag.
Meier, D. (2004). Solution Circle für Teams. In C. Rauen (Hrsg.), *Coaching-Tools.* managerSeminare.
Messerschmidt, J. (2015). *Das Selbst im Bild. Eine empirische Studie zum Einsatz von Bildmaterialien zur Förderung von Selbstreflexions- und Selbstveränderungsprozessen im Einzelcoaching.* Peter Land.
Miedaner, T. (2002). *Coach dich selbst sonst coacht dich keiner.* mvg Verlag.
Migge, B. (2013). *Schema-Coaching.* Beltz.
Minuchin, S. (1997). *Familie und Familientherapie: Theorie und Praxis struktureller Familientherapie.* Lambertus-Verlag.
Mollbach, A., Studer, T., & Bergstein, Held, D. (2017). Future Management Development Studie 2017. ► http://assets.kienbaum.com/downloads/Future-Management-Development-Studie-2017-Kienbaum.pdf?mtime=20170222151305.(eingesehen am 25.09.2017)
Montag, C. (2016). Lässt sich aus unseren Datenspuren im Internet ablesen, wer wir sind? In *Persönlichkeit–Auf der Suche nach unserer Individualität* (pp. 137–141). Springer.
Moreno, J. L. (2008). *Gruppenpsychotherapie und Psychodrama: Einleitung in die Theorie und Praxis.* Georg Thieme Verlag.
Mücke, K. (2004). *Hilf Dir selbst und werde, was Du bist.* Klaus Mücke Öko Systeme Verlag.
Offermanns, M. (2004). Gestaltung von Transfermeetings. In C. Rauen (Hrsg.), *Coaching- Tools.* managerSeminare.
Petzold, H., & Orth, I. (Hrsg.). (2005). *Poesie und Therapie. Über die Heilkraft der Sprache. Poesietherapie, Bibliotherapie, Literarische Werkstätten.* Aisthesis.
Peus, C., Frey, D., & Braun, S. (2011). Einsatz von Gruppenworkshops in Kombination mit Individualcoaching zur Förderung von Führungskompetenzen. In B. Birgmeier (Hrsg.), *Coachingwissen* (2. Aufl.). VS Verlag.
Pfisterer, B. (2016). Falldokumentation (unveröffentlicht) im Rahmen des Coaching Lehrgangs „Business-Coach für Wirtschaft und Verwaltung" bei der Führungsakademie Baden-Württemberg und dem Karlsruher Institut für Coaching.
Patrzek, A. (2015). *Systemisches Fragen, essentials.* Springer.

Pietschmann, D. (2009). *Das Erleben virtueller Welten. Involvierung, Immersion und Engagement in Computerspielen.* Werner Hülsbusch.

Ploil, E. O. (2009). *Psychosoziale Online-Beratung.* Ernst Reinhardt.

Poepsel, M. A. (2011). The impact of an online evidence-based coaching program on goal striving, subjective well-being, and level of hope (Unpublished Doctoral dissertation), Minneapolis, MN. Harold Abel School of Social and Behavioral Sciences. ► http://gradworks.umi.com/3456769.pdf. Zugegeriffen: 20. Juli 2016.

Prior, M. (2004). *MiniMax-Interventionen. 15 minimale Interventionen mit maximaler Wirkung.* Carl-Auer-Systeme.

Prior, M. (2006). *Beratung und Therapie optimal vorbereiten.* Carl-Auer-Systeme.

Radl, J. (2016). Demografie, Coaching Jüngerer, Lernverhalten der Zukunft. Ein Projekt der Fachsäule FCIO des DBVC. Vortragsunterlagen. ► http://www.coaching-kongress.com/wp-content/uploads/Radl_Der-Einfluss-derDemografie-auf-das-neue-Lernen_Coaching_CKED16.pdf. Zugegriffen: 4. Juni 2016.

Rauen, C. (2002). Der Ablauf eines Coaching-Prozesses. In C. Rauen (Hrsg.), *Handbuch Coaching.* Hogrefe.

Reindl, R. (2015). Psychosoziale Onlineberatung-von der praktischen zur geprüften Qualität. *E-beratungsjournal.net, 1*(6), 55–67.

Reindl, R., Engelhardt, E., & Zauter, S. (2016). Online-Supervision–Systematische Bestandsaufnahme eines neuen Arbeitsfeldes. *E-beratungsjournal.net.*

Resch, K., & Tomaschek, M. (2014). Wissen und Fähigkeiten weiterentwickeln. In A. Ryba, D. Pauw, D. Ginati, & St. Rietmann (Hrsg.), *Professionell coachen. Das Methodenbuch: Erfahrungswissen und Interventionstechniken von 50 Coachingexperten* (S. 308–320). Beltz.

Ribbers, A., & Waringa, A. (2015). *E-Coaching. Theory and practice for a new online approach to coaching.* Routledge.

Risau, P. (2009). Die Wahl der Technik. Standards und Anforderungen an technische Lösungen zur Online-Beratung. In *Handbuch Online-Beratung. Psychosoziale Beratung im Internet* (S. 201–211). Vandenhoek & Ruprecht.

Rogers, C. R. (1972). *Die nicht direktive Beratung.* Kindler.

Rosenberg, R. S., Baughman, S. L., & Bailenson, J. N. (2013). Virtual superheroes: Using superpowers in virtual reality to encourage prosocial behavior. *PloS one, 8*(1), e55003.

Roth, G. (2003). *Aus Sicht des Gehirns.* Suhrkamp.

Schein, E. H. (2003). *Prozessberatung für die Organisation der Zukunft.* Bergisch-Gladbach EHP.

Schermuly, C. C., et al. (2014). *Zu Risiken und Nebenwirkungen lesen Sie…–Negative Effekte von Coaching.* Zeitschrift für Arbeits-und Organisationspsychologie A&O.

Schermuly, C. C., & Graßmann, C. (2015). *Erfolgreicher Einsatz von Coaching in der Führungskräfteentwicklung. Handbuch Mitarbeiterführung: Wirtschaftspsychologisches Praxiswissen für Fach-und Führungskräfte* (S. 1–13). Springer.

Schmidt, G. (2004). *Liebesaffären zwischen Problem und Lösung.* Carl-Auer, Auer-Systeme.

Schmidt-Tanger, M. (2014). Coachingfehler-zwischen Hoffnung und Haltung. In A. Ryba, D. Pauw, D. Ginati, & St. Rietmann (Hrsg.), *Professionell coachen. Das Methodenbuch: Erfahrungswissen und Interventionstechniken von 50 Coachingexperten* (S. 438–446). Beltz.

Schreyögg, A. (2015). Bewertung eines Coachingprozesses aus tiefenpsychologischer Sicht. In H. Geißler & R. Wegener (Hrsg.), *Bewertung von Coachingprozessen.* Springer.

Schulz von Thun, F. (2013). *Das innere Team und situationsgerechte Kommunikation: Kommunikation, Person, Situation.* Rowohlt Taschenbuch.

Schütz, A., & Rentzsch, K. (2007). Selbst und Kommunikation. In U. Six, U. Gleich, & R. Gimmler (Hrsg.), *Kommunikationspsychologie-Medienpsychologie.* Beltz Verlag.

Schwan, S., & Buder, J. (2007). Informationsaufnahme und –verarbeitung. In U. Six, U. Gleich, & R. Gimmler (Hrsg.), *Kommunikationspsychologie-Medienpsychologie.* Beltz Verlag.

Seel, N. M., & Ifenthaler, D. (2009). *Online lernen und lehren.* Ernst Reinhardt Verlag.

Shazer, S. (1989). *Der Dreh. Überraschende Wendungen und Lösungen in der Kurzzeittherapie.* Carl-Auer.

Sherpa Coaching Survey. (2015). The Tenth Annual Executive Coaching Survey. ► http://www.sherpacoaching.com/pdf%20files/2015_Executive_Coaching_Survey_Pblic-Report.pdf. Zugegriffen: 21. Aug. 2015.

Six, U., & Gleich, U. (2007). Kommunikationskompetenz, Medienkompetenz und Medienpädagogik. In U. Six, U. Gleich, & R. Gimmler (Hrsg.), *Kommunikationspsychologie-Medienpsychologie.* Beltz Verlag.

Six, U., Gleich, U., & Gimmler, R. (2007). Kommunikationspsychologie. In U. Six, U. Gleich, & R. Gimmler (Hrsg), *Kommunikationspsychologie-Medienpsychologie.* Beltz Verlag.
Steils, N. (2013). Identität durch Avatare in virtuellen Welten. ► http://www.checkpoint-elearning.de/article/12804.html. Zugegriffen: 20. Juli 2016.
Steinke, I. (2012). Qulitätsbegriff und Qualitätsmanagement. In *DBVC-Deutscher Bundesverband. Leitlinien und Empfehlungen für die Entwicklung von Coaching als Profession* (4., erw. Aufl., S. 114). DBVC-Geschäftsstelle.
Storch, M. (2014). Ressourcen aktivieren mit Mottozielen. In A. Ryba, D. Pauw, D. Ginati, & St. Rietmann (Hrsg.), *Professionell coachen. Das Methodenbuch: Erfahrungswissen und Interventionstechniken von 50 Coachingexperten* (S. 334–347). Beltz.
Storch, M. (2005). *Das Geheimnis kluger Entscheidungen. Von somatischen Markern, Bauchgefühl und Überzeugungskraft.* Goldmann.
Storch, M., Cantieni, B., Hüther, G., & Tschacher, W. (2011). *Embodiment.* Huber.
Storch, M., & Krause, F. (2007). *Selbstmanagement-ressourcenorientiert.* Huber.
Strikker, H., & Strikker, F. (2013). Coaching studieren? Akademisierung im Business-Coaching. *Coaching-Magazin, 2,* 36–41.
Süss, D. (2008). Mediensozialisation und Medienkompetenz. In *Medienpsychologie* (pp. 361–378). Springer.
Szabo, P. (2015). Bewertung von Coachingprozessen: drei Sichtweisen mit unterschiedlichen Vorannahmen von Nützlichkeit. In H. Geißler & R. Wegener (Hrsg.), *Bewertung von Coachingprozessen.* Springer.
Theeboom, T., Beersma, B., & Vianen, van A. E. M. (2013). Does coaching work? A meta analysis on the effects of coaching on individual level outcomes in an organizational context. *The Journal of Positive Psychology: Dedicated to furthering research and promoting good practice, 9*(1), 1–18.
Thiery, H. (2014). Telematisierung des Alltags und der Beratung. Philosophische und mediensoziologische Skizzen zu den Möglichkeitsbedingungen digital vermittelter Beratung und Therapie. *E-beratungsjournal.net Fachzeitschrift für Onlineberatung und computervermittelte Kommunikation, 2*(2), 54–82.
Topan, A. (2011). *Teamcoaching.* Boorberg.
Trepte, S., & Reinecke, L. (2013). Auswahl und Gestaltung von Avataren in Computerspielen. Hamburg Media School. ► http://www.hamburgmediaschool.com/forschung/forschung-an-derhms/forschungsprojekte/auswahl-und-gestaltung-von-avatarane-incomputerspielen/. Zugegriffen: 20. Juli 2016.
Trepte, S., Reinecke, L., & Bruns, C. (2008). Psychologie in den Medien. In B. Batinic & M. Appel (Hrsg.), *Medienpsychologie* (S. 556–581). Springer Medizin.
Varga von Kibéd, M., & Sparrer, I. (2009). *Ganz im Gegenteil: Tetralemmaarbeit und andere Grundformen Systemischer Strukturaufstellungen.* Carl Auer.
Vieweg, M. (2013). Auch virtuelle Rucksäcke sind schwer. ► http://www.wissenschaft.de/technik-kommunikation/technik//journal_content/56/12054/914362/Auch-virtuelle-Rucks%C3%A4cke-sind-schwer/. Zugegriffen: 20. Juli 2016.
Vogel, I. (2007). Emotionen im Kommunikationskontext. In U. Six, U. Gleich, & R. Gimmler (Hrsg.), *Kommunikationspsychologie-Medienpsychologie.* Beltz Verlag.
Vogelauer, W. (2010). Coaching spürt keine Krise-vermehrte Nachfrage-steigende Professionalität. ► http://www.trigon.at/aktuelles/pdf/downloads/Coaching_Befragung_2010.pdf. Zugegriffen: 20. Aug. 2015.
Wagner, B., Horn, A., & Maercker, A. (2014). Internet -based versus face-to-face cognitive behavioural intervention for depression: A randomized controlled non-inferiority trial. *Journal of Affective Disorders,* 152–154, 113–121.
Weber, G., & Drexler, D. (2002). Familien-Stellen bei Psychosen. *PiD-Psychotherapie im Dialog, 3*(03), 243–247.
Wegener, R., Fritze, A., & Loebbert, M. (2014). *Coaching-Praxisfelder.* Springer Fachmedien.
Weger, U. W., & Loughnan, S. (2013). Virtually numbed: Immersive video gaming alters real life experience. *Psychon Bull Rev.*
Weiß, J. (1990). *Selbstcoaching.* Junfermann.
Whitmore, J. (2006). *Coaching für die Praxis.* allesimfluss-Verlag.
Wolf, C. (2014). *Systemisch-lösungsorientiertes Coaching als unterstützter Lernprozess. Untersuchung von Änderungen des Musterzustands als förderlicher Initiator des Lernens.* AV Akademikerverlag.
Wolf, C. (2014). Musterzustände im Coaching erkennen und verändern. *Organisationsberatung, Supervision, Coaching, 21*(4), 469–482

Wuppertaler Kreis e. V. (2013). Trends in der Weiterbildung, Verbandsumfrage 2013. ► http://www.wkr-ev.de/trends13/trends2013.pdf. Zugegriffen: 30. Okt. 2014.

► www.portal-gesundheitonline.de= Portal des Dachverbandes der BKK, bietet Suche nach Onlineberatung in der Region und zu bestimmten Themen, sowie Chats zu bestimmten Themen, wie z. B. Mobbing-Beratung, Ehe-Familien-Lebensberatung. Angebot: Emailberatung, Einzelchat, Gruppenchat.

Yaghoubzadeh, R., & Kopp, S. (2015). Spoken Language, Conversational Assistive Systems for People with Cognitive Impairments? – Yes, If. In *ASSETS'15: Proceedings of the 17th International ACM SIGACCESS Conference on Computers & Accessibility.* ACM.

Zezula, P., & Beer, R. (2012). Theratalk: Ein Online-Portal für Paare und Partnerschaft. In H. Geißler & M. Metz (Hrsg.), *E-Coaching und Online-Beratung. Formate, Konzepte, Diskussionen.* VS Verlag.

MIX
Papier aus verantwortungsvollen Quellen
Paper from responsible sources
FSC® C105338

If you have any concerns about our products,
you can contact us on
ProductSafety@springernature.com

In case Publisher is established outside the EU,
the EU authorized representative is:
Springer Nature Customer Service Center GmbH
Europaplatz 3, 69115 Heidelberg, Germany

Printed by Libri Plureos GmbH
in Hamburg, Germany